UFOs

The Final Answer?

UFOs

The Final Answer?

Ufology for the 21st Century

Towards an Explanation of Flying Saucers,
Ufology and Alien Abduction

EDITED BY
DAVID BARCLAY &
THERESE MARIE BARCLAY

BLANDFORD

A BLANDFORD BOOK

First published in the UK 1993
by Blandford, A Cassell Imprint
Villiers House
41/47 Strand
LONDON WC2N 5JE

Reprinted 1993
Copyright © 1993 Blandford Press

Distributed in the United States
by Sterling Publishing Co., Inc.
387 Park Avenue South, New York, NY 10016-8810

Distributed in Australia
by Capricorn Link (Australia) Pty Ltd
P.O. Box 665, Lane Cove, NSW 2066

Cataloguing in Publication Data for this title is
available from the British Library

ISBN 0-7137-2362-9 (pbk)

Typeset by Litho Link Ltd, Welshpool, Powys, Wales

Printed and bound in Finland

CONTENTS

To all ufologists past, present and yet to come: the only people with the courage to consider the possibility that there are more things in Heaven and Earth than are dreamed of in any extant philosophy.

EDITORS' NOTE

It was originally intended to illustrate this work with photographs. However, it soon became clear, due to the breadth of content, that to do so would probably lessen the impact of the ideas contained in the various contributions. In any case, it was agreed that, in ufology, it is always assumed that the camera can lie, and it was deemed more productive to the debate to avoid the usual controversy regarding UFO photos.

LIST OF CONTRIBUTORS

David Barclay has over 45 years' experience in ufology as both an investigator and a percipient. Founder of the British Earth Mysteries Society, he was also the original Editor of *The UFO Debate*. He put forward the virtual reality hypothesis, and is the author of *Fatima: A Close Encounter of the Worst Kind*?

Therese Marie Barclay has been active in ufology for 12 years. She is Assistant Editor of *The UFO Debate*. A founder-member of the British Earth Mysteries Society, she has recently returned to full-time education to obtain a science degree.

Joseph Dormer B.Sc. has been in ufological investigation for many years. He is President of Fylde UFO Research Group and a contributor to *The UFO Debate*.

Roger Ford is a freelance UFO writer who has contributed to both national magazines and UFO group publications since 1970.

Robert Moore has been an active member of the British UFO Research Association (BUFORA) since 1982. He is currently BUFORA's Special Projects Officer and co-ordinator for the Association's LIGHTBALL research project. He is also BUFORA's official investigator for the Somerset area. He has been closely involved with *The UFO Debate* magazine since its inception in 1990.

Charlotte A O'Conner is a cosmologist whose main interest is the origin of man. She has contributed articles to *The UFO Debate*.

K W C Phillips B.Ed., B.A. has worked for 20 years as a BUFORA investigator, including being Investigations Co-ordinator 1971–75. He is currently Assistant Editor of *UFO Times*. In 1983, he became the leader in England for the Anamnesis Protocol.

Arthur Tomlinson B.Sc. has spent 40 years in ufology. He is now a full-time lecturer on the subject.

FOREWORD

IF UFOs DID NOT EXIST, IT WOULD BE NECESSARY TO INVENT THEM

Dr R W Shillitoe Ph.D.
Clinical Psychologist

Most of the people who do not believe in UFOs regard the evidence for their existence as immeasurably weak. It is an act of faith. Most of the people who do believe in the existence of UFOs, and especially that this presumed existence implies extra-terrestrial intrusion, regard the evidence as crushingly overwhelming. This, too, is an act of faith. How is it that people can hold such passionate views about a phenomenon for which there is little or no empirical evidence – according, that is, to conventional science? How is it that diametrically opposed conclusions can be derived, with equal certainty, from the same body of inconclusive data?

Human beings pride themselves on their ability to think rationally and logically. In reality, however, this ability is badly flawed and most people neither behave rationally nor take into account available evidence before arriving at conclusions. Using an experience as a starting-point (seeing lights in the sky; watching the value of investments increase), they then draw conclusions about them (the lights were caused by interplanetary visitors; the rise in stock values was caused by shrewd investment). Statistical analysis, however, shows that there is no such thing as a shrewd investor on the stock market. Up or down, it is all a matter of good or bad luck. Or, to be more scientific, to the manifestation of unpredictable statistical probabilities. In the long run, investors and market analysts perform at the chance level: major profits are wiped out by major losses. But, such is human nature that, when things go well and investments show a profit, the conclusion is drawn that skill and ability were responsible. On the other hand, when things go badly and the company invested in crashes, the occurrence is more likely to be blamed on external factors, such as bad luck, or unpredictable events. The human need to impose order on the world and to see ourselves in command of our destiny ensures that we take credit when things go well, and offload the blame when they do not. We try to believe what we want to believe, and 'logically' order sensory input to this end. In ufology, is this tendency accentuated by the indeterminateness of the data being dealt with?

Allied to this is the question of how well (or rather, how badly) people are at using statistical information to estimate accurately how likely a given event is. Ufology is very much at the mercy of statistical sleight of hand. Believers, and non-believers, using the same body of data, will inevitably arrive at different conclusions; conclusions supported by their interpretation of the statistics involved. But try to answer this: if you go to a meeting of, say, ufologists (or for that matter, of the British Association for the Advancement of Science), how many people must be in the room before the chances are even that any two of them will share the same birthday (date and month, but not year)? The correct answer – 23 – always surprises people, and it is interesting that ufologists are more likely to give significantly worse estimates than orthodox scientists. Could this represent an active willingness to be deceived on the part of ufologists? If so, then a great many people want to be deceived. Surveys suggest that up to 50 per cent of the population believes in UFOs as evidence of visits to Earth by extraterrestrials. The 'evidence' these individuals point to is monumental in quantity if not in quality, so why does orthodox science remain unconvinced and insist that reported 'sightings' are at best hallucinations or indicative of feverish imaginations or, at worst, lies and deliberate deceptions. There are a number of reasons.

First and foremost is the fact that UFOs in their reported manifestations are incompatible with the 'laws of science', as they are subscribed to at this time. Furthermore, the belief in the extraterrestiality of UFOs assumes a yet-unproven absolute – that life exists elsewhere in space; that planets (yet to be discovered) are capable of sustaining the kind of life we are familiar with, and that this life is capable of travelling immense distances at extraordinary speeds. Scientifically, the alternative is equally unpalatable: that these manifestations emanate from some uncharted and ill-defined 'inner space'. Orthodox science can have no truck with concepts such as these and still remain true to its brief. Secondly, scientists rightly point out that the burden of proof is on ufologists, and that it has been repeatedly demonstrated that explanations compatible with textbook science – comets, meteors, flares or well-meaning misperception of other mundane stimuli by witnesses – have, can and do account for a great many UFO reports. Even worse is the fact that some reports, even those given by ostensibly bona-fide, 'serious' ufologists, have been deliberate hoaxes. This alone is enough to contaminate the possible validity of all other reports, and casts serious doubts – from a scientist's point of view – upon the whole body of reported sightings from day one. Thirdly, it is admitted, even by those dedicated to the ufological interpretation, that the description of the objects seen almost always reflects the technological sophistication of the witness, or the period in which the sighting occurs. Thus, reports have developed over the course of this century from sightings of large 'balloons' or 'airships' which allegedly travelled at anomalously high velocities, to reports of fast-moving 'space vehicles', the 'design' of which kept pace with human expectations in the matter of 'space technology', and would have been familiar to the NASA scientists or Russian cosmonauts. Such changes in description, paralleling the actual advancement of terran transportational systems, would not, it is claimed, occur if the reports were of 'genuine' products of non-terrestrial technologies. At the moment, these scientific arguments are unanswerable, and only the ongoing achievements of our own space technology will ever be capable of resolving the matter. Or so science believes.

Clearly, however, the desire to believe in the UFOs exerts great psychological power on vast sections of the populace. Carl Jung's notion that round objects in the sky symbolize the order and wholeness that is longed for in times of doubt and stress, may or may not be true in its specifics, but it cannot account for the fact that, despite the many benefits of modern living, many people would dearly love to prove orthodoxy wrong, and see science humbled. They point gleefully, and with a marked degree of anticipation, to the great scientific blunders of the century – the 'proof' of the existence of N-rays which were later shown to be imaginary; or to the use of insulin coma therapy for the treatment of serious mental illness, which turned out to be completely ineffective. They point, with some justification, to the way in which science, for all its apparent power and ability to harness the forces of nature, has despoiled the planet and is presently bringing its survival as a life-sustaining environment into doubt. They point to the way in which the gap between our common-sense view of the world and the view of the world promoted by physicists, with their talk of the Uncertainty Principle and of the Unified String Theory, no longer seem to be in harmony or share any common ground. There is a gut feeling in the ordinary individual, even in those not ufologically inclined, that, science has got it wrong in a big way and that, perhaps, a *deus ex machina*, in the form of UFOs, might come to our rescue.

In the end, people tend to believe what makes them feel comfortable: this gives them hope and reaffirms their individual worth in a society which values them not. Why some of these people feel comfortable with a world view that includes the existence of UFOs in their 'classic' interpretation, and why others do not, is of deep psychological interest. If our beliefs happen to coincide with what is objectively demonstrable, then that, perhaps, is a bonus; certainty is gained, but something also, perhaps, is lost.

Consider this: a stage magician, wanting to debunk the claims of mediums, spiritualists and parapsychologists, was demonstrating his skills before a large audience. Ectoplasm, spirit writing and bent cutlery followed each other in quick succession. Suddenly, a man jumped up from the audience; 'You're a fraud!' he shouted. 'Of course,' replied the magician. 'That's my point – it's all trickery and sleight of hand.' 'No, no,' said the man. 'It really is magic; you're just trying to convince us it's all only sleight of hand!'

Reach your own conclusions.

CHAPTER 1

A TANGLED WEB

David Barclay and
Therese Marie Barclay

U fology is not quite as simple as it would first appear. According to Allen J Hynek, who spent a lifetime studying the subject:

> The UFO Phenomenon, in its totality, is surprisingly complex. Understandably this is not recognised by the general public. . . . The man on the street's simple opinion that either UFOs are all nonsense or that visitors from outer space do exist is brutally destroyed by close study.[1]

Of the paradigms proposed to explain, or explain away, ufological phenomena, all have a greater or lesser statistical probability in their favour. But as any ufologist who has been in the study for any length of time can tell you, almost all of the explanations – from ETs to DTs – can only be 'proven' as correct, when evidence to the contrary is either ignored or devalued. The dilemma facing ufologists now is the same one that has faced them all along: how much of the, now mountainous, documentation is factual; how much the result of honest misperception; how much the result of hoaxing; and how do you start to discern which is which? If ufologists are unable to reach a consensus on the mystery they have set themselves to study, then the general public cannot be blamed for favouring the one paradigm that could subsume all the others, and which is in keeping with presently extant cultural expectations. For some reason, probably the fact that it was in the middle of our science-fiction century that the UFO phenomenon went public, the problem has been seen by all concerned as a 'scientific' one. That one assumption was probably a mistake. If ufology is anything, it is an investigation based on deduction, rather than empirical experimentation. Sherlock Holmes would have loved it. For, as he was made to say by his creator Conan Doyle, there is nothing more certain than: 'When the impossible has been eliminated then, whatever you have left, no matter how improbable, must be the truth.'

Logically, all mysteries must have a solution. It can, and will, be no different with the UFO mystery. All that is presently wrong is that there are too many ufologists trying to force the available evidence into the constraints of preconceived paradigms, rather than attempting to evolve an inclusive hypothesis from the evidence available to them. Those ufologists who see the study in simplistic terms of whatever paradigm they are pursuing should refer to the words of Allen Hynek, arguably the most informed ufologist of all, who injected a cautionary note into ufology when he wrote:

> In the area of UFOs, deeper acquaintance reveals a subject that has not only potentially important scientific aspects but sociological, psychological, and even theological aspects as well.[2]

The great psychologist, C G Jung, when he addressed the problem from the viewpoint of his own discipline, came to almost the same conclusion. He clearly defined the disturbing dichotomy inherent in UFO manifestations when he wrote in reference to his own 'Archetype' hypothesis: 'Unfortunately, however, there are good reasons why the UFOs cannot be disposed of in this simple manner.'[3] This statement would seem to indicate that Jung remained unconvinced by his own 'psychological' explanation regarding the genesis and maintenance of what has turned out to be this century's most intractable mystery. Why should this be so? Seemingly, in his own investigations Jung had come up against the classic conundrum posed by ufological data – How much is true? How much is false? And how is one supposed to tell the difference? Like many before and after him, Jung found that he could not dismiss, even the most strange, accounts of ufological interactions out of hand, because the reports came from persons, and sources, he had no option but to accept as authoritative, even though many of the reports were 'so bizarre that they tax our understanding and credulity to the limit'.[4] The conclusion he eventually drew was unpalatable to him, in that it implied that the UFO phenomenon was something so paradoxical in its operations that were it 'true', it might threaten the very existence of the human race by destroying the world view that our race has cherished since time immemorial. In view of this, he felt that he had no option but to pursue other lines of, perhaps less socially destabilizing, enquiry, because in his view 'the notion of a materialized psychism opens a bottomless void under our feet.'[5] Instead, he fell back on a, not altogether unfamiliar, alternative: 'that UFOs are real material phenomena of an unknown nature coming from outer space'.[6]

Without doubt, everyone who comes into ufology brings with them expectations of what they think it is all about. Or, perhaps more accurately, what they are prepared to tolerate in the area of explanations for the phenomenon. Sometimes, it is equally certain that they are unaware of this. Such attitudes are unavoidable, given the effects of enculturation, which is why there are as many true disbelievers as there are true believers, and why – some 44 years on – ufology is in exactly the same position as the one in which it started out: trying to 'prove' or 'disprove' the existence of something to be investigated. The issue is now so emotionally overloaded that tempers sometimes fray, to the detriment of the study as a whole.

An impartial eye can immediately see from the documentation that there is certainly something begging an explanation; either that or it must be assumed that millions of credible witnesses, world-wide, have taken leave of their senses. There is a school of thought within ufology that does consider this option as a serious possibility. It is an easy way out. All you have to say to any witness is 'you're barmy' and the mystery is solved. If you are attracted by the simplicity of this option, please bear in mind that there, but for the grace of god, go you. Sightings of UFOs are now (and have been for a long time) pandemic. Reports of them have emanated from all sections of society, with a noticeable predisposition to that section of society (pilots, the police, astronomers, the clergy et al.) whose testimony about any other observation would be considered unimpeachable. Because of this, it is perhaps much better to keep your options open and accept that there is a phenomenon to be explained without, of course, leaping to any premature conclusions as to what that solution is likely to be.

The major cause of all the ufological umbrage is the fact that the phenomenon seems to be multiform. It can be perceived as balls of light, either high or low level, or as monstrous machinery that bears no resemblance to anything yet produced by the technologies of this planet. To complicate the issue further, there are now innumerable witnesses claiming various types of intercourse with non-human beings who accompany the ufological manifestations. More disconcertingly, perhaps, it would seem that once 'entities' appear on the scene, the whole thing takes on undeniable aspects of Jung's feared 'materialized psychism'. This aspect of ufological endeavours is sufficient to upset the ufological applecart. If *they* are 'psychic' then *they* can't be 'scientific', and battle commences. No one is interested in solving the mystery, only in proving themself right and the other person wrong. It is much ado about nothing. As with a lot of issues, it is human chauvinism that is ufology's Achilles heel. Life, the universe and everything are not necessarily defined in human terms. It is far more logical to suppose that human life is defined in terms of life, the universe and everything. And on this basis it must be contemplated that the phenomenon might be such that we will never solve the UFO mystery. But, as it's early in the game, perhaps that is being unduly pessimistic.

So, after all that, what *is* ufology? Well, for one thing, it is probably the last great public investigative enterprise wherein the gifted amateur is not at any disadvantage. In fact, anybody can be a ufologist, providing they have the necessary streak of curiosity, and the stamina to follow where it leads, because, at this point in time and despite the protestations of the proponents of the various paradigms, there still are more questions than answers about the manifestations of the phenomenon. As Jung discovered, much to his apparent dismay, the phenomenon encompasses elements that are hard to reconcile by recourse to the presently extant parameters of consensus reality. In a way that is almost occult, the UFO phenomenon has, since its public début in 1947, managed to maintain not only its essential mystery, but to expand and enhance it by apparently drawing to itself other mysteries formerly thought to be separate enigmas in themselves. This evolution of the mystery has been endlessly disconcerting to those who set out to solve it, as time and again possible solutions have been invalidated in the process. In an effort to get some idea of the kind of conceptual problems faced when trying to come to terms with the various manifestations, and strategies, attributed to the UFO phenomenon in the literature, we can do no better than look to the dolphin and understand the possible interactive precedents set by mankind's relationship with it. In the dolphin, we have a creature which many feel is our intellectual equal, but which is still quite alien to us. As far as marine zoologists can ascertain, the natural organization, or 'civilization' if you will, of the species is quite complex. There is even a strong possibility that it has a language, or means of individual-to-individual communication, which is equal – or even superior – to its human equivalent. Yet, because of the constraints imposed by its genetic inheritance, which maintain the species's form and attributes that enable it to live in its natural environment – its 'niche' – it has never produced, perhaps never even felt the need to produce, a technology of any kind – at least, as we understand that word. Due to these same natural constraints, it is unable to leave its watery 'reality' to expand the area of its operations. We, as a species, suffer from no such constraints and, although our hydrographic technology is cumbersome when compared to the natural expertise of the dolphin, it does enable us to make our land-based superiority felt in other areas. Presently there is no way of telling what dolphins in the wild make of our various surface craft and submersibles with their accompanying 'entities'. Perhaps in some strange way, we are the UFO (Unidentified Floating Objects) phenomenon of the dolphin reality. For the sake of argument, it is an analogy worth the drawing. Fishermen, scientists, even showmen, have all had a go at the dolphin, and all for very different purposes. Even with their presumed intelligence, it is hardly likely that dolphins have been able to deduce, from their various though necessarily limited contacts with sundry members of the human race, the complexity and diversity behind the various 'intrusions' into their reality. They are further hampered in any hypothetical attempt to investigate these intrusions by their inability to leave their watery reality of their own volition. They can only do so when 'contacted' or 'abducted' by us. Even then, their perception of the 'reality' into which they have been brought is only peripheral, and their understanding of it conditioned by their experience of whatever purpose they have been abducted to serve. Although no real good has accrued to dolphins in these transactions, it is on record that dolphins in the wild seem predisposed to human contact, in much the same way as some humans are seemingly predisposed to 'alien' contact. It is arguable that neither party knows what it is they are getting themselves into. As the supposedly 'superior' lifeform, we are able to enter at will into the dolphin reality to contact, abduct or even ignore them, depending on the reason for any given intrusion. This similarity between the way the human race interacts with the dolphin, and the way in which the UFO phenomenon interacts with the human race is strangely synchronous – to say the least. But what if it is more than that? What would be the ramifications for our race?

Quite rightly, there will be those who will be quick to point out that the foregoing speculations are only germane *if* the UFO phenomenon does indeed represent a human – non-human interaction. There is, presently, no irrefutable evidence that any intelligence, let alone a non-human intelligence, is operating on planet Earth, but there are indications. Our introduction to the woman who, in deference to her request for anonymity as a precondition to having her experience mentioned publicly, we are obliged to identify by the pseudonym 'Mrs B', came when she wrote to us regarding a UFO sighting she had from the back garden of her house in a suburb of Bradford, in West Yorkshire.[7] Her purpose in writing was to discover if, as investigators, we had come across any other reports of the object she had sighted. Enquiries were made, but, as is frustratingly usual, we were unable to find any further witnesses, so went to see Mrs B to inform her of our failure. She took it very well, and we began discussing her sighting in more detail than she had been able to put into her original letter. She now told us that on a sunny Sunday afternoon in July 1986, she had been seated out in her garden, reading a book. The book in question had nothing to do with UFOs, but was about Klaus Barbie. So any kind of self-inflicted auto-suggestion seems to be ruled out. She described the day as being typical of fine Sunday afternoons that are filled with 'the sound of children's voices as they played, dogs barking, and what sounded like a lawn-mower being used not too far away'.[8]

Although absorbed in her book, she felt a sudden impulse to look up into the sky, to see what she initially thought was a kite. Silver in colour and oblong in shape, it was apparently moving in her direction, and as it came closer, she realized that there were no strings attached to it. Also, as it came towards her in a trajectory that would take it directly overhead, she became aware that its movement was too steady and purposeful for something wind-born. In any case, as far as she could recall, there was no wind to speak of on that day. Now thoroughly intrigued, Mrs B waited for it to pass directly above her so that she could get a better look. But then something occurred which completely surprised her:

> As it got nearer, it seemed to me it must have suddenly become aware of me, because it veered to the left and turned back, moving quite fast now, and went behind a large white cloud.[9]

The witness seemed quite certain that the anomalous object was aware of her scrutiny, and that it was this that had caused it to alter course. To compound her feelings of 'the watcher being watched', the object – from behind the cloud – seemed to play a strange game of peekaboo with her, before it finally exited at tremendous speed up into the sky, where it was lost to sight. It would have been quite easy to dismiss Mrs B's testimony as 'wishful thinking', and to have 'explained' her sighting as being of

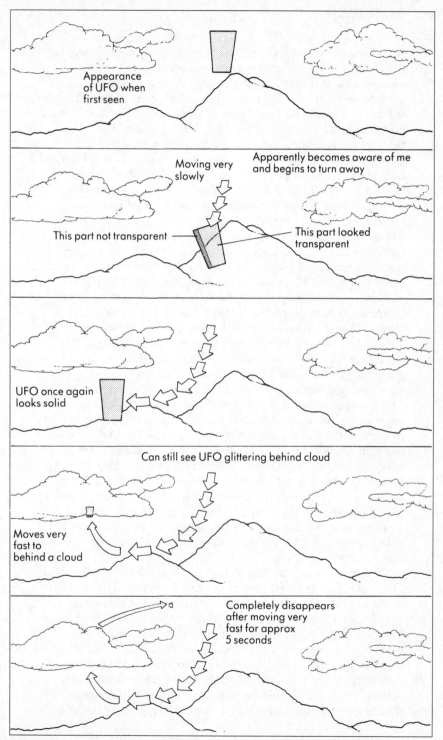

Figure 1 Progress of a UFO seen by Mrs B in July 1986 – taken from sketches made by her.

something mundane, its apparent 'manoeuvres' being caused by the vagaries of air currents in the atmosphere. However, we discovered that the cloud cover on the day in question was at considerable altitude, so for the object to have 'gone behind it' and still be seen argues for something of fairly large dimensions. Based on the subjective data volunteered by the witness, we estimated that, whatever it was, it must have been at least the size of a Boeing 747 for its angularity to have been evident to her. Had it been even further 'behind' the cloud cover than Mrs B estimated, then its size would have been appreciably larger. So what was it? Trying to answer such a question is where the ufological heartaches begin. Those who disbelieve in the mystery would be within their rights to claim misperception. Others who fear imminent interplanetary attack could equally well claim 'alien spaceship on patrol', while those with a scientific bent could cry Meaden Vortex. We would be unable to disagree convincingly with any of them. In our view, the only really interesting piece of information in this report was that the witness claimed 'observer effect': which is to say that the object's apparent behaviour appeared conditioned by the fact that she was watching it. It is a claim that is made by witnesses to all forms of Fortean phenomena, even when, as in this case, it is unclear how their scrutiny could have been noticed by a seemingly inanimate object. Mrs B was adamant that the object's actions persuaded her that it knew it was being watched, and being watched specifically by her. Accepting this witness's testimony at face value (and who are we to doubt her when we weren't even there at the time), there seems only one way that an inanimate object can respond interactively: its actions had to be informed by intelligence. The thought is so shocking that even we are inclined to rule it out of court, even though we know from a statistical viewpoint it has as much chance as all the other options for an explanation of being the correct one. Even so, we must point out that 'non-human intelligence' does not necessarily imply ET.

Some years ago now, John A Keel published his seminal work, *Operation Trojan Horse*, which expanded ufological investigative horizons almost to infinity. One of the chapters in that book was called 'Never mind the answer – what's the question?'. It is probable that Keel – a Fortean of good standing – was being a little facetious, in which case it might well turn out to be 'many a true word spoken in jest'. It has been proposed, with some justification, that to know which are the right questions to ask to solve any particular problem, you must necessarily know most of the answer anyway. As no one presently seems to know even a small portion of the answer to the UFO mystery, how can we be sure that the questions that are being asked about it are the right ones? Here is a pertinent parable to illustrate the point. Consider, if you will, the plight of a monkey who has lived all his life in the jungle. He has no reason to suppose that 'reality' is anything other than that which he supposes it to be. He's doing OK. Then, one day, he finds an anomalous object. Let us say it is a half-empty Coke can. Well, being a half-way intelligent monkey, he soon discovers how to enjoy the tasty dregs left in the can, but after that he has problems; problems which, because of his enculturation, he has no idea even exist. Having quite enjoyed the drink, he would probably want more and, in monkey terms, he is bound to ask himself where grows the tree from which such succulent fruit can be picked; then spend the rest of his life in a fruitless search for a non existent Coca-Cola tree – forever unaware that he is asking the wrong question about obtaining cans of Coca-Cola. For the monkey, the search might well be both exciting and intellectually stimulating, and he might conceive of any number of persuasive hypotheses along the way. In the end, the exercise would be unproductive, and he would never locate the Coca-Cola tree of his limited imagination.

Is it possible that we ufologists have been making this same basic, but unavoidable, error in the way we have set out to solve the mystery of the Coca-Cola cans from space – or wherever? Are we erring too much in our own favour by assuming that our anthropomorphic initiatives are equal to the task of solving a mystery that Allen J Hynek once admitted he found both shocking and paradoxical in its manifestations? Perhaps the real solution to the UFO mystery is beyond the conception of our enculturation. For our hypothetical monkey properly to have confronted and solved the Coca-Cola can mystery, realize the full ramifications inherent in the existence of that one can, and then take full advantage of that knowledge, he would have had to be born human. We must now hope that a similar precondition does not apply to us in our effort to solve the UFO mystery, and that to appreciate fully the UFOs' 'reality', we do not have to be born 'ufonauts'. As the monkey and Coke can analogy is somewhat inexact, the odds are probably still in our favour, and we are not being over-optimistic in believing that the mystery is solvable by human ingenuity – providing we don't overdo it by insisting that the eventual solution must make the kind of sense we feel comfortable with. It must always be borne in mind that in confronting the unconventional, which the UFO phenomenon unarguably is, conventional solutions are most likely redundant.

Probably the best thing to do now is to start again from the beginning (if there ever was such a point), and without expecting UFOs to turn out to be anything in particular, see if Holmesian deduction from the available evidence can indicate if they are, after all, interesting enough to justify further attention being paid to their multiform manifestations. If, as the majority of ufologists seem to suspect, there is an intelligence behind it all, perhaps all we are really witnessing is something else's ongoing attempts to discover if there is intelligent life on planet Earth.

Bearing all this in mind, it is hoped that readers of this book really will dispense with all and any preconceptions, or mis-apprehensions, they might have about UFOs and what they might or might not be doing in their various appearances on this planet. In the final analysis, it might well be that whatever they are doing, it has nothing whatsoever to do with us, except insofar as they have to distract our attention somehow while they get on with the real business at hand. If, indeed, it is a *they* and not an *it* we are dealing with. . . . Well, we told you ufology wasn't quite as simple as it might first appear . . .

REFERENCES

1 Fowler, R E   *The Andreasson Affair.* Introduction by Allen J Hynek (Bantam Books, 1980)
2 ibid.
3 Jung, C G   *Flying Saucers: A Modern Myth of Things Seen in the Sky* (Routledge & Keegan Paul, 1987)
4 ibid.
5 ibid.
6 ibid.
7 Authors' personal files
8 ibid.
9 ibid.

CHAPTER TWO

LOOK BACK IN ASTONISHMENT

Arthur Tomlinson B.Sc.

It has become almost an article of faith that ufology had its beginnings in 1947, when businessman Kenneth Arnold, from Boise, Idaho, made his seminal report of the objects he allegedly saw over the Cascade Mountains in America. In fact, this is not so. All that really happened was that a phenomenon with a long pedigree was finally described in such terms by the media that it caught the public's imagination. It is demonstrable from many sources that the phenomenon that has come to be known in this latter half of the twentieth century as 'UFOs' has been endemic throughout history, and probably even before that. In some way yet to be determined, it can only be that the UFO phenomenon has an interface with human society as it developed on this planet. In support of this contention, attention can be drawn to the Bible, both the Old and New Testaments, and many other ancient books and documents that contain material amenable to ufological interpretation. Renaissance paintings by Carlo Crivelli, Raphael, Ghirlandaio, and Jean-Pierre Muzard contain ufological images that contribute nothing to the main subject of the painting. Some of these show strange craft in the sky, a good number of which have detailed structures quite out of place in the paintings of artists living in pre-scientific cultures. That these anomalous images in the paintings should correlate exactly with what has come to be recognized as the 'classic' UFO configuration is singularly synchronous – to say the least. There are so many examples of similar synchronicities in ancient literature that the study suffers from an embarrassment of riches, and it is only possible to scratch the surface of this evidential material in a chapter of this length.

EARLY UFOs AND FLYING MACHINES

From a document written in hieroglyphics during the fifteenth century BC, during the reign of Pharaoh Thutmose III, the following translation is taken:

> A circle of fire coming in the sky, noiseless, one rod long with its body and one rod wide. After some days these things became more numerous, shining more than the brightness of the Sun.

What could they have been? At such a remove in time, it is impossible to say. Yet from the description in the papyrus, it can be surmised that – whatever they were – they bore a remarkable resemblance to objects described by witnesses to the modern UFO phenomenon.

Alexander the Great, an almost mythical figure in his own right, had several experiences which were blatantly ufological in nature, if the ancient records are to be believed. For instance, while he and his forces were in the process of crossing the River Jaxartes into India, in 329 BC, he was startled to see two 'shining silver shields' diving repeatedly on his army, causing horses and elephants to panic – and the soldiers also, one would presume. Seven years later, in 322 BC, during Alexander's seige of Tyre, a large 'flying shield' leading a formation of four 'smaller shields' circled over the city, and while the encamped army watched in amazement, the 'large shield' shone a beam of light on to the city walls which caused them to crumble. More beams were fired which destroyed the remaining walls, and the attackers, not ones to look gift horses in the mouth, poured into the city. Almost immediately, the flotilla of 'flying shields' departed at high speed. Another incident, immortalized in the Mogul painting in the British Museum, involving Alexander the Great, is the story of his 'flight to the heights of Heaven on the back of an eagle'. Apparently, the 'eagle' carried him so far aloft that he was able to study the topography of the earth from the vantage point of a modern-day spy satellite, and plan his world conquest. Granted these accounts come down to us from an age that we consider to be rife with myths and legends, and pre-scientific, and must therefore be considered as fanciful. For did not our ancestors shake and tremble in their boots before a plethora of 'gods' which we in our wisdom now know to be only personified natural occurrences? Like you, I am still waiting to witness the natural occurrence that takes the form of 'flying shields' or an 'eagle' so powerful that it can put itself into orbit. But, wait a minute, perhaps such a thing has come to pass, for did not an 'eagle' land on the moon? Should our own civilization pass away, to be lost in the antiquity of another, what will those people then make of the statement 'the eagle has landed' contained in the mythology of our times concerning our leap to the moon on the back of Apollo? You tell me. If they are as intellectually arrogant as we are, there can be only one answer.

Closer to us in time – but still from those days during which conventional scholarship insists that even the educated were fantasy prone – come reports of incidents that one can only suspect have ufological ramifications. In *The Anglo-Saxon Chronicle*, which is a collection of documents written independently in various English monasteries between AD 450 and 1150, there are several references to astronomical phenomena, such as eclipses, comets, and mock suns (parhelia), all correctly identified. This makes the following two references of more than passing interest. The first, in the *Laud Chronicle*, referring to the year AD 1105 states:

> On the eve of Cena Domini, the Thursday before Easter, two Moons were seen in the sky before day. One to the East and the other to the West, and both at full, and that same day the moon was a fortnight old.

What could these ancient chroniclers have been describing? It hardly seems likely that it was the moon. Another entry from the *Laud Chronicle*, written *circa* AD 1108, states:

> On the fifth day of May the Moon appeared in the evening shining brightly, and afterwards little by little its light waned, so that as soon as it was night it was so completely extinguished that neither light, nor circle, nor anything at all could be seen of it: and so it remained until almost daybreak when it appeared at the full and shining. On this same day it was a fortnight old. All night the sky was very clear, and the stars over all the heaven were shining brightly.

One can only wonder if the chronicler had been at the 'moonshine' produced in many monasteries in those days. To do otherwise is to give rise to speculations of a very disturbing kind. What was the moon doing: suffering from celestial schizophrenia in one case, and fading out completely in the other? What, in fact, were the chroniclers describing? Rare, never to be repeated, natural occurrences – or something else?

A report – perhaps familiar to those who followed the fortunes of the Bermuda Triangle – is the one given by no less a person than

Columbus who, from the deck of the *Santa Maria*, while it was in the vicinity of the 'vexed bermooths', observed 'a light glimmering at a great distance'. He apparently was impressed enough by it to call one of the crew to witness it with him. The light was observed to disappear and reappear several times during the course of the night. What was it? At this remove in time, your guess is as good as anybody else's. The point is that anomalous lights in the sky were spotted and documented by competent observers well before there was any black technology to blame them on.

Returning to Europe, in particular to France in the ninth century, it seems from his writings that Agobard, an archbishop at that time, was witness to the return of 'abductees'. Three men and one woman were seen to alight from an 'aerial ship'. They were immediately surrounded by an angry mob, from whom the intervention of Agobard delivered them. The strangers were compatriots who all claimed to have been carried off by 'miraculous men' who had shown them 'unheard of marvels' – hence the antagonism of the crowd. Obviously the fate of 'abductees' at the hands of their fellow humans has not changed all that much over eleven centuries.

THE CHINA–TIBET BORDER

This area has always been a hotbed of anomalous events: a land filled with demons and other non-human creatures, and the preserve of that most enigmatic of individuals, Rigden Jyepo, King of the World and ruler of the Hidden Kingdom of Schamballah. Little wonder, then, that it too has its undeniable ufological affiliations. Allegedly, in recent times a group of archaeologists exploring the caves in the Bayan-Kara-Ula region, near the border between China and Tibet, unearthed 716 stone discs, together with material displaying hieroglyphics and various drawings. These apparently dated back thousands of years, and had a very strange tale to tell. The discs, in particular, were the subject of much speculation, as they resembled a modern phonograph record, in that they had a hole in the middle from which a double groove spiralled out to the edge. Fortunately, for everyone's peace of mind, the groove was not a sound-track, but a form of writing which took the archaeologists many years to decipher. Even then, what the discs said was considered so startling that the Peking Academy prevented its publication for some time. Finally, for some inscrutable Chinese reason, the work was published under the title of *The Grooved Script Concerning Spaceships Which As*

Recorded On The Discs Landed On Earth 12000 Years Ago.
Which just about tells it all. Some of the discs were sent to Moscow,
where it was discovered that they contained anomalously large
amounts of cobalt. In part, the text discovered on the discs states:

> The Dropa descended from the clouds in their craft
> while the native Ham people (a Tibetan tribe) hid
> in caves. However when they had communicated
> by sign language they realized that the Dropa
> meant them no harm.

The writings go on to describe the grief of the Dropa at the loss
of their spaceships during a dangerous landing. So it would seem,
in the recovery of these discs, that even 'crash retrieval' is nothing
new. It is also possible that the Dropa were somewhat previous in
their lamentations regarding lost spaceships, if the testimony
contained in the writings of the explorer, mystic and all-round
adventurer, Nicholas Roerich, is to be believed. The story
appeared in his book *Altai Himalaya*, which concerned the
vicissitudes undergone by an expedition he had led into Tibet
during the years 1926–1928. The authenticity of the account is
enhanced by the fact that when the book was first published, the
event recorded in it was seen as merely an 'interesting' occurrence. It was not until the flying-saucer Fifties that the ufological
ramifications inherent in the Roerich sighting were recognized. If
it is that 'one white crow proves that not all crows are black',
then the event witnessed by the Roerich expedition, and recorded
non-committally by him in a book about the expedition, must be
regarded as the white crow of ufology that proves beyond a
shadow of a doubt that there are things flying about the Earth
that have no connection with human technologies. The expedition
consisted of Roerich himself, eight other Europeans and a com-
plement of local guides and bearers. In 1926, while it was crossing
an isolated part of western China, the group camped near Ulan-
Davan. Here, Roerich's attention was drawn to what appeared to
be a 'great black vulture' circling in the sky above the tents. While
watching the vulture, as related by Roerich: 'We notice something
shiny, flying very high from the north-east to the south.' Unable
to resolve the matter satisfactorily with the naked eye: 'We bring
three powerful field glasses and watch the huge spheroid body
shining in the sun, clearly visible against the blue sky and moving
very fast.'

This recourse to technology did little to demystify the matter, and
as they were watching, the object abruptly changed the direction of
its flight to south-west, and was soon lost to sight. Now this report

has much in common with those that have surfaced since 1947 concerning UFOs. It stresses the size, shape, speed and refractive index of the object observed. Had Roerich made this report today, there is no doubt it would have been immediately classified as an encounter with a 'daylight disc'. The files of ufology are stuffed to capacity with similar reports, the majority of which, like Roerich's, are without convincing explanation. In fact, the Roerich report conforms to the most stringent requirements of modern ufology, in that it was a multiple-witness report by credible witnesses whose observations were aided by the use of powerful binoculars. At the time, no attempt was made to interpret the sighting in accordance with any scientific hypothesis. However, as Roerich's narrative goes on to explain, there was an explanation, of sorts, forthcoming. Just before the observation, the expedition had been joined by a group of Lamas, also heading for Tibet, who informed the startled Europeans that what they had all been watching was: 'The sign of Schamballah.'

To us, and perhaps even to the members of Roerich's expedition, this must seem like invoking a mystery to explain an enigma. However, it does at least demonstrate that the Lamas were sufficiently familiar with this kind of celestial event to identify it confidently in terms of their cultural consensus reality. Once again, it seems evident that the solution to the modern UFO mystery might lie in the past, rather than in the future.

THE FLYING MACHINES OF OLD ATLANTIS

There are some doubts as to whether or not Atlantis ever existed, at least in its 'fabulous' form. Nevertheless, there are many myths and legends about an ancient civilization that got a bit too clever for its own good, and for whatever reason, it has come to be known to students of ancient mysteries as Atlantis. And many are the legends about its technological prowess. W Scott Elliott, in his book *The Story of Atlantis*, describes Atlantean flying machines, called Vimanas, as being made of wood or metal. The wooden ones had a substance injected into the thin wood to give it a leather-like toughness. When metal was used, it was an alloy of two white-coloured metals and one red metal. The legends indicate that these Vimanas were self-luminescent. Also, the description of their movement through the atmosphere is interesting. The author writes: 'The course of their flight never being in a straight line, but always in the form of long waves, now approaching and now receding from the Earth.' Like a saucer skipped over water? It might also be likened to those modern descriptions of UFO movements that use 'falling leaf', or 'pendulum-like' to describe the motion of the object reported. Concerning this kind of 'Vimanic' motion, I will now recount two incidents of which I have personal knowledge, which include descriptions of the kind of movement attributed to Vimanas, as well as similar elements of self-luminescence.

The first occurred in 1958. One evening I received a phone call from a woman who asked if I would speak with her 16-year-old daughter. Apparently, the daughter had seen a 'craft' that had frightened the wits out of her. So frightened was she, as I later discovered, that she had not spoken a word since the morning after her strange experience. From what I know of teenage girls, I find this silence even more remarkable than the existence of flying saucers. On the following Monday I went to see the young lady in question. She lived with her mother, five storeys up, in a high-rise in Salford, Lancashire. Seeing where she lived, with the view it commanded, I expected to be given a report that would probably be amenable to an explanation involving the aircraft that fly in and out of Manchester Airport. In the event, whatever it was that she saw, it certainly wasn't a conventional aircraft. After the introductions, I learned of the girl's strange silence since the time she had viewed the object, and it was with some difficulty I got her to recount the details of her experience to me. Apparently, the previous Friday night, or to be more precise at 3.50 a.m. of the Saturday morning, she had awoken and gone to the toilet. As she was getting back into bed, she became aware of a high-pitched whine coming from outside. Curious (a typical teenage trait), she went to the window and looked out. I don't know what it was she expected to see, but what she did see frightened the wits out of her. At the base of the block opposite, she saw 'on the ground' a 'circular craft'. The object was luminescent, but two brighter 'orange' lights could be seen shining from underneath it. As she watched, it took off, 'wobbling like a pendulum'. It proceeded straight up the side of the flats, its movement steadying the higher it rose. When it reached the top, it tilted slightly and took off at speed in the direction of a nearby main road, and was lost to her view. Alone, this girl's testimony would be rejected as a possible phantasmagoria, or waking dream, of some kind, based on the fact that she had experienced it during the hours of sleep. It would have been a fair assumption. We have all taken similar trips to the toilet during the course of the night, and know that we make the necessary journey almost 'in our sleep'. However, in this case, such an explanation is invalidated because I was able to find other witnesses to the object's appearance near the flats. This second observation was made by two boys, aged 7 years and 9 years respectively, who had been camping out that night. (Camping out in the middle of a built-up area? The behaviour of small boys is even more of a mystery to me than that of teenage girls.) From where they were camped, they could see the high-rise in question, and told me that they saw 'this big light go up into the sky from the foot of that skyscraper flat. It was round and mixed up with oval.' To the best of my belief and knowledge, the witnesses were unaware of each other's existence, so some kind of juvenile collusion can be ruled out. In any case, I am certain the girl's 'fear reaction' was genuine; her mother's understandable anxiety certainly was.

The second incident came to my attention in October 1984, when I received a letter from man living in Norwich in which he wrote about an object which had allegedly been photographed at Tacolneston. The description he gave was of a large, circular craft with 16 red lights around its top periphery and which, as it sped away, noticeably wobbled from side to side – a movement that increased as it passed a nearby radio mast. Once beyond this possible source of man-made interference, it soon steadied itself, and disappeared into the distance. It is only an assumption on the part of the witness that the craft's wobble was caused by the radio waves emanating from the mast. If the report has any validity, it seems more likely that, like the object near the flats in Salford, its wobble was caused by the engaging of the means of its propulsion, as it was evident to witnesses before the craft came near the radio mast.

VIMANAS IN ANCIENT INDIA

If indeed the Vimana is an Atlantean device, then it seems certain from several ancient sources that it was probably manufactured under licence in ancient India. Sanskrit texts are filled with references to gods who fought battles in the sky using Vimanas equipped with weapons as deadly as any we can deploy in these more enlightened times. For example, there is a passage in the *Ramayana* which reads:

> The Puspaka car that resembles the Sun and belongs to my brother was brought by the powerful Ravan; that aerial and excellent car going everywhere at will . . . that car resembling a bright cloud in the sky.

The narrative continues:

> . . . and the King [Rama] got in, and the excellent
> car at the command of the Raghira, rose up into the
> higher atmosphere.

The translation of these ancient texts by Maharishi Bharadwaja is unambiguously entitled *Aeronautics*. Published by the International Academy of Sanskrit Research, in Mysore, India, it is described as 'a manuscript from the prehistoric past'.

In the *Mahabharatra*, an ancient Indian poem of enormous length, we learn that an individual named Asura Maya had a Vimana measuring twelve cubits in circumference, with four strong wheels. The poem is a veritable mine of information relating to conflicts between gods who settled their differences apparently using weapons as lethal as the ones we are capable of deploying. Apart from 'blazing missiles', the poem records the use of other equally deadly weapons. 'Indra's Dart' operated via a circular 'reflector'. When switched on, it produced a 'shaft of light' which, when focused on any target, immediately 'consumed it with its power'. In one particular exchange, the hero, Krishna, is pursuing his enemy, Salva, in the sky, when Salva's Vimana, the *Saubha* is made invisible in some way. Undeterred, Krishna immediately fires off a special weapon: 'I quickly laid on an arrow, which killed by seeking out sound' – a variation on our own heat-seeking missiles? Many other terrible weapons are described, quite matter of factly, in the *Mahabharata*, but the most fearsome of all is the one used against the Vrishis. The narrative records:

> Gurkha flying in his swift and powerful Vimana
> hurled against the three cities of the Vrishis and
> Andhakas a single projectile charged with all the
> power of the Universe. An incandescent column of
> smoke and fire, as brilliant as ten thousand suns,
> rose in all its splendour. It was the unknown
> weapon, the Iron Thunderbolt, a gigantic
> messenger of death which reduced to ashes the
> entire race of the Vrishnis and Andhakas.

The after-effects of this Iron Thunderbolt have an ominously recognizable ring. Apparently, those killed by it were so burnt that their corpses were unidentifiable. The survivors fared little better, as it caused their hair and nails to fall out. Could these incredibly old documents really be describing a prehistoric pre-emptive nuclear strike? For those who would comfort themselves with the notion that these accounts are a form of prehistoric fable or science fiction, it is as well to remember that our own science fiction did not emerge until there was science on which to base its speculations, and that these days science *fact* has outstripped science *fiction*. We now have our own Indra's Dart (the laser), Vimanas (attack aircraft), Iron Thunderbolt (nuclear bomb) and 'smart' weapons capable of seeking out their own targets by various programmed methods of identification. It all makes the old adage about 'nothing new under the sun' take on a whole new meaning. Perhaps the most disturbing, and challenging, information about these allegedly mythical Vimanas in the ancient records is that there are some matter-of-fact records describing how to build one. In their way, the instructions are quite precise; it is not the fault of the ancient writers if our own technology is still not at a sufficiently advanced stage for advantage to be taken of their instructions. In the Sanskrit *Samarangana Sutradhara*, it is written:

> Strong and durable must the body of the Vimana be made, like a great flying bird of light material. Inside one must put the mercury engine with its iron heating apparatus underneath. By means of the power latent in the mercury which sets the driving whirlwind in motion, a man sitting inside may travel a great distance in the sky. The movements of the Vimana are such that it can vertically ascend, vertically descend, move slanting forwards or backwards. With the help of the machines human beings can fly in the air and heavenly beings can come down to earth.

According to other, equally ancient, texts, the Vimanas could travel to the solar regions (*Surymandala*), or even out to the stellar regions (*Naksatramandala*). As a matter of interest, the word Vimana is still in colloquial use in India: it now means aircraft; perhaps it always did. Even more startling, there is a very ancient document which apparently describes, in technical rather than mythical terms, the materials and method of constructing a 'flying saucer'. It is one of two written relics from 7,000 years ago. Drawing on data given in an article by Y N Iban Aharon, authoritative scholar in ethnology, arch-aeology and early civilizations, we learn that one of the documents, the *Hakatha* (Laws of the Babylonians) states quite unambiguously:

> The privilege of operating a flying machine is great. The knowledge of flight is among the most ancient of our inheritances. A gift from 'those from upon high'. We received it from them as a means of saving many lives.

More fantastic still is the information given in the ancient Chaldean work, *The Sifrala*, which contains over one hundred pages of technical details on building a flying machine. It contains words which translate as graphite rod, copper coils, crystal indicator, vibrating spheres, stable angles, etc.: none of which would seem out of place if found in a modern non-fiction technical manual.

For those who care to look with their eyes open, the evidence tending to indicate that some form of flying machine existed in ancient times is overwhelming, going far beyond mere coincidence. There are two Tibetan books, the *Tantjua* and the *Kantjua*, in which specific references to prehistoric flying machines can be found. In these texts they are described as 'Pearls-in-the-Sky'. And it can only be seen as synchronous that many who witnessed the 'Dancing Sun' at Fatima in 1917 described it as looking as if made of mother of pearl. Perhaps, equally evidential, is the religious document, *The Sophia*, preserved in the St Petersburg National Library, which refers to a process whereby 'God' keeps in touch with his 'Angels' when they are not in his presence. The process described can hardly be considered miraculous, in view of our own global telecommunications technology. Apparently, according to information in *The Sophia*:

> An Angel has a projection above his eyes where a sacred cloud rests. He also has a thing that receives sounds on his head where he receives an order where to go from his Lord. He also looks at the mirror in his hand and gets in the mirror something on which an instruction from God is given.

Where do you suppose the ancients, who according to orthodox archaeology had no technological knowledge, got the idea that some kind of hardware would be necessary for a supposedly omnipresent, all-knowing, all-seeing deity to keep in touch with his minions? These days the word miracle is often used in the context of our own technology. Perhaps it was just the same in the days of the ancients and that, without technology of some kind, no miracles are possible.

FLYING SAUCERS IN THE BIBLE

No review of ancient ufology would be complete without at least one good look at Biblical material. This one document alone has sufficient material to convince that something occurred in the distant past that begs a better explanation than 'personification of natural forces'. Put yourself in the place of an individual living in the days of the Old Testament, and ask yourself how you would describe even the products of our own technology using the descriptive metaphors available to you? The only things available to you for comparison would be the various animals you had seen, and celestial objects like the sun, moon and stars, with the occasional bolide and comet, and phenomena like whirlwinds, thunder and lightning, and, of course, clouds. How much more difficult then to describe your sighting of a high-technology flying craft piloted by non-human beings? There are many indeterminate references to possible technological devices in the Old Testament where the object being described is either called the 'Glory' of the Lord or likened to a 'Cloud'. The greatest number of these references appear in the Book of Exodus, in connection with the flight from Egypt of the Jewish people. To understand properly what is meant by these references, we would have had to see for ourselves: something not possible this remove in time. Or is it? In modern ufology, Aime Michel has drawn attention to appearances of what he describes as the 'cloud cigar', which, from descriptions extant, would seem to resemble a large cylinder-like craft hidden within a cloud, possibly of its own creating as a means to camouflage. Also, at Fatima, during the series of 'apparitions' that took place in 1917, the one constant phenomenon, viewed by all who were at the site, was the appearance of a 'cloud' that took station over the holm oak over which the Blessed Virgin Mary was allegedly seen by the main percipients. The connection of UFOs to clouds is further enhanced by modern reports, such as the one given by Aime Michel in *The Truth About Flying Saucers*. In May 1950, the 20th to be exact, Professor Hall of the Lowell Observatory, Massachussetts, observed, both with the naked eye and through binoculars, a 'silvery disc'. The object sighted was strange enough, but Professor Hall also told of how it apparently used a cloud as a form of camouflage, writing that it was 'surrounded by a white froth like whipped cream'. The assumption must be that, as this 'froth' accompanied the object in its manoeuvres, it was something generated by the object itself, either as a deliberate attempt at camouflage, or as a by-product of whatever system propelled it. Even so, the possibility of an airborne technology similar, and perhaps superior, to that presently extant in this closing decade of the twentieth century will not gain easy acceptance merely by pointing up strongly coincidental material. It does not matter that our own airborne devices, from Shuttle to commercial aircraft, also produce cloud-like phenomena: condensation trails in the case of high-flying planes, and anyone who has seen a Space

Shuttle launch will know what I am referring to. In view of this 'will to disbelief' on the part of sceptics, perhaps it is more likely to convince if I now draw attention to one particular Biblical reference, the study of which by a modern scientist has enabled him to take out several patents on the strength of it. I refer, of course, to Joseph F Blumrich and his technological interpretation of the object reported by Ezekiel. As an engineer at NASA who had spent most of his life designing rockets, including the gigantic Saturn V, Blumrich was naturally sceptical that the material in the Bible represented any description of anything that was 'objectively real'. He, therefore, set out to debunk scientifically such material, and chose the Ezekiel account as the one most suited to a scientific hatchet job. In the event, the opposite occurred and he became convinced that Ezekiel, despite his pre-scientific terminology, was indeed describing an actual object. Blumrich 'reconstructed' the said object from its Biblical description, and in passing, obtained several patents from the design. Even more persuasive of Blumrich's reconstructive accuracy is the description of the object allegedly seen by Cash and Landrum – the similarity extending even to the probable method of propulsion. It is also somewhat convincingly coincidental that, although Ezekiel's description of what he saw has been interpreted by others over the years according to their particular bent, it took a modern-day scientist steeped in the technology of our era to recognize it for what it really was and to produce patentable ideas from the narrative.

Moving on to the New Testament, there are many episodes which are amenable to a ufological interpretation. However, the most piquant of these must be the 'star' that announced the birth of Jesus to the 'three wise men'. Theology points out that magi is a name for astrologers and magicians with which the world abounded at that time, and that, therefore, the 'star' was probably an unusual astrological conjunction of some sort, if indeed it was anything at all. However, it can be argued that such a conjunction would have been equally visible to the astrologers employed by Herod, and he would not, therefore, have needed to rely on the three wandering magi for his information. The Bible narrative clearly indicates that the 'star' moved: not as the other fixed heavenly bodies do, but under its own steam, to 'come to rest' above the birthplace of Jesus. A fifteenth-century Russian translation of an even more ancient document states that this 'star' was watched by many astronomers/astrologers in many Eastern countries, and that one particular night it lit up the whole sky as though it were the sun. It goes on to reveal that this 'star' then hung over Mount Vans for a complete day, after which it landed on the mountain like an eagle. It is alleged that those texts also refer to others which go so far as to claim that Christ 'came down' from that 'star'. This would seem quite probable if we are to believe the New Testament when it says that Christ returned to 'heaven' in a 'cloud'.

UNIDENTIFIED FLYING OBJECTS IN RELIGIOUS PAINTINGS

Perhaps disturbingly, there is a, presently unadmitted, interface between religion, particularly Christianity, and the UFO phenomenon. Without taking an intransigent stand either way, I would now draw attention to the anomalous, and very flying saucer-like images that have appeared, for no apparent reason, in paintings of religious themes. The most evidential of these come from Renaissance times, and all are extant to this day in various venues, where they can be viewed. The question that these images pose is not whether or not spaceships were abroad in those days, but why – out of all the other anomalies they could have included in their paintings – did these artists choose the only one that would be recognizable as a flying saucer in the twentieth century? Coincidence hardly covers it. Of particular interest in this context is a fresco in the Dechany Monastery, in former Yugoslavia, which apparently depicts angels, not with wings, but looking as if they are the pilots of some unknown type of craft. The monastery was built in the early part of the fourteenth century and had to wait until the Yugoslav magazine *Svet* published photos of the frescoes (with the legend 'Spaceships on the Dechany Crucifix, Sputniks in our frescoes') to achieve international notoriety. And yet again, it has to be pointed out that the world had to wait for the advent of modern space technology, and the concomitant expansion of ideas, before images left by our pre-scientific ancestors could be given a less than supernatural interpretation. It is enough to make one wonder about how much that has heretofore been taken as fiction might in the end turn out to be fact.

An example of fiction that did turn out to be fact is the information contained in Jonathan Swift's account of one of Gulliver's travels. While most readers will be familiar with his adventures in Lilliput and Brobdinag, as these are the two stories which have been told and retold in the various media, they may be unaware that a third travel, to a place called Laputa, was recounted by Swift, and that it is in this account that synchronously ufological material can be found. The story opens with Gulliver sighting a 'flying circular

Table 1 Tables demonstrating Jonathan Swift's amazing accuracy when describing the Martian moons.

PLANET	No.	DISTANCE	NAME	FOUND
VENUS	0			
EARTH	1	384,405	MOON	BC
MARS	?			
JUPITER	4	421,600	Io	1610
		670,800	Europa	1610
		1,070,000	Ganymede	1610
		1,882,000	Callisto	1610
SATURN	5	294,500	Tethys	1684
		377,400	Dione	1684
		526,700	Rhea	1672
		1,221,000	Titan	1655
		3,558,400	Iapetus	1671

Having the above data, and if one wanted to give Mars some moons in a fictional story, then it would be no surprise to put a figure of two into the above table, although a figure of three would not be amiss. However, what to put for the distance of the moons from the planet? Based on the above table, which was all he had to go on, Swift should have picked distances between say 250,000 km to 2 million km. If he had, he would have been totally wrong and out by a factor of 10 to 20 – as the table below shows.

PLANET	No.	DISTANCE	NAME	FOUND
VENUS	0			
EARTH	1	384,405	MOON	BC
MARS	2	9,380	Phobos	1877
		23,500	Deimos	1877
JUPITER	4	421,600	Io	1610
		670,800	Europa	1610
		1,070,000	Ganymede	1610
		1,882,000	Callisto	1610
SATURN	5	294,500	Tethys	1684
		377,400	Dione	1684
		526,700	Rhea	1672
		1,221,000	Titan	1655
		3,558,400	Iapetus	1671

island'. As with its more modern counterparts in ufology, this island is driven by some form of 'magnetic motor'. This strange island lands, and Gulliver is 'abducted'. It is the vehicle, or island, that is named Laputa. One is left to wonder where Swift got the idea of a circular island from. There are no circular islands on the earth from which he could have drawn his inspiration. Even more mystifying is the information he got from the inhabitants of this strange island in the sky regarding the moons of Mars.

We all now know that Mars has two moons, but these were not discovered by Asaph Hall until 1877, there being no telescopes powerful enough until then. As Swift's account was published in 1726, 151 years before Asaph Hall's discovery, we are left to wonder where Swift got his information. It was not just a matter of a lucky guess, as the information was too exact. The Laputians told Gulliver that the Martian moons orbited the parent planet at three and five diameters respectively. Swift calculated the orbits and came up with figures of 16,970 km (10,521 miles), and 30,152 km (18,694 miles). The actual figures are 9,380 km (5,816 miles), and 23,500 km (14,570 miles). But it has to be remembered that Swift was working from the figure for the Martian diameter known in 1726, which was inaccurate. By comparing the two sets of figures, it can be suspected that had Swift had the correct figure to work with, his results would have been even more startling. Was this book of *Gulliver's Travels* faction, and was Swift the beneficiary of knowledge gleaned from an actual encounter with aliens? The speculation will be unacceptable to the modern scientific mentality, yet the synchronicity remains, and is compounded if it is taken in the context of the other writings referred to in this chapter.

So, where does that leave us in regard to the modern UFO phenomenon? Can any insights be gleaned from reassessing ancient and legendary material? Fanciful though some of these accounts might appear to present-day readers, it must be stressed that this is no reason to dismiss them out of hand. With the upsurge of human science, they seem infinitely less fanciful today than they were even 50 years ago. Someday the future might look back in astonishment at our pre-scientific superstition that there were no such things as flying saucers.

BIBLIOGRAPHY

Adamski, G and Leslie, D   *Flying Saucers Have Landed* (Werner Laurie, 1953)

Barclay, D   *Fatima: A Close Encounter of the Worst Kind?* (Mark Saunders, 1987)

Blumrich, J   *Spaceships of Ezekiel* (Corgi, 1974)

Dione, R   *God Drives a Flying Saucer* (Corgi, 1973)

Downing, B   *Flying Saucers in the Bible* (Lippincott, 1968)

Drake, R   *Gods and Spacemen* series (Sphere, 1974–76)

Drake, R   *Cosmic Continents* (Sphere, 1986)

Evans, H   *UFOs: The Greatest Mystery* (Albany Books, 1979)

Jessup, M   *UFOs and the Bible* (Citadel Press, 1956)

O'Brien, B J & C   *The Genius of the Few* (Turnstone, 1985)

Scott Elliott, W   *Story of Atlantis* (Theosophical Press, 1954)

Stemman, R   *Visitors From Outer Space* (Aldus Books, 1979)

Story, R   *Encyclopedia of UFOs* (NEL, 1980)

Swift, J   *Gulliver's Travels* (1726)

Temple, R   *The Sirius Mystery* (Sidgwick & Jackson, 1976)

Thomas, P   *Flying Saucers Through the Ages* (Spearman, 1965)

Trench, B leP   *The Eternal Subject* (Spearman, 1973)

Vallee, J   *Passport to Magonia* (Regenery, 1969)

CHAPTER THREE

THE PSYCHO-SOCIOLOGY OF UFOLOGY

K W C Phillips B.Ed., B.A.

It has been pointed out, much to the chagrin of any number of ufologists, that what is being studied are *reports* of UFOs – not UFOs in their own right. This is still as true today as it has ever been during the past frustrating 40 years or so. Even in those most 'physical' of cases which have been interminably dissected in the interim by both military and civilian UFO groups set up to study the bewildering nature of the UFO enigma, ambiguities and contradictions are omnipresent. The Delphos (Kansas, USA) case exemplifies this dilemma. Indeed, those scientists who were brave enough to risk their reputations by studying the ground residue which, according to the witnesses, was caused by a close encounter (CE), hovering UFO, did, in fact, find chemical anomalies in the soil samples taken from the Delphos site. One of those scientists, Dr Errol Faruk, who at that time was an organic chemist at Nottingham University, in England, almost compromised his credibility when he concluded from the samples he had studied that the allegedly mysterious ring formed at the site had: 'either got to be of biological origin, something like a fungal ring, or its got to be an authentic case.'[1]

Many more such cases could be cited to confuse the issue further, but suffice it to say that any really inexplicable UFO report is usually characterized by its strangeness, its ambiguity, and its elusiveness in terms of susceptibility to scholarly investigation. In addition to this triple categorization, it can be shown that the UFO phenomenon has a religious, historic and folkloric dimension, the implications of which are only just beginning to be appreciated by those who are willing to sift the evidence. It would appear that there is more to the UFO phenomenon than is accounted for in any simplistic extraterrestrial hypothesis. Moreover, by inspection of the tens of thousands of reports from all over the world, it would seem that – paradoxically – while the UFO phenomenon gives every indication of being impossibly remote from us, at the same time it displays facets that indicate that it is intimately close.

Given that the foregoing declaration is valid, and we conclude correctly that there has never been any meaningful funding and resourcing of UFO research at the scientific level (leaving aside the largely discredited Condon Committee of 1969, the results from which ostensibly ended official interest in ufology in America, and the *public* records of which were eventually destroyed), then it is hardly surprising that no progress has been made in understanding the UFO phenomenon. Given the public attitudes of contemporary Establishment science, which will be discussed later, it is highly unlikely that any real attempt will be made to enlarge our understanding of the mystery in the foreseeable future. The prevailing 'scientific' attitude seems to be: 'It can't be – therefore it isn't'. Given the ongoing intellectual attrition these factors generate in ufology, is it any wonder that our understanding of UFOs is virtually *nil*? Despised and ridiculed by science as being 'unscientific', misrepresented and abused by media 'silly season' journalism, and totally ignored by society at large, it should come as no surprise to learn that ufology (the amateur and unofficial study of UFO reports by mostly unqualified individuals) is largely a matter of intransigent attitudes confronting unwarranted assumptions. Apparently only the UFO witnesses are able to really sit and ponder the meaning of what has happened to them. Furthermore, due to the ambiguity and absurdity endemic in the subject, even those in the 'softer' disciplines of psychology, sociology and theology regard the subject with indifference. These, and all the other vested interests, dismiss the subject of UFOs by that age-old and most effective method: devastating ridicule.

Despite this rather depressing prognosis, the UFO phenomenon continues to persist, with no real sign of abatement. So, why is it then, given its pandemic omnipresence, we have failed to take up the challenge and carry out a thorough and systematic appraisal on an ongoing basis in order to relieve future generations of the onerous task of starting from the beginning? Is the Scientific Study of Unidentified Flying Objects (the Condon Committee) carried out at the University of Colorado, and which expended the princely sum of $300,000 on its now discredited efforts, going to be the sum total of scientific endeavours to confront this mystery?

Whatever happened to scientific curiosity? The answer is simplicity itself: scientists are as vulnerable as anyone to the socially destabilizing effects of ridicule, and very few of them are going to risk compromising their scientific credibility (or their research grants) by seeming to take seriously a subject that has been designated non-science by their peers. This is not to say that no work is being done; there are some who are doing excellent work in field research and investigation. Two British researchers spring to mind. One is an aerospace engineer, Roy Dutton, who has apparently developed a testable 'UFO Global Circle Hypothesis', the parameters of which, it is claimed, determine the extraterrestrial nature of the UFOs.[2] Even if one is unable to accept Dutton's conclusions, surely, if the hypothesis is testable, it should be scientifically tested? The other researcher is Paul Devereux who, together with colleagues, has developed an equally testable hypothesis which demonstrates that UFOs are primarily a light phenomenon generated by seismic activity. Forgetting for one moment the paradoxes and ambiguities which will inevitably occur when one applies phenomena to any theoretical model, based on the foregoing observations, it goes without saying that UFO characteristics will readily adapt themselves to both these hypotheses, even though, logically, they both can't be right, since their respective concepts seem mutually exclusive. After all, it was this sort of duality that made a universal description of the nature of light so difficult to define. The dichotomy was that light was either a particle or a wave, and for a time those two concepts seemed irreconcilable. Well, as we now know, the paradox proved itself, and it's now accepted that light possesses *both* characteristics! Which is no big deal, as it has now been discovered that so do other, heavier moving objects: for instance snooker balls, but their wave motion is so small as to be undetectable by the human eye. How is it then that two such diligent and perceptive researchers as Dutton and Devereux – as well as dozens of others equally diligent and perceptive who have developed such wide-ranging hypotheses as birth trauma and ball lightning to explain UFOs – have ended up on extreme ends of the spectrum of conclusions when they are all drawing their inspiration from the same phenomenon? The answer would seem to be that both researchers (as well as the others) have elements of truth in their philosophies, but seem to lack essential data in one or more essential areas that would give their work a universal (dual) application.

It was this apparently missing data (which seemed to be the underlying reason for the generation of paradoxes within the respective hypotheses) that, in the 1980s, stimulated an Austrian UFO researcher, Dr Alex Keul, to search for these crucial yet elusive factors. Like so many others in the field, he too had come up against the same frustrations instigated by the seemingly dual nature of the UFO. Because Dr Keul's formal education was Vienna-based he, like many other researchers there, was influenced by the psycho-analytical school of thought. It was somewhat fashionable in those days (and still is in certain circles) to apply psychological hypotheses to the phenomenon of UFOs. Naturally, because the phenomenon is riddled with ambiguities and absurdities, and causes such peculiar reactions within certain sectors of society, the conditions became ripe, if one leaves out the embarrassing physical paradoxes, for the evidence to mount up gradually to the point where it seemed to indicate unequivocally that everyone who saw UFOs was crazy! In other words, as in every other country in the world, reductionism reigns supreme. Nevertheless, although Dr Keul was a meteorologist, and was thus firmly grounded in the physical sciences, he could not ignore some of the salient mental factors outlined in the psychological hypothesis: to have done so would have devalued some important research work in this field. It was at this point in his career that Dr Keul switched from a hard, physical science to the softer science of psychology and eventually settled in an academic career in this field, based at Salzburg University. In the early 1980s in Salzburg, Dr Keul began to ponder about the psychological factors of the UFO experience but, like his colleagues in Vienna, he began to reduce the solution to the whole phenomenon to everyone being crazy! This conclusion was incompatible with the trans-cultural and omnipresent nature of the UFO phenomenon, as well as, of course, those awkward physical characteristics. Yet, the more he looked into the psychology of the UFO witness, the more he began to realize that there was something 'different' about them. Was it, perhaps, some form of aberrant enculturation which was causing all these UFO reports? Or was it some Jungian archetype arising from the collective unconscious of mankind? However, such theories had been mooted before, yet the physical paradoxes still remained; thus there had to be some factor that was being overlooked.

Now, as already mentioned, Dr Keul himself was a reconciliation of opposites, a duality, in that he had been schooled in both the hard and the soft sciences. So, with hindsight, it now seems inevitable that he should begin to apply the two disciplines to the problem of the UFO in order to develop a working model which interfaced the physical environment of the UFO event with the inner world of the UFO percipient. In other words, he now saw the problem in terms of a mind versus physical environment hiatus caused by our cultural grounding in Descartian principles which, simply put, means that we consider the external world and the internal world of the human mind as two separate and unrelated entities: one is 'real' and the other 'imaginary'. According to this model, mind could never influence matter, or vice versa. Or could it? The more he studied the reports, the more Dr Keul began to notice bizarre factors which couldn't be put down to mere chance alone. These factors, overlooked by most researchers, included, among other things, strange synchronicities and odd out-of-place events reported by the witnesses which seemed to indicate that there was a deeper level of meaning to the UFO experience. Therefore, seeing these oddities and applying them to the whole of the mind–environment model, Dr Keul slowly began to work on the missing element in all the various and contradictory reports which came to his attention and, in so doing, came to the somewhat shocking conclusion that the missing factor was *the human witnesses*: that is, we knew next to nothing about them, let alone the enigmatic UFOs they were wont to report in large numbers. Even more fundamentally, we knew nothing of the void between the witness and the object perceived.

When Dr Keul came to Britain in 1981, he outlined his plans for a detailed and comprehensive witness study, which he called the Anamnesis Protocol (*anamnesis* being the Greek for life memory).[3] He argued that, even in the most classic and inexplicable cases, we still knew next to nothing about the witness(es) or, indeed, their life history. To illustrate this problem, a brief reference is made here to the ambiguous Delphos case, mentioned earlier. In this instance, we have both a full description of the event as told by the witnesses to the investigators at the actual location of the alleged UFO event, as well as a detailed analysis by qualified scientists of the chemical composition of the residue claimed to have been left by the object at the landing site. However, apart from the fact that the witnesses were a seemingly sincere farming family living in the mid-western state of Kansas, we know practically nothing about them, or their life histories. More importantly, we know nothing about their post-UFO-event lives!

Consequently, in order to explore the 'unidentified witness', a pilot scheme, using the Anamnesis Protocol was carried out by Dr Keul in both his home state and in the Bedfordshire–Buckingham-shire area of the Home Counties in England during 1981–82. The results of this study were later evaluated by him and, noting the apparently close parallels between both sets of witnesses, he decided to introduce a modified version of the Anamnesis in 1984. The Protocol proved to be an outstanding success in the witness-study field, but the unexpected and additional bonus was that it was readily accepted by witnesses as being meaningful to their experience. Thus it was both an effective reporting medium, as well as a sympathetic *counselling method* – the latter being of particular value in CE cases where the witness suffers severe post-event trauma. Encouraged by this initial success, the Protocol was modified in 1987, in order to cope with developing theories, and again in 1990, after the intermediate version had been applied to other countries, notably in South America and Germany. Despite this success, it is timely here to remind the reader that this method of investigation does not make a study of UFOs as objects (whatever one conceives them to be) but of the *witness within the UFO experience*. So what, in the final analysis, does it show? Table 2 should help to indicate the overall perspective.

To enable the reader to obtain a firm grasp of the overall witness profile, it is first necessary to ignore all non-significant and moderately significant figures (i.e. those figures which are roughly in line with the results obtained from the control sample). Given this remit, we shall concentrate on those areas where there was a significant, positive response and relegate the remaining data to the 'quiescent' aspects of the witnesses' lives. Let us now select these salient points and see what we come up with in terms of profiling the life of CE/UFO witnesses.

From this approach it can be seen that the strongest and most persistent characteristic to emerge is that the overwhelming majority, 12/3 (12 out of 15), of witnesses surveyed gave a high incidence of self-reported ESP phenomena; in many cases these reports went right back to early childhood (leaving aside for one moment the results of those persons tested who reported ostensible 'psychic' phenomena to the Association for the Study of Anamolous Phenomena [ASSAP, second column], since this would not be surprising in the least). Moreover, since this early study was computed, this ESP factor was found to be omnipresent and to a much more profound degree *in those cases where very close approaches of anomalous objects were said to have occurred*! Sometimes, it is even present in the more distant approaches, but at much weaker intensity. Hence we can now construct our first hypothesis from the Anamnesis data, tabled on the next page.

Table 2 Evaluation of the British Anamnesis Project, June 1987

NUMBER OF CASES	CE UFO n=15	ESP n=15	CONTROL n=10
CASES UNDER 3 YEARS	2	12	N/A
FEMALE/MALE	9/6	10/5	6/4
AGE RANGE: UNDER 20	1	0	2
20–29	6	2	3
30–39	3	8	1
40–49	1	4	3
50–59	4	1	0
OVER 60	0	0	1
NON-INTACT FAMILY ORIGIN (BROKEN HOME)	5	7	1
'UPROOTED' (MOVED HOME >5 TIMES)	7	5	4
SIBLINGS >3	2	2	1
EMPLOYMENT: MANUAL	3	4	2
OFFICE	3	3	2
SELF-EMPLOYED	0	1	1
HOUSEWIFE	2	2	0
STUDENT	0	0	2
UNEMPLOYED	7[1]	4	2
RETIRED	0	0	1
SICK/INVALID	0	1	0
SATISFIED WITH HOUSING/NOT	4/3	9/2	10/0
SATISFIED WITH WORK OR STUDIES/NOT (CUMULATIVE)	2/13[4]	6/9[3]	8/2
MARITAL STATUS: SINGLE	5	7	4
MARRIED	4	6	4
COHABITING	5	0	0
DIVORCE	0	1	1
WIDOWED	1	1	1

NUMBER OF CASES	CE UFO n=15	ESP n=15	CONTROL n=10
CHILDREN: NONE	8	8	5
1–2	5	4	4
3–5	1	3	1
6+	1	0	0
SATISFIED WITH FAMILY OR SOCIAL LIFE/NOT	3/6	7/5	9/1
NO CLOSE FRIENDS	2	2	0
CLUB, SOCIAL MEMBER	6/3	5/6	5/5
SATISFIED WITH CASH SITUATION/NOT	2/5	6/5	5/5
SERIOUS ILLNESS OR HANDICAP	6	3	1
INSOMNIA	6	5	4
DREAM RECALL	14[3]	13[2]	5
FLYING/UFO DREAMS RECALLED	8[4]	6[1]	1
NIGHTMARES	5	9	6
VIGILANCE MINIMUM IN THE EVENING	3	4	2
'HABIT BREAKING' BEFORE OBSERVATION	6	2	N/A
ACCIDENT PRONENESS	5	2	3
'LIFE EVENT' AROUND OBSERVATION TIME	4	4	N/A
RELIGIOUS/MYSTICAL EXPERIENCES	5	7[1]	2
MEANING TO LIFE	9	10	6
MEDICAL TREATMENT FOR SEVERE REASON	5	9[1]	3
TAKING DRUGS FOR ILLNESS	4	1	1

NUMBER OF CASES	CE UFO n=15	ESP n=15	CONTROL n=10
NON-RIGHT-HANDED	3	1	2
WEAR SPECTACLES	8	8	6
HEALTH: DEPRESSION NERVOUSNESS DIZZINESS FAINTING FITS HIGH/LOW BLOOD PRESSURE	3 7[3] 1 1 1 3	5 7[3] 6 2 1 1	3 2 2 3 0 3
OBSERVATION AFTER-EFFECTS	7	7	N/A
NARCOTICS TAKEN	1	0	2
EXPERIENCED ESP/NOT	12/3[4]	14/1[4]	1/9
FAMILY, FRIENDS EXPERIENCED UFO/ESP	6/2[2]	7/3[2]	2/8
MEMBER OF CHURCH OR RELIGIOUS GROUP/NOT	2/13[1]	2/13[1]	3/7
IMPORTANCE OF LIFE SPIRTUALITY	11/3[1]	9/2[1]	6/4
READ UFO BOOKS BEFORE READ SCI-FI BOOKS BEFORE	11[2] 5	7[1] 3	3 6
SUPPORTIVENESS OF FAMILY, FRIENDS WHEN TOLD/NOT TOLD	7/7	4/5	N/A
SELF-MOTIVATED REPORT	9	6	N/A
CHANGE IN LIFE AFTER OBSERVATION	10[2]	4	N/A
PREVIOUS 'PARA-NORMAL' EXPERIENCES	1[3]	8	N/A
INTEREST & BELIEF SYSTEMS/NOT: ASTROLOGY PARAPSYCHOLOGY SPIRITUALISM BERMUDA TRIANGLE ANCIENT ASTRONAUTS ANCIENT CULTURES	 9/2[1] 7/0[1] 6/5[1] 10/1[2] 6/2[1] 7/2[1]	 6/3[1] 10/0[1] 9/2[1] 9/1[2] 2/3[1] 6/8[1]	 3/4 4/1 2/4 2/4 1/4 3/7

NUMBER OF CASES	CE UFO n=15	ESP n=15	CONTROL n=10
NOT SUPERSTITIOUS	13	5	6
NEGATIVE TO CURRENT STATE OF SOCIETY	14	12	8
VISIONS/NONE	5/2[1]	8/2[1]	6/4
HEARD ABOUT UFOS BEFORE OBSERVATION	14[4]	10	N/A
BELIEF IN UFOS FROM OUTER SPACE	6	5	5
BELIEF IN ET LIFE BELIEF IN LIFE AFTER DEATH	7[1] 8[2]	9[2] 9[2]	5 3

[1] – not significant
[2] – slightly significant
[3] – moderately significant
[4] – highly significant

It is appropriate here to mention that, as well as the Anamnesis Protocol being carried out with these early 1980s' cases, the Rorschach Test was also applied, but this latter test had to be abandoned due to the lack of international standards.

Editor's note: We are sure that readers will appreciate that the foregoing table is of necessity a limited exposition of the complexity of the Anamnesis Protocol. Readers wishing more details, or wanting to take part in the Protocol, are invited to contact the editors at the address on page 190.

Hypothesis No. 1

The self-reported ESP proneness of a witness varies according to the 'perceived' distance of the UFO.

The second most positive response given by the witnesses was that a sizeable majority of UFO witnesses, 3/22, suffer from status inconsistency (i.e. dissatisfaction with work, career, interpersonal relationships and studies, etc., or experience career/status 'mismatch' in terms of their inherent intelligence or abilities). In plain English 'status inconsistency' means that a witness feels that he or she has never realized their full potential in life and is therefore at the 'wrong level'. Now, whether this status inconsistency is directly attributable to the UFO experience itself, or its aftermath, or vice versa, is still a matter of debate, but there is strong evidence to show that a witness's ambitions are very often knocked off course through the emergence of 'irrational' forces which seem to be inherent within the UFO experience; sometimes these irrationalities can have a devastating effect on the life of the witness. This second strongest characteristic enables us to formulate our next hypothesis:

Hypothesis No. 2

The status inconsistency of a witness varies inversely according to the 'perceived' distance of the UFO.

The third strongest response was that just over half of the number of witnesses tested claimed to have had UFO/flying dreams. Because this response is not as strong as the first two above, a hypothesis will not be ventured here, except to say that the dreamscapes of CE witnesses need to be studied carefully in all future evaluations of the witnesses's lives.

Could the foregoing hypotheses be said to be testable? Certainly, any wide-scale application of the Anamnesis Protocol should have some validity when testing the above hypotheses, since Anamnesis is a culture-free method of testing and thus, in the fullness of time, should tell us whether or not we have struck gold here. And if the hypothesis does not hold up under strict scrutiny by referees, could it be said that the UFO phenomenon is nothing but an extrasensory phenomenon? Most certainly not! Such a conclusion would once again amount to reductionism (that great slayer of progression): a 'nothing but' syndrome which has often set back the cause of ufology with its blinkered approach and the bending of data to fit whatever paradigm prevails. Such ufological 'square pegs' as the ETH, mirages, ball lightning and the psycho-social hypotheses, to name but four which have emerged over the past 40 years, just come around and go around with no end in sight and simply sweep under the carpet any unwelcome paradox that threatens to dent their theories. In any event, to claim UFOs are nothing but ESP is simply explaining one unknown by invoking another. Nevertheless, from the figures shown in Table 2 and from those gathered from a subsequent and more comprehensive Anamnesis study, *the ESP factor remains dominant* and convincingly shows that, as far as the CE witness is concerned, we do seem to be dealing with a very special subset of human society, but it will only remain convincing once a *wider* study is made of an appropriate sample of non-sighters of UFOs in society.

Perhaps by setting out a brief outline of a case history, I can help the reader to obtain a useful mental snapshot of the UFO experience as perceived through the eyes of the witness, rather than merely looking at a collection of figures. The case is typical of the medium-distance UFO encounter as profiled by the Anamnesis Protocol – and there are many other similar ones. The witness is male, in his late thirties, and now living and working in London as a science teacher at a comprehensive school. He is intelligent, with qualifications in the science/engineering field. He holds no extremist ufological views, and is in no way seeking notoriety or financial gain by disclosing his UFO experiences. In the investigator's view, he is psychologically stable, and were his testimony about anything other than UFOs, there is no doubt it would be taken very seriously indeed by society at large.

JOHN'S STORY

While living on the Isle of Skye, off the coast of Scotland, John witnessed, in the company of three other people, a huge, silver metallic-like, cigar-shaped object passing above the nearby Isle of Rhum, just to the south of Skye. The object came from the direction of Mallaig, on the Scottish mainland, and seemed to pass right over Rhum itself and, as it did so, the witnesses were able to estimate its size. Since, at its widest part, Rhum is nearly eight km (five miles) across, and the witnesses noticed that the object was about one quarter of the island's length, it seemed logical to assume that the object was about one and a half km (one mile) long. The object itself was about ten times as long as it was thick, and along a horizontal section – of a different colour to the main fuselage – there appeared to be portholes emitting a yellow light. The surface of the object appeared very silvery and *reflected the prevailing sunlight very brightly*. It took about ten minutes to go from the mainland to Rhum and, once the island had been reached, the object passed into a cloud. John and his party eagerly awaited its re-emergence but, strangely, this did not happen, and the object was never seen again. With his scientific and technical training, John is now convinced that, on that day, he and his companions were watching the 'product of some form of technology' (*sic*). The details of this sighting – multiple witnesses, incredibly large object, inexplicable disappearance – leave us bereft of a ready explanation. To compound the issue even further, there were no other reports about this encounter from either the local Press or radio, the authorities, such as the police, or the coast guard. But let's look at further strange episodes from John's life.

Ball lightning

While working as a deck-hand with three other crewmen on a fishing boat off the coast of Skye on an overcast day in 1972, John, hearing the winchman, Jim, scream, looked around and saw at the top of the mast that formed the radio aerial a 'ball of lightning'. It was about the size of an orange and of the same colour. It was emitting sizzling/crackling noises and, after a few moments, began to work its way slowly down the mast, across the deckhead of the wheel-house (the boat was listing at the time as the catch was being hauled aboard), down the side of the wheel-house, emitted a 'pop' as it hit the metal gunwale, and finally fizzed as it went into the sea and dissipated. When the crew looked at the side of the boat, they saw that the ball had left a peculiar deposit on the section where it had made contact. This residue was similar to a teastain or resinous deposit, but not in the least like a scorch mark. The mark was very noticeable because the side of the vessel had recently been painted white. To quote John: 'It looked as though someone had thrown a tea-bag at the side of the boat.' The time taken for the ball to traverse from the masthead to the surface of the sea had been about 13 to 14 seconds. Because the ball had followed the cant of the deckhead in its descent, John felt that it was definitely being influenced by the pull of gravity. But the most curious comment about this, probably natural, manifestation was that John insisted that while viewing the phenomenon *it was very difficult for him to co-ordinate the visual information with the thinking processes of his brain*. Despite this perceptual difficulty, however, he said that the ball reminded him of the sphere of a van de Graff generator giving off an electrical discharge.

Ghost experience

In a shared house in Ealing, John was in his room finishing an essay when he suddenly saw the room door opening. Thinking it was one of his flatmates playing a practical joke, he prepared himself to take the prank in good part. However, when the door was fully open, John could see no one there. Yet he distinctly heard footsteps cross from the open door and come to a stop by his chair. Suddenly, John felt two bony, ice cold 'fingers' jab into his shoulder, a sensation described by him as 'most horrible'. Panic-stricken, he fled out of the room and did not experience this phenomenon again.

OOBEs

John has also had a number of out-of-the-body experiences. The first one occurred when he was about 14 years old. He was relaxing on his bed when he suddenly became aware that he was 'looking' at himself lying in bed from a viewpoint that seemed to be located high up in one of the corners of the room. He remembers thinking: 'Good Lord, I can see myself lying on my bed.' The next instant, he found he was back on the bed again. This sort of experience happened quite frequently over a twelve-month period, and John found the whole thing very unnerving, since the very process by which this happened was totally spontaneous and outside his control. The phenomenon always happened while he was in his own room, and never outside it. The 'viewing' location never varied, and always seemed to be from one of the top corners of the room, and never directly above his body. Each of these experiences lasted about four or five minutes and he did not tell anyone at the time. At 14 years old who can you tell, without risking ribald comment?

THE HUMAN WITNESS: THE MISSING FACTOR IN OTHER, SEEMINGLY DISPARATE PHENOMENA?

The above cited case, which would not be considered particularly spectacular nowadays, is but one of many (the true figure is not known) which are surrounded by self-reported, psychic phenomena, and it would make an interesting study if ufology were to go back to those classic, historical cases and ask some pertinent life questions about the witnesses. Who knows, we might turn up some highly relevant dimensions to the case which would throw new light on some of the internally inconsistent factors which ufologists have been unable to resolve over the years. Having said this though, the shocking truth is that certain ufologists have known of these sorts of human dynamics in UFO cases for many years but, apparently due to a deep desire on their part to present UFO reports to the public within the framework of a rigid belief system, they, aided and abetted by the more uncritical ministrations of the media, allowed a very narrow concept of UFOs to propagate within society. Perhaps the most important of the human factors thus hidden from the general public was the psychic factor, the persistence and embarrassingly regular emergence of which within CE reports has been regularly swept under the table. Even more shocking than this cover-up is the realization that the same censorship principles have been widely applied to other fields of phenomena, notably the field of cryptozoology. Think of all the money and time which have been lavished on the study of, for example, the Loch Ness Monster, when not a penny or a minute is devoted to the study of the lives of the witnesses. Again, life studies applied to the many thousands who have reported sightings of anomalous lake creatures on a world-wide basis – if the Anamnesis Protocol is valid – would certainly reveal a wealth of detail which would give us an even more powerful insight into the nature of these seemingly disparate phenomena.

We shall highlight this point with an incident which occurred in a Norwegian lake in the sixteenth century, and cited in the *Hamar Chronicle* of 1540:

> It happened once at midnight, that all the bells starting ringing in Hamar Cathedral, and the organ began playing by *itself* . . . During the night *there were so many ghosts in the episcopal residence*, looking as if two armies had come into battle, that the watchman and everyone was terrified. *At the same time*, on Lake Mjosa, a terribly large [lake] serpent appeared.[4]

As in the case of UFOs, many other examples are to be found in the various archives but, like certain ufologists, and presumably for equally profound psychological reasons, cryptozoologists prefer to sweep these embarrassing psychic factors under the rug. Thus, yet again, the general public receives a very narrow and inaccurate view of the phenomenon. This must ultimately pose in the mind of the reader the question: 'Do all disparate phenomena have a basis in objective consensus reality?' The answer must be yes, and the reasons for this answer will follow shortly. Indeed, in the Delphos case, actual residues were discovered, but in all of these physical cases we will inevitably find internal inconsistencies and absurdities which fly in the face of reason, and often defy physical laws; to use the words of Jacques Vallee: 'UFOs are a real phenomenon, but they are a window to another reality.'[5]

It is very difficult to draw all these physical and non-physical threads together but, if we are ever to gain a comprehensive understanding of what is going on, we must begin to look at the various physical studies which have been carried out by the few intrepid researcher/investigators all over the world, and then interface this work with the inner life of the witness. Therefore, given the constriction of resource availability under which everyone in the field works when studying the following main areas, people would be well advised to take account of the human factor in their respective appraisals.

EARTHLIGHTS

From empirical work and field studies carried out by Devereux, Merron, McCartney, Persinger and Lafreniere et al., it is now beyond doubt that seismic/tectonic processes within the earth itself are producing light phenomena in the atmosphere.[6] An excellent example of this is the long-term outbreak of aerial lights, from 1981 onwards, in the remote, mountainous region of Hessdalen, Norway. This episode was one of those rare occasions when a small team of volunteers was able to operate an instrumental survey of the phenomena and, indeed, was able to obtain many excellent photographs of amorphous blobs of pulsating lights. The lights remain a mystery to this day and it is puzzling why the established sciences have not shown more interest than they have: what more physical proof does one need? But an even greater mystery is to be found in the eyewitness accounts given by the people of Hessdalen. What, then, did these witnesses report? By now you should be guessing correctly that it was metallic-looking, cigar-shaped objects, structured discs, and other shapes which, they insisted, seemed to be of artificial origin. How could such a well-attested phenomenon possess such a seemingly dual character? Could it be because, despite all the sterling efforts carried out by those who took part in the Hessdalen survey, they inadvertently neglected to investigate a vital component in the whole scenario – the human witnesses?

EXTREME CLOSE ENCOUNTERS/ABDUCTIONS

This area of our study has always been highly controversial (more so than UFOs themselves), but, despite the rigid belief systems which have been generated in the wake of the abduction scenario, there remain some physical symptoms within the bodies of 'abductees/experients' which have yet to be explained adequately. Moreover, according to the US-based organization Treatment and Research of Experienced Anomalous Trauma (TREAT), witnesses to CE phenomena who have been traumatized by their encounter have *suffered profound shock and display symptoms and trauma which, according to current psychology and practitioners associated with the treatment of abductees, could not have been caused by hallucination alone*! Hopefully, the following account of the repercussions affecting a witness after an incident in Essex, England, will illustrate the problem. The report concerned the observation of a large, structured flying object which was seen to pass over the town of Witham, and a later 'landing' of an anomalous object with 'entities'. The event was a multiple-witness case, but the following transcript relates to the illnesses suffered by the main witness subsequent to his UFO experience:

> I've been trying to find somebody who will listen to me, because there has been a lot of things happen to me that I can't explain; a lot of things like, I mean to say . . . just after that time when I did see the big ship . . . that's the only way I can describe it . . . and these other things that I can't explain . . . I became ill, drastically ill. I have had specialists sort my body out in every direction, in every way. I've never been pulled, pushed, prodded so much in my whole life. I'm still under the doctors now and I still get the . . . symptoms of things. I've had my kidneys pack up on me, or virtually pack up on me, I've had my lungs, my heart, every organ in my body . . . can you imagine something . . . inside you?

[Something wrong inside you, or what?]

> No, actually inside you. Now, my illness started with a very, very bad sore throat . . . it felt like to me . . . that it felt like, you know what I had described to the doctor and he said it was an infection of some sort,

but he didn't know what. It was like somebody had got a red-hot torch and branded my throat with it, you know, pushed it right down. Well, this burning feeling went in every organ in my body; every organ. Well, the latest instance, well that's why I'm wearing dark glasses now.

[Your eyes are affected as well?]

They are now, but this is because I . . . I've been OK for a few months, you know. When I spoke to you the other night.

[Soreness, watering of the eyes, or what?]

No, I got burns.

[Witness lifts glasses to reveal what look to be areas of red patches around the eyes and lower forehead.]

My face is like this because I spoke to you on the phone the other night.

[Really?]

Really!

[So you feel that something is trying to stop you from communicating your experience to me?]

Yes. Whether you believe it or not. I mean, I don't mind whether anybody believes this, but I know I believe it. Now, I went out that night after I spoke to you. Don't ask me where I went because I don't know; I just went out. The next morning I woke up and I've got this [the red patches around the eyes]. Now whether you believe it or not . . . I can't explain where I went, I can't explain how I got there, all I know my boots were muddy . . . and I can't remember anything about it. I just don't know where I'd been.

[Have there been other times in your life when you lost your memory?]

Yes, there have been several times in my life when I've gone out and I don't know where I've been.

[You can't remember at all?]

No. Anyway, getting back to my illness . . . it started off with my throat, then it went to my chest and it went to my stomach and my bowels. I've had every ache and pain in my body. I've had different things happen to my eyes that I can't explain . . . I can prove that because my wife has actually seen it [change of colour to the iris of the eyes] . . . and that's why we got divorced, and separated and everything else because of it. Well, my children are terrified of me because I do things . . . very strangely; that's the shortest way of putting it. My eyes . . . whether you believe it or not, as I said, you know, my eyes change colour; they do actually change colour.

[The irises or the general eye?]

The irises . . . the middle bit changes colour.

[Can you describe the colour change?]

Well, sometimes they go black, jet black. Sometimes they go red and sometimes they go bright white. They actually do it.

[This tended to upset your kids?]

All depends . . . all depends if I'm in a good mood, I'm normal as normal could be. But if you upset me, my eyes start to go black. And if you *really* upset me, they go bright red . . . like glow, you know . . . which I've explained all this to the doctors and that and they said, yeah, OK . . . and I've had me eyes tested and that and they can't find anything wrong.

Other physical characteristics include those cases where impressions are left on the ground by anomalous objects which were reported to have touched, or nearly touched, the ground. The following South American case, researched by British investigator, Bill Dillon, is typical.

On 31 October 1963, a UFO, estimated at being 8 m (25 ft) in diameter and shaped like a wash basin, was observed in broad daylight by several persons at Iguape, south-west of Santos, in Brazil. The slow-moving UFO, which was making a roaring noise, collided with a palm tree before falling into the nearby Peropava

River. The observers watched as the river bubbled and boiled at the point of entry of the object. This was followed by an eruption of muddy water, then one of pure mud. The authorities, using divers, initiated a search for the, presumed wrecked, flying saucer, but the divers could find nothing in the water, 5 m (15 ft) deep. Finally, engineers searched the area with mine detectors, but they, too, found nothing. Speculating about the incident, Jim and Coral Lorenzen suggested that the object may have departed the scene while submerged underwater. Again, one could cite cases such as these *ad nauseam*, and they, as well as those (admittedly fewer) cases where truly inexplicable photographs were taken of strange aerial phenomena, would point to no real solution. However, they do pose an interesting question: why is it, if UFOs are as real as these cases would seem to indicate, that no progress has been made in our understanding of at least the physical aspects of the UFO?

The answer to this perplexing question must reside in the fact that there is little or no cross-disciplinary study of the phenomenon, so that all the internal inconsistencies and absurdities of these thousands of reports can be resolved into a cohesive whole. Historically, the past 40 odd years have seen a catastrophic piecemeal approach to the UFO problem by the confining of the respective efforts within the framework of one hypothesis only. For example, just two of these approaches have resulted in a dichotomy that seems unreconcilable: ETH versus Bah! Humbug! It is not very scientific on either side, but the real tragedy is seeing the proponents of these, by now totally rigid, viewpoints trying to overcome the inevitable and relentless paradoxes in the material they are 'investigating' by either denying or distorting those parts of it that do not support their various paradigms. Admittedly, other initiatives have emerged recently, and have been applied to the UFO study; some of which, like earthlights, have been highly enlightening. But disciplines such as folklore, theology, mythology and anthropology have not yet even recognized that ufology is a subject well worthy of their attentions. In fact, in the wake of the Anamnesis results, as well as some of the work produced by researchers like Keel and Vallee, it is absolutely vital that these disciplines scrutinise UFO reports very carefully, because only their respective studies have the distinct advantage of knowledge of the irrational forces which seem to have persistently dogged mankind over the millennia. Make no mistake about this connection between the nature of mankind and those forces which have totally overwhelmed him throughout history: it is the very essence of the UFO experience.

Carl Sagan once surmised that, on the face of it, there should have been a man on the moon by the Middle Ages. Such a speculation is not so *outré* as it might first appear. Many ancient civilizations – most noticeably ancient Greece and China – obviously had very good, basic knowledge of the properties of matter, astronomy, mathematics, natural philosophy and so on. Therefore, assuming those societies should have progressed in some exponential form, one *would* have expected a global, technological society by the thirteenth or fourteenth centuries of our era. History shows that it did not happen – why not? Why is it that not one ancient civilization has survived to go on to greater things? The answer has to be: *we are being controlled and manipulated by an unidentified consciousness, the nature of which is to provoke mankind into adopting irrational and rigid belief systems.* This statement is really quite shocking, and destructive of all that we hold dear to our hearts; but even more shocking than this is the fact that this control is still being exercised today in the guise of the UFO phenomenon. From the abduction of Enoch, either at the end of the fourth or the beginning of the third millennium BC, to that of Ezekiel, to the contact of Joseph Smith in New York State in the last century (an incident that gave rise to Mormonism), right up to the various abduction and contactee UFO witnesses of the late twentieth century, the rationale behind all these absurdities is always seemingly the same: the control of the hearts and minds of humanity.

Many readers of this chapter will no doubt be saying to themselves now that such an outrageous suggestion cannot possibly apply to the civilization of the late twentieth century. After all, man *has* gone to the moon, and plans are already well in hand for a manned Mars mission by early in the next century. Our technological progress, on all fronts, now seems virtually unstoppable – especially not by the irrationalities of the past. Surely our race has outgrown the superstitions of pre-scientific societies? Don't you believe it! Even if the thesis of an unidentified consciousness is not totally correct, there is plenty of evidence extant that ancient irrationalities are alive and well in twentieth-century society, and are being joined daily by others contemporary to our culture. The only issue to be resolved is if it is all just cosmic coincidence, or if it is malice aforethought. The proof of the pudding will be in the eating, for if the thesis of unidentified consciousness is totally wrong, then our civilization will advance exponentially, and our technology-assisted abilities will make us truly godlike: the second apple of Eden is there for the taking – perhaps. It is logical to assume that if our experience is the natural progression of life as we know it – is perhaps part of the evolutionary principle – then we might even interface with other planetary civilizations which have achieved the same progress as ourselves. It is in hopes of this, perhaps, that the industrialized nations of the world are investing billions of dollars in listening to the universe via radio telescopes in a search for extraterrestrial intelligence (SETI). Notwithstanding this effort, there is something odd here if one considers the time and money spent on SETI and the nil returns so far gained. This oddity is generally known in relevant circles as the Fermi Paradox (FP). Simply put, the FP is this: given that planetary formation is universal, and conditions for the emergence of intelligent life are also universal – where is everybody? Unless the operators of SETI are keeping very quiet about it, there has not been *one* recorded instance whereby the earthbound listening antennae have detected alien radio signals of an artificial nature. This total failure can mean only one of three things.

1. Mankind, representing intelligent life, is alone in the universe.
2. Other intelligent species have arisen elsewhere in the Universe but have failed, because of nuclear war, resource depletion or natural calamity, to stay the course, and are even now sitting in the ruins scratching their behinds and wondering what the hell happened. Judging from our own experiences the 'life' of a technological civilization seems to be about 200 years (yes, in case you hadn't noticed, time *is* rapidly running out for us). If this is the case, then earth's scientists would be hard put to find ETI, as the statistical chances of two or more civilizations with a maximum life in the 200-year range coinciding in time are one billion to one – if you want to be optimistic about it.
3. There exists intelligent life elsewhere in the universe but, like us here on earth, these alien species are vulnerable to the intrusion of the same irrational forces; the intrusions of which arrest the host species's progress, or radically modify the way it embarks on a course of development, which renders it undetectable within the Newtonian or Einsteinian systems.

For our own peace of mind, let us assume that options one and two are non-starters, and concentrate instead on option three. How then could these irrational forces operate? The answer has to be: through a process which presents the host species with a series of inexplicable, and ambiguous, phenomena, which are designed to play upon cultural prejudices. In our own circumstances, the many manifestations of the UFO phenomenon fit this bill exactly. And it is as well to remember that it is entirely possible that UFOs are only one of many manifestations in this process of control. New irrational initiatives are always coming along to keep us wrong-footed – as is probably the case with the phenomenon of the crop circles, which, though attributed in some quarters to the UFO phenomenon, seems to be presently superseding it in popularity as a cause of endless argument. Let us call these various irrational manifestations, including the UFO phenomenon, unidentified consciousness (UC). How can UFOs be a form of UC? The very idea sounds preposterous. Surely such competently observed, unknown objects, which unexpectedly manifest in the way they do (for example, at Delphos), cannot possibly have a conscious relationship with the observer . . . or can they?

THE 'CONSCIOUS' UFO

The following reports emanate from opposite ends of the earth: one from London, England, and the other from Piedmont, USA.

Case No. 1
On several evenings, the witness, who lives in south London, would look out of her bedroom window and observe a bright light in the sky. This light would approach her house, stop, emit secondary lights which would go off then light up again some time later. However, what later amazed this witness was the apparent fact that when she mentally instructed the light to 'go back', it would comply; and when she thought 'come forward', it would immediately approach her position. *This process would happen two or three times a week!*

Case No. 2
In 1973, a professor of physics, Harley Rutledge, decided to investigate lights in the sky (LITS) which had been appearing, in numbers, near the town of Piedmont. Therefore, he assembled a team of specialists and set off for Piedmont, confident that a few weekends with his team, utilizing scientific measuring instruments, would be sufficient to resolve the mystery. It just goes to show how wrong you can be. It was not until seven years later that his report on the incidents experienced by him and his team was published. The events in themselves were trivial, but one certain aspect of the UFOs' behaviour puzzled everyone. Apparently, whenever the UFOs came within range of measurement, they would either move,

change course or halt. *It was almost as if the UFOs were detecting the investigators' intentions, voices – or thoughts*!

Somebody up there knows us intimately!

Extending our universal model to include all such disparate phenomena, we can now declare with some certainty that UC works on humanity in such a way as to cause its progress to be halted, or to be altered in some radical way. But what is the vital link in this process? Can the Anamnesis results – assuming they are valid – give some clue here? The answer is yes, and the clue suggested is quite unambiguous in its inference. *The UC is operating on the ESP-prone individuals in our society*. It is they who are receiving the absurd messages during close encounters with anomalous phenomena. It is an ongoing pandemic process which, thankfully, does not always result in the message taking societal root; but on those occasions when it has, it spreads like wildfire and its theme is always culturally calamitous. This UC is demonstrably monolithic in intellect, impregnable, unstoppable, and – if deduction is not a defunct discipline in dealing with it – would seem to be the originator of all the world's major religions.

So, you are entitled to ask, if we are up against such an undefinable and ungraspable form of consciousness, what is the point in sending good money after bad in trying to comprehend what is quite obviously incomprehensible? After all, if the USAAF, with all the resources at their command, could not come up with anything better than the Condon Committee (Colorado University, 1969), what chance do under-resourced individuals and organizations have to solve the mystery? About as much chance as me trying to swim the Atlantic with one hand tied behind my back.

So, if we can't study *it*, what can we do? Pretend it isn't there? No, that's not working. Accept it on its own terms? No, that way leads to the return of the Dark Ages. Perhaps if we can't study *it*, we can at least study the social effect it has – by their fruits shall ye know them, so to speak – by carefully monitoring the way mankind responds to these 'signs' in the sky, or for that matter, on Earth. For a start, by carefully documenting the life profiles of CE witnesses, we can begin to ascertain whether the ESP-prone individual continues to be the 'chosen' one of the CE experience. We also need to study those members of the population who do *not* have UFO experiences to find out whether there are any ESP-prone individuals among them. For if there are, then the ESP hypothesis is called seriously into doubt, and we are in genuine danger of being left truly bereft of a universal theory.

Another equally important area of study are the major religious manifestations, and their witnesses, who seem to form the main attraction for persons seeking the 'supernatural', in much the same way as UFO contactees form the focus for individuals seeking contact with 'spacemen'. The comparison would seem to be that major religious events seem to embody much that can be correlated with what occurs in ufological interactions: from the bright lights in the sky and ground-level entities, to the doom-and-disaster messages seemingly beloved of contactees and visionaries alike. The last major religious event with unarguable ufological affiliations took place in Portugal in 1917.[7] But there have been other 'lesser' events since, and even before, then, such as the one that took place in Wales in 1904–5.[8] We must then examine the way in which these powerful social messages, symbols and themes are propagated through human society, giving rise to the setting-up of irrational religious and cultist groups. Finally, we must study the effects of clashes between the established order, which in itself is only a remnant of a previous 'revelation', and the 'heretical' viewpoints emanating from the various 'contacts' which are endeavouring to assert the 'new order'; the most recent manifestation of this struggle against the established order are the aspirations of New Age proponents.

These social developments, caused by confrontations with the UFO monolith, can be studied with effectiveness, and at moderate cost, which always helps. Thus, although we will probably never discover the true source of the UFO, we will certainly discover much about the way societies arise, structure themselves, and eventually fall. Who knows, we might even learn something nice about ourselves . . .

REFERENCES

1 Chalker, Bill   'UFOs 1947–87', BUFORA [FT]: p. 185
2 Dutton, T R   'We are Definitely not Alone', BUFORA paper, 2 May 1987
3 Anamnesis (Keul, A G 1981, Keul & Seymour, C 1987, Keul & Phillips, K W C 1990): now a 69-question, time-invariant, culture-free, protocol covering the demographic, medical, spiritual, educational and belief orientation components of the UFO witness.
4 Meurger, M & Gagnon, C   'Lake Monster Traditions – A Cross-cultural Analysis', FT, London: p. 23
5 Vallee, J   *Confrontations* (Souvenir Press)
6 Barclay, D   *Fatima: A Close Encounter of the Worst Kind?* (Mark Saunders, 1987)
7 ibid.
8 Devereux, P   *Earthlights Revelation* (Blandford, 1990): pp. 64–77

CHAPTER FOUR

SCIENCE v. SAUCERY

Robert Moore

ILLUSION – AND REALITY

To most people, the term UFO conjures up an image of a
domed, plate-shaped object with riveted hull, and bedecked
with aerials, portholes, landing-gear, and flashing lights.
Remarkable really, as only a very small proportion of UFO reports
claim confrontations with such exotic forms. More than 70 per
cent of the reports concerning night-time observations of UFOs
refer only to 'nocturnal meandering lights', which have been
described variously as pin-points of light, blobs, squiggles and
vague luminous shapes – nary a 'saucer' to be seen.[1] Behind the
dramatic 'space alien' headlines, backed by sensationalist
suppositions, there lurks the hidden, or more likely deliberately
ignored, phenomenon of *misperception*: that is, when a given
mundane stimulus, due to various physical and psychological
factors, is mistakenly perceived as something other than what it
actually is. In the world of Sporty UFO speculation, this perceived
'difference' is translated immediately into 'alien spaceship'. When
examined in sufficient detail, it becomes obvious that rational
solutions can be found for most of these reports: the ratios being
9 out of 10,[2] and 19 out of 20,[3] having demonstrable prosaic
causation. There are many who cannot accept that such a high
percentage of sightings are the result of misperceptions. They
point to those reports submitted by 'expert observers', such as
policemen, pilots, astronomers, etc., whom they feel to be so
reliable that it is virtually impossible for them to make an
observational error of this nature. Unfortunately, anyone –
expert or otherwise – can be deceived by optical illusion.
Susceptibility is due neither to low intelligence, gullibility nor
unreliability, but rather to the way our brain processes incoming,
confusing information. Many mundane objects can present

unfamiliar aspects when seen under adverse observational conditions. But why, in these circumstances, do persons predictably perceive flying saucers? This public propensity would seem to be attributable to the UFO tradition which exists within the subculture of most westernized societies. The saucer shape established its predominance after the Kenneth Arnold report of June 1947. All Arnold said at the time was that the anomalous objects that he saw flying over the Cascade Mountains in America, which in fact were crescent shaped, moved 'like a saucer skipped over water', and the freedom of the Press did the rest.[4] The public inclination to perceive this mandala of misperception is now pandemic, and any indeterminate stimulus is likely to be described as a 'disc' or a 'saucer' by the witness. This would seem to indicate prior knowledge of the subject on the part of the witness, despite any disclaimers to the contrary on their part. Certainly, the vast majority of witnesses cannot be accused of being UFO enthusiasts – however, a ufological education can be subliminally acquired from media presentation. Such mass-media presentations are usually simplistic in their approach, and are, therefore, probably the main source of the inexact information that now contaminates even 'raw' UFO reports.

Natural causes of 'UFOs'

The number of mundane phenomena able to generate a false UFO report is estimated to be in excess of 150[5]. Around 90 per cent of all reported UFO incidents have detectable natural causes. Some phenomena predominate, while others generate sighting reports only rarely. Almost 65 per cent of sightings are instigated by only six different kinds of natural stimuli, of a kind which are extremely common in the contemporary environment. The remainder of the reports are induced by much rarer man-made objects and natural happenings. Of the vast majority of incidents that generate spurious reports, 85 per cent occur during the hours of darkness.

Around 25 per cent of spurious UFO reports involve the misperception of quite ordinary aircraft and helicopters.[6] Of these, 75 per cent relate to nocturnal sightings of aircraft running lights. Depending on its attitude (e.g., banking, climbing, descending, etc.), and the witnesses' angle of view, an aircraft can display anything from one to four or more lights to the ground-based observer. In addition to their normal running lights, aircraft can also be fitted with very bright strobe-type flashing lights. Aircraft also have landing-lights which they turn on before take off and landing. These are similar to, but many orders of magnitude brighter, than car headlamps (which, by the way, have also caused their share of UFO reports).[7] In low cloud or ground fog, the eerie effect of switched-on landing-lights can be seen for miles around. Some special kinds of planes have further illumination in the form of drogue advertising signs.[8] When these are lit up at night, they can, when seen at a distance just out of range of naked eye resolution, convey an impression of anomalousness, and they have been reported in terms of 'rotating discs'. Military inflight refuelling exercises, carried out at night, have had much the same effect because of their very bright and non-standard modes of illumination. In fact, any aircraft-lighting pattern, when observed at night by the uncritical witness, can result in spaceships that pass in the night, for the simple reason that the unwary observer is inclined to 'impose' their expectations on the sighting by, in effect, playing dot-to-dot with the lights. Or, perhaps more scientifically, by conducting their very own version of the Rorschach ink-blot test. Even aircraft observed in broad daylight can occasionally generate UFO reports. When reflecting sunlight, they can appear at a distance to be discoid or elliptical in shape, their tailplane and wings hidden, either by the viewing angle or the dazzle of the reflected sunlight: astonishingly, around 30 per cent of aviational misperceptions occur during the day.

Reports based on the misperception of stars and planets are responsible for 20 per cent of *all* false UFO reports.[9] For some reason, planets seem to be mistaken in this way more than stars. The majority of astronomically based reports relate to observations of apparently stationary stellar objects that appear to the witness to be either a single point of light, a disc or a triangle, or just a vague luminous oval. These sightings usually have a duration in excess of ten minutes. Stars and planets are vulnerable to a range of little-known perceptual or atmospheric effects. Atmospheric turbulence causes those bodies nearest the horizon to flash anomalous spectral colours due to a prismatic effect compounded by the composition of the atmosphere through which their light passes. Autokinesis also causes bright stellar bodies to appear to move erratically in a confined area of sky. Hand-held binoculars, or telescopes, have much the same effect. Another optical illusion of movement is generated when viewing takes place from a moving vehicle. The effects of parallax make the observed stellar object appear to pace the car in which the observer is sat. Inevitably, meteors cause their share of spurious UFO reports. Around 10 per cent of reports relate to fireballs, spectacular giant-sized shooting stars, seen at night.[10] Sightings usually last ten seconds or less, but during that time witnesses have 'seen' cigar-shaped objects with window lights, and sometimes the now almost obligatory 'rotating disc'. An increasing number of spurious reports are generated by the re-entry of man-made meteors (e.g., expended rocket boosters, decaying satellites). An additional 5 per cent pertain to misperceived weather balloons.[11] Most of these sightings occur during daylight, and account for at least 50 per cent of all reports of daylight UFOs. The majority of incidents do not involve the small, and relatively more common, radiosonde, but refer to those very large, high-altitude balloons which are infrequently launched to gather data from the upper atmosphere. The smaller radiosonde bursts within hours of launch, but the skyhook variety can persist for many weeks, and travel great distances during that time. These balloons can appear as a spherical, tear-drop, triangular or discoid shape, depending on their altitude. Their colour is dictated by prevailing light conditions: appearing bright white or silver on sunny days, and dull grey when the day is overcast. Their prime time for causing UFO reports is around sunset, when the westering sun can make them appear to change colour. This effect is even more startling if the sun has just gone below the viewer's horizon, but is still reflecting off the balloon at high altitude. Such balloons can also give the appearance of travelling against the wind if the air current that is carrying them is diametrically opposed to the one at ground level, which it often is. They can even convey the impression of climbing under power, if caught in a strong thermal.

Orbiting hundreds of miles above our heads is the junk-yard in the sky.[12] This is composed of a myriad of man-made satellites. When seen from the ground, they seem able to fool most of the people all of the time, and are certainly responsible for at least 5 per cent of all spurious reports. Birds, parachute flares, model aircraft, airships, toy balloons with shiny Mylar surfaces, spotlights and laser displays all contribute to the incidence of reports, as do, more infrequently, ball lightning, mirages, unusual clouds and sundogs (ice crystals in the atmosphere refracting sunlight). When combined, these various mundane phenomena are responsible for 25 per cent of reports.[13]

Most spurious reports accurately describe what was seen, even if the witness includes their own subjective conclusions in the report. A star, for instance, might be reported as a brilliant object hanging motionless in the sky. This can be easily identified as such by comparing the known attributes of the suspected cause (a star) with that attributed to the observed 'UFO'. The correlation will close the case – for the investigator at least. Yet other instances are more complex, involving factors other than observer subjectivity when

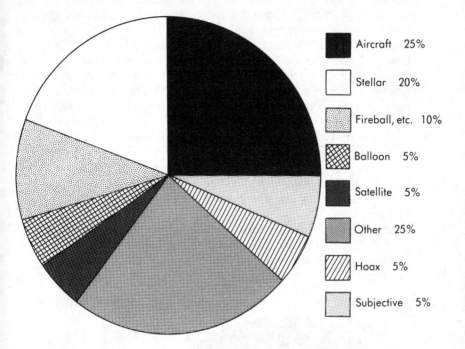

Aircraft   25%

Stellar   20%

Fireball, etc.   10%

Balloon   5%

Satellite   5%

Other   25%

Hoax   5%

Subjective   5%

Figure 2 IFO *stimuli (low strangeness).*

faced with the unfamiliar. The following play their part in distorting the appearance of an otherwise normal looking phenomenon.

1. Misleading light effects, unusual viewing angles, atmospheric and perceptual factors.
2. False cause and effect: any sighting of an 'anomalous' aerial form could be linked by the witness with unconnected natural background noise, or radio interference during the incident, or with marks on the ground afterwards.
3. Two or more normal and unconnected stimuli subjectively linked to produce a perception of a single phenomenon. Thus, a meteor and a star would be reported as a fast-moving light that suddenly halted and then hovered until sighting termination.
4. Defective memory: a major factor when an incident is reported days, sometimes even months, after it has occurred. All parameters can be modified beyond recognition by this human failing – especially if the person was inattentive during the observation of the stimulus.

Instances where a UFO experience has no basis in objective reality are fairly uncommon. When occurring, they can involve anything from spots before the eyes (e.g., the unusually persistent after-images after a bright light source has been glanced at), to a genuine hallucination. They are much rarer than many realize, accounting for only 5 per cent of reports.[14] Few subjective-based UFO events involve the use of narcotics or alcohol, and most hallucinatory incidents apparently develop from the individual concerned falling into an unsuspected state of altered consciousness: a mental condition similar to that experienced at the interface between sleeping and waking. It is probable that some alleged encounters with UFO entities are generated in this way, as the UFO imagery has much in common with the distorted human and animal imagery that appears frequently in clinical based hallucinations.[15]

An additional 5 per cent of reports of airborne lights and forms are fraudulent in nature.[16] The number of hoaxes radically increases in relation to the incidence of so-called 'high strangeness'

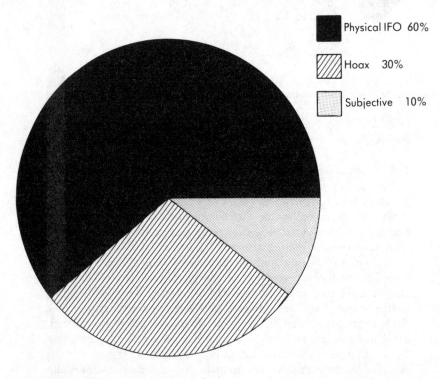

Physical IFO 60%

Hoax 30%

Subjective 10%

Figure 3 High strangeness UFO incidents.

events (i.e, alleged close-quarter observation of UFOs and their 'occupants').[17] Around 60 per cent of this type of report are attributable to physical stimuli, but a staggering 30 per cent are the result of deliberate hoaxes. The remaining 10 per cent have subjective causes.

Thus, as it would appear that *every* report has a *potential* mundane causation, the first thing we have to consider is the possibility that those remaining – the 'true UFOs' – do *not* represent unique phenomena. The determination of whether or not these reports do represent encounters with exotic phenomena (i.e., spaceships, could be achieved by objectively comparing the attributes of the solved reports with those of the unsolved ones. If similar, their claim to uniqueness would be rendered doubtful. But if differing, the possible existence of true UFOs would seem that more probable. In the absence of *watertight* results from such a study, can the possibility of true UFOs be ascertained from the existing evidence? From the body of evidence in existence, it would appear that some reports are of phenomena admitting to *no* obvious mundane solution: either all possible prosaic causes were demonstrably absent, or the attributes of any and all natural stimuli present were totally dissimilar to those of the reported UFO. Many UFO reports undeniably have rational explanations, but with the admitted existence of a body of 'unknowns', should we consider the possibility that some reports might, after all, relate to bona fide observations of alien spacecraft?

The Extraterrestrial Hypothesis (ETH)

The distances between the stars are immense. It takes light, the fastest known medium, moving at 300,000 km/sec (186,000 miles per second), years to traverse even the smallest of interstellar distances. The light from our sun takes about four years to reach our nearest stellar neighbour – Alpha Centauri. The estimated distance between stars presently thought capable of supporting life-bearing planets is 30 light years – or more.[18] So you can well appreciate why it might be necessary to take more than a packed lunch if you intended to go where no man has gone before. Light, being practically massless, has no difficulty in achieving light speed. But the same would not hold true of even the most advanced of spacecraft which, presumably, must have greater mass than a photon. Because of this it would acquire infinite mass as it approached light speed, and to drive it beyond that point would require more energy than is contained in our entire universe. It's like this: the faster the ship moves, the more inertial mass it accumulates, until it reaches a level outstripping the ability of even theoretical modes of power, such as fusion or anti-matter drives, to supply enough thrust to move it.[19] But that's not all.

Then there are the twin problems of time dilation and catastrophic impact.[20] Anyone who has ever had a car accident knows the disproportionate amount of damage that is caused to one's car when striking an object even at moderate speed. How much more then if the speed had been in the order of thousands of miles per second? At that speed, an object the size of a pinhead would cause complete destruction. On an interstellar vessel undergoing such impact, you would hardly have time to glance at your watch to discover that you were too young to die, having only aged a couple of years while the universe at large slid into senility. That's the trouble with time dilation. You nip off for a few years at a reasonable fraction of light speed, and you return to find your great, great grandson has absconded with the family jewels in your absence. And it is his great, great, grandson who is at the spaceport waiting to tell you all about it. Obviously, stellar travel has some definite drawbacks. To be serious, though, journeys involving approaches to light speed to make them viable within one person's lifetime, result in the phenomenon of time passing at different speeds inside and outside the moving vessel. Inside the ship, time would pass more slowly than on the planet of your departure, but you would not notice this until journey's end. At which time you would discover that the world you were contemporary with had passed away, leaving you to be a stranger in a strange land. The initial ages of any pilots being trained for such missions will be a limiting factor on the length of journey that could be undertaken. They would probably have reached a quite mature age before they were considered competent, as were the pilots involved in the American moon missions, whose average age was around 32 years.[21] The obvious facts of human biology would necessarily limit any theoretical maximum distance which could be covered by such a relativistic vessel. This would apply equally to any aliens thinking of journeying to earth from light years away. So if, as some never tire of maintaining, they are already here, how did they do it without falling foul of relativistic realities?

Science-fiction literature has often featured the hyperdrive.[22] This is a hypothetical spaceship-propulsion system which negates relativism by allowing any vessel so fitted to circumnavigate the universe by travelling 'outside' it – in another dimension. By such means, interstellar journeys take only days, and time dilation is not involved. Once entirely fictional, this concept now has a valid theoretical basis.[23] Scientists perceive such journeys as involving the 'linking' of one part of space with another by 'warping' the fabric of space/time. Natural space/time warps are permitted by contemporary astrophysics. They are called black holes, and the theory is that these super dense remnants of collapsed stars cause a kink in the continuum. Although there was much speculation in the Seventies as to their possible use as a means to rapid interstellar travel, many scientists today are sceptical because of the hypothesized effects a journey through a black hole would have on the spaceship – not to mention its pilot and passengers.[24] The only rapid travel available by going through a black hole is – into oblivion. The titanic gravitational forces at the heart of these holes, strong enough to prevent even the escape of light, would compress the spaceship, and everyone in it, into a pinhead-sized piece of super dense matter. And after that it really would not matter. There is still some speculation that interesting things might be possible at the 'event threshold', known scientifically as the Einstein-Rosen Bridge, encountered just before the point of no return. Some scientists believe that it could be used to travel great distances within seconds. So could mankind, or another intelligent species, develop a technology capable of generating an artificial event threshold? It seems unlikely, as any spaceship so fitted would not only have to generate an Einstein-Rosen Bridge, but also shield itself from the adverse gravitational forces associated with its creation. In modern physics, black holes can only be created by the implosion of stars approximately ten times the size of our sun. So there would seem to be no way to create artifically a side-effect that needs such a colossal collapse to generate it. Black holes, must, therefore, be ruled out as a means to rapid interstellar travel.

Although science accepts that the probability of life existing elsewhere in space is statistically almost certain, it still remains sceptical that any of that presumed 'life' has found its way – by technological means – to Earth. As detailed above, the obstacles seem insurmountable. So where does that leave UFOs? The UFO evidence, although mountainous, does not encourage great confidence that it represents sightings of extraterrestrial activity on our planet. It is a case of quantity rather than quality. The 'proof' so far put forward in support of ETH can safely be described as unconvincing. Physical 'evidence' has turned out to be foundry slag, fragments of pure (terrestrial) metals, plastics, soot, hoaxed artefacts constructed from cannibalized pre-solid state radios, and cardboard flavoured cookies. Rumours of 'crashed saucers' containing dead aliens have remained just that – rumours.[25] The alleged 'alien implant' recovered from the innards of abductee claimants have mostly turned out to be variously mundane objects.[26] There is also a noticeable lack of definitive photographic evidence, despite ongoing claims to the contrary.[27] Not one picture extant conclusively shows a nuts and bolts UFO. It is one of the facts of ufology that pictures depicting 'alien craft' have the lowest survival rate of any other class of UFO photograph. The verdict on them has always been either 'inconclusive' or 'hoax'.

Despite this distressing tendency of 'evidence' to fail to carry conviction, there still are reports which seemingly have no rational solution. So, if an extraterrestrial origin is rendered invalid, and the well-understood natural order fails to give answers, could it be that what is being reported are manifestations of rare, and as yet unrecognized by science, forms of natural phenomena. Given the diversity of 'true UFOs', it seems the height of folly to expect that only *one* type of phenomenon is responsible for all the inexplicable reports. Thankfully, the search for plausible causes need not be a directionless shamble in the dark. Research conducted within, and independently of, the UFO movement has discovered various concepts which, if valid, will account for much that is presently deemed 'unexplainable' – and I don't just mean those 'true UFO' reports. For the purposes of rational ufology – as opposed to flying saucery – much could be gained from a detailed examination of these theories.

Anomalous mirages

Mirages are images distorted by the action of compact air layers of differing temperatures (inversions) located between the affected stimulus and the observer.[28] The perceived image succumbs to refraction (bending of light rays) which causes a displacement in space. Refraction can also distort the image until it bears no resemblance to its stimulus, and it may also display a striking diversity of false colours. Self-luminous objects (e.g., the sun) directly transmit light (photons), but other objects – from human beings to the man in the moon – are only rendered visible by their ability to reflect light. As all optically perceived images consist only of an object's transmitted or reflected light, it follows that the image of any of them can be adversely affected (distorted) by inversions. The orientation of an inversion's hot and cold air layers is dependent on local weather conditions, and the effect that inversions have upon light passing through them is dependent on the orientation of the layering. An inferior mirage is one where the warm air is beneath the cooler air, which causes light rays passing through it to be displaced *downwards*. Inferior mirages can often be seen during the summer, as a shimmering fuzzy patch, on tarmac roads. Superior mirages, where the cold air is underneath the warmer air, refract light *upwards*; the image of any object refracted by it is seemingly elevated as a result.[29] Superior mirages are often created when a high-pressure weather front moves into one dominated by a low-pressure one. A mirage can only form during calm meteorological conditions where strong winds and rain are absent.[30] Good visibility is also required. It is known that a rare positioning of the inversion layers can render visible to an observer, objects normally hidden below the horizon. It is termed the Novaya Zemlya effect after the Russian island where the first recorded instance occurred in 1597. It is important to remember that only phenomena positioned a short distance from the horizon are susceptible to inversion effects.

Mirages have considerable potential as a possible cause for any number of 'true UFO' reports.[31] The work of Steuart Campbell details the special attributes that inversions with *curved* thermoclines (the sharp temperature gradient of an inversion) may possess. The thermoclines of most superior mirages are known to be vertical, which limits image refraction to a maximum arc of 0.5°. However, in the case of an inversion with a curved thermocline, there is a strong possibility that the refracted mirage image could attain greater apparent 'altitude'. So what kind of UFO report could superior mirages account for? This phenomenon might explain that class of reports which refer to low-level luminous objects known as 'spooklights'. Spooklights are normally reported as seeming to 'float' a short distance from the ground.[32] So could they be explained as a product of flat thermocline inversions? It is certainly true that some spooklight incidents have been identified as mirages. Despite this, many researchers in this field eschew a blanket meteorological solution for the phenomenon.[33] So, what then of the ubiquitous 'true UFO'? Most reports locate the object a considerable distance from the horizon. Could these 'true UFO' incidents be caused by witnesses reporting observations of curved thermocline mirages? It is certainly possible; although the validity of this concept has been questioned by various critics. The required level of refraction need not be as great as that indicated in 'true UFO' reports.[34] The vast majority of witnesses are very poor at deducing elevations, and an object's actual height is often half that claimed by the observer. It is accepted that a mirage consists of an inverted and a non-inverted image.[35] Steuart Campbell suggests that, depending on the extent of merging of these two images, any number of 'UFO Shapes' could be formed. Some atmospheric physicists suspect that mirage images are composed of compacted 'clusters' of smaller images which look to any observer like a speckled, fuzzy blob. In this context, it is interesting to note that a number of possibly authentic 'UFO photographs' depict such forms.[36] Even those ufological 'erratic movements' could be the result of an ancillary effect of the mirage.[37] A dynamic wave within the vertical part of a curved thermocline can theoretically allow the mirage to appear to traverse along a wide arc, back and forth, by a process known as light ducting. Campbell proposes that many such mirages of stars and planets are responsible for generating spurious UFO reports.[38] If valid, his proposal would explain why 80–90 per cent of 'true UFO' incidents occur during the hours of darkness. The most controversial aspect of Campbell's mirage hypothesis is the proposal that astronomical mirages, under rare conditions, can become sufficiently visible to be seen in daylight, and so be the major cause of the daylight 'true UFO' reports as well.[39] Although the possibility of daylight astro-mirages is rejected by many, the possibility of their existence, with its necessary rarity, certainly explains the ufological 'reality' of diurnal reports being much scarcer than nocturnal ones. Objects visible during the day (i.e., aircraft, ships, human beings, etc.) would also be susceptible to refraction, and have been demonstrably involved in many striking instances of mirage phenomena.

IONIZATION PHENOMENA

So, does our quest for ufological solutions end in a mirage? Hardly, as we still have to account for those UFOs that have been reported as traversing along constant, wide arc trajectories without any sign of 'backtracking'. And what of the alleged UFO-induced bio-effects, such as anomalous tanning, swelling and burning of skin tissue? All these factors present difficulties for mirage phenomena as an explanation for *all* reports. Because humming sounds and ozone-like odours have been repeatedly encountered in a UFO context, this immediately raises the suspicion that some UFOs might be electrical in origin. This possibility is enhanced by allegations of UFO partiality towards power lines or electricity generators. It has been postulated that all these attributes are consistent with various forms of ionization phenomena. I have designated diverse energy forms 'ionization phenomena' because, although the various types have different processes of generation, they all involve direct or indirect ionization of air molecules to give them form. Furthermore, postulated meteorological/geological/tectonic activity could result in such forms becoming luminous by raising their energy content to sufficient levels. Ball lightning, described as being a soccer ball-sized glowing mass, is a good example of a scientifically accepted phenomenon that is possibly ionization phenomena.[40] The vast majority of ball-lightning incidents occur during thunderstorms. After displaying various forms and colours, the 'ball' can either explode or just fade away. The motions, colours and physical effects attributed to ball lightning have much in common with those attributed to many 'true UFOs'.[41] A point of disparity is that 'true UFOs' seem to have longer lifespans than ball lightning: 2.5 minutes on average, as opposed to 15 seconds for ball lightning.[42] But such similarities as do exist give good reason for surmising that some 'true UFO' reports could well be of a more enduring form of ionization phenomena that is similar to ball lightning.

The plasma vortex

As UFOs do not seem to be restricted to manifesting themselves during thunderstorms, this might seem to exclude ball lightning as an explanation.[43] Its much shorter visible lifespan, possibly due to a limited energizing process dictated by the various components that make up a thunderstorm, also make it less viable as ufological report source material. However, not all observations of ball lightning-like manifestations have occurred during thunderstorms. Some reports of these non-thunderstorm related phenomena have quoted life durations of up to ten minutes. Therefore, it must be possible that what has been reported is a more enduring form of ionization phenomena, similar to – but not the same as – ball lightning.

Dr Terence Meaden, as a result of his work on the ancillary mystery of corn circles, has proposed the existence of a phenomenon he has called plasma vortex.[44] The correlation between the plasma vortices' predicted atributes and those ascribed to light-form UFOs is tantalizingly consistent. When a plasma vortex reaches a sufficient degree of rotation, it is possible that cascade ionization (i.e., a sustained series of ion collisions) takes place, causing the ions to contract and to induce a 'pinching' effect in the magnetic field around them. This, in turn, would result in the formation of a low-pressure cavity: a vacuum where the air's electrical resistance would be lower than normal. Under these conditions, the air within the affected area could fluoresce. Meaden predicts that such vortices could display conical, cigar, spheroid or discoid forms, depending on rate of spin and ion content.[45] The manifestation would be maintained by a continuous input of air being drawn through a conducting tunnel formed by rotation. This would ensure that consumed ions would be replenished with new ones, a process that would sustain this phenomenon, and result in it enduring for much longer periods than are possible for ball lightning.[46] Dr Meaden predicts that such plasma vortices would generate electromagnetic fields strong enough to interfere with vehicle ignitions. How a conglomeration of ions could produce such an effect is not clear, even theoretically. What is certain is that it is not caused, as many UFO buffs believe, by powerful magnetic fields. Some UFO researchers suggest that the cut-off is induced by energy emissions interrupting the timing of an engine's spark plugs.[47] So the predicted electromagnetic effects of plasma vortices are certainly consistent with long standing ufolore.[48] It is also probable that a phenomenon capable of emitting sufficient energy to stall car engines would also impede radio reception, and probably radiate ultra violet in sufficient quantity to produce symptoms identical to alleged UFO-induced bio-effect, from feelings of warmth or nausea to actual skin damage.

Earthlights

Observational and experimental evidence indicates that it is possible that natural tectonic processes within the earth's crust could generate ionization phenomena.[49] This possibility was initially indicated by observations of unusual light emissions occurring during earthquakes. During the 1970s and 1980s, the theories of Michael Persinger[50] and Dr Bryan Brady,[51] modified by Paul Devereux,[52] proposed that very low levels of tectonic stress on earth faults could produce spectacular luminescences. The viability of this concept is enhanced by the fact that such areas play host to long-term, high-level UFO activity – as is the case in Hessdalen, Norway,[53] and the Pennines in England.[54] Indeed, many reports from these, and other similar regions, describe the UFO as appearing to follow the direction of the earth fault, or to have appeared directly from the earth itself.[55] Also potentially explicable in this context are those UFOs that apparently direct continuous beams of light down on to the ground. Earthlight proponents, especially Persinger, who initially proposed this, believe these light beams to be luminous discharges of energy from a fault line: its upper extremity acquiring a rudimentary shape by means yet unclear. It seems curiously coincidental that such speculations echo Dr Meaden's plasma vortex hypothesis which proposes that through rapid rotation, a funnel of energy (in the case of earthlights, an atmospheric vortex) can acquire a basic form. All of this would seem to bear out the contention that electromagnetic emissions are typical of other forms of ionization phenomena, and not just those of a telluric origin.

The physical processes involved in the creation of earthlights are presently uncertain. Dr Brady believed he had discovered a viable means when samples of quartz rock he was crushing gave out tiny, short-lived luminous blobs.[56] However, critics cast doubts on this method's viability in nature, pointing to the very high pressures required by the process, and the very short lifespans of the phenomena produced. Devereux, recognizing the flaws in the peizoelectrical hypothesis, has produced rock-originated lumines-cences in the laboratory by other means.[57] However, the light emanations so far produced by Devereux are devoid of both broad-band radiation spectra and microwave emissions. This would appear to preclude earthlight phenomena from producing the 'true UFO' type of biological injury.

Artificially generated ionization phenomena

Mankind may also be responsible 'for the artificial creation of ionization phenomena' as a side-effect of the operation of technological devices which are now an indispensable part of civilization.[58] Philip Klass, who now rejects *all* extraordinary solutions to the UFO mystery, once suggested the existence of plasma, defined by him as a cluster of ionized air created by the electrical discharges associated with high-voltage power lines and generators. Klass went on further to suggest that static accumulation in the air, caused by the frequent passage of air traffic, could, under certain conditions, generate a similar phenomenon.[59] If correct, this would certainly go a long way in explaining UFOs' apparent predilection for 'tagging' aircraft.

Other factors

Specific weather conditions may play an important part in the creation of all classes of ionization phenomena. A number of studies indicate that UFO incidents seem to occur more frequently during winter.[60] This could be due to the longer hours of darkness which increase the time for casual observation of the sky. Or it might have something to do with the fact that severe barometric pressure changes are more likely at this time of year. The passage of weather fronts occurs even prior to the manifestation of suspected earthlight phenomena.[61] Other environmental factors may also contribute towards ionization-phenomena induction. Electrical resistance is very low around pointed objects (i.e., hills with a pronounced apex, mountains, etc.). In confirmation of this, holy mountains around the world have legendary light phenomena associated with them: balls of light that traverse from one mountain top to another, which are known scientifically as mountain peak discharge.[62] Similar topographical features are also thought to be important in the formation of plasma vortices, which are thought to be created by air eddies induced by hills.[63]

But none of these theories can fully explain how a collecion of luminous air particles can be perceived as craft-like objects, complete with darkened hull, running lights and portholes. Steuart Campbell suggests that low-altitude ionization phenomena could become infused with dust and other wind-blown detritus, as is the case with the better-known vortex phenomena, like tornadoes.[64] This could explain reports of 'structured discs' very much like those from Trinidad in 1957[65] and Livingston, Scotland, in 1979.[66, 67] Campbell suggests, with some justification, that these incidents could just as easily have been generated by astronomical mirages.[68]

Drawbacks

However, unlike mirages, all forms of ionization phenomena are presently only theoretical, their existence yet to be demonstrated empirically. This despite the proposed processes of their creation resting firmly on well-accepted scientific laws and principles. All that luminesces is not necessarily ionization phenomena. Peter Day's movie, which shows a luminous phenomenon in the sky over Oxfordshire, England, was once thought to be prime UAP evidence.[69] It now seems more likely that the luminous object was aviation fuel which had spontaneously ignited after being ejected from an F-111 aircraft that was in difficulties in the area and preparing for a possible crash landing.[70] Similarly, a German UFO group (CENAP) discovered that the cause of a spate of suspected plasma reports was handmade fire balloons.[71] So caution is a necessary adjunct to speculation in this area, especially since Klass and Campbell, both former plasma advocates, have now abandoned these concepts in favour of more naturalist solutions.

UNCONVENTIONAL AIRCRAFT

In the days of seminal saucery, when the outbreak seemed confined to the United States, there was speculation among that country's military that flying saucers originated back in the USSR.[72] The fear was expressed that the Soviets had acquired, or developed, high-performance, disc-shaped aircraft based on captured Nazi designs.[73] Reinforcing these suspicions, drawings surfaced in the 1950s allegedly depicting saucer-shaped aeroforms developed by the Third Reich. At this remove in time, it is clear that this was not true, and the pandemic nature of the UFO phenomenon is now a matter of history. However, there is a case for arguing that technologically advanced terran aeroforms have, at one time or another, been responsible for their share of UFO reports.[74] The American Stealth aircraft, because of all the secrecy surrounding it, attracted considerable ufological mystique. Even though the existence of these planes is now admitted, former attitudes still leave lingering doubts about UFO sightings relating to other secret, unconventionally designed aircraft under development.[75] Some even allege that some sightings relate to actual UFOs, rebuilt by the Americans after they had retrieved the crashed saucer. Such fantastic claims aside, it is clear that diverse types of exotic aviational hardware exist that could originate UFO reports.

Remotely Piloted Vehicles (RPVs)

The RPV is a missile-sized, remotely controlled aircraft, often equipped with powerful infra-red cameras. RPVs possess a marked night-flying capability, and can remain airborne in most adverse weather conditions. Their designs are various and include missile-, glider-, tub- or disc-shaped configurations. These devices are driven by a variety of propulsion systems: jet, turbo-prop, rotor blade or rocket; the type of propulsion dictated by the function they are to serve. Though normally used for reconnaissance, once stripped of surveillance equipment, they can be used as decoys to confuse heat-seeking missiles, or to test the airworthiness of new body designs intended for eventual manned operations.[76] A small number are used for civilian purposes, some even being employed by local councils in Britain to enforce drought orders. RPV development is mostly the preserve of the military, and tests are carried out over areas reserved for military exercises. These robot aircraft are designed to be capable of carrying out manoeuvres similar in all respects to those accredited to UFOs: sudden stops and starts, tight turns and fast acceleration are all well within the capabilities of the RPV. An observer misperceiving a nearby RPV as a large object at considerable distance, would be suitably astonished by any of the above manoeuvres, as he or she would see them as being carried out by a large object at anomalously high speeds.

Non-standard aircraft

'Flying wings' (boomerang-shaped aircraft) were developed in both the USA, by the Northrop Company, and in Germany, by the

Horten Brothers, during the late 1930s and early 1940s.[77] These devices had considerable problems with aerodynamic stability, which were subsequently overcome by advances in aviational technology.[78] The USAAF's saw-winged Stealth bomber is a direct lineal descendant of the Horten and Northrop designs. Both companies also flirted with oval-shaped aircraft. The USA used the prop-driven 'flying flapjack' in the 1940s. Then, in the early 1950s, in conjunction with the Avro Corporation of Canada, it developed a prototype jet-driven 'saucer'.[79] As with the early 'flying wings', this device was aeronautically unsound and was eventually abandoned. But despite early failures, work continued to develop a viable saucer-shaped aircraft. Recently, a man-carrying, disc-shaped device, constructed by the Moller Company of America, has reached an advanced state. The Moller Disc uses a number of VTOL engines distributed around its circumference.[80] One can only wonder, given the inherent aerodynamic instability of such a design, whether the idea would ever have been considered viable, were it not for the appearance of flying saucers? However, problems of airworthiness do not apply to lighter-than-air vessels, resulting in a number of operational oval- or saucer-shaped airships. The Hystar – a small, highly manoeuvrable, disc-shaped, mini-airship – is currently helping to fell lumber in British Columbia, Canada.[81]

Trojan horses

In 1953, the Robertson Panel (a scientific committee sponsored by the CIA to assess the UFO evidence extant then, suggested that the Soviets could, in any future superpower conflict, jam US military communication channels by generating a 'wave' of false UFO reports.[82] In the 1950s, Leon Davidson alleged that the CIA had created the UFO mystery for the sole purpose of obscuring classified tests and exercises.[83] More recently, in the 1970s, W A Harbinson went one better by alleging that UFOs were extremely advanced terrestrial devices piloted by cybernetically altered humans.[84] Scaling down these wild suggestions, it is possible to surmise that, on occasion, public belief in UFOs has been manipulated to cover in confusion the existence of secret military exercises. An extreme example occurred in the Soviet Union in September 1977, when a spy-satellite launch caused a spate of sensational UFO stories to emanate from the town of Petrozavodski.[85] These accounts were not dismissed by the Soviet authorities, usually hostile to such outbursts, as they hoped to use them to cover up the actuality of the launch. In the West, it is interesting to note that the vast majority of 'crashed flying saucer' stories originate from America; more specifically, from areas close to American military installations involved in missile experiments or work on classified aircraft.[86]

Reviewing the foregoing, it is probable that some 'true UFO' reports do concern sightings of unconventional aircraft. However the more extreme possibilities also referred to, like ETH, lack any solid supporting evidence. Reports potentially explicable in these terms (i.e., spaceships) are those referring to sightings of distant crescents, cross-, delta-, and missile-shaped UFOs. It is possible that RPVs and classified aircraft account for only a minority of sightings, compared with other causes. One would expect UFO reports originated by these devices to be more common around proving grounds, exercise zones and military establishments. It is equally possible that malfunctioning RPVs occasionally drift from these regions, giving rise to shock-horror stories of crashed saucers and aliens on ice.[87] It is unlikely, even in the present international climate, that further aerial experimentation will be discontinued. And so it is to be expected that the products of this, always clandestine, enterprise are likely to keep their status as prime ufological entertainment for generations of ufologists yet unborn.

SUBJECTIVE PHENOMENA

The term 'flying saucer' is a misnomer: a media misrepresentation of the crescent-shaped machines Arnold allegedly saw and described as 'moving like a saucer skipped over water'. Therefore, what can we make of claimed sightings of discoidal UFOs? Why do forms actually resembling those mistakenly attributed to the Arnold sighting appear in only a few reports? To be fair to an army of UFO percipients down the decades, Meaden's plasma vortex hypothesis and Campbell's astro-mirage hypothesis both allow for the appearance of 'saucer' forms. However, the dominance of the image of a circular spaceship, the 'flying saucer', is likely to be rooted in subjective preconceptions. Natural theories trying to account for its pre-eminence in flying saucery could well be at a disadvantage in that they would be trying endow a subjective supposition with a physical causation. Indeed, in every aspect of ufology, it is often difficult to deduce exactly what science's physical laws should be applied to, and what is simply due to subjective factors.

The 'Domed Disc' conundrum
The difficulty, and importance, of distinguishing between reality

and illusion in ufology becomes starkly apparent when reviewing the strange evolution of the 'domed disc'.[88] Numerous reports from the late 1940s and early 1950s describe flat-based, cupola-crowned discoids.[89] However, another version of this UFO form materialized in the wake of *Flying Saucers Have Landed*, a book published in 1953.[89] The relevant section was the one authored by George Adamski, who claimed to have had conversations with the occupants of a saucer (a Venusian scout ship) and to have photographed the machine.[90] His photographs show an extravagant-looking object, adorned with spherical 'landing gear', and benefiting from a cupola reminiscent of a gazebo with portholes. Despite the slings and arrows of outraged 'scientific' ufologists in the interim, Adamski's claims have never been categorically refuted.[91] The findings of the Russian Venus probes have undermined his claims somewhat, and have made it obvious that someone was lying about the spaceman coming from Venus. But who? Adamski or the long haired Ufonaut? A solution is made all the more difficult by the fact that UFOs closely resembling the Adamski 'Venusian Scout Ship' were reported by witnesses *before* the Adamski narrative was published.[92, 93] What option do we have, other than to consider the possibility that everyone is lying? Is it possible to suspect that those reports, including Adamski's, originated in the subjective assumptions of the witnesses? In which case, everybody was telling the truth – as they saw it.

As the UFO form has undergone radical change over the years, apparently staying just ahead of, but linked to, the advance of mankind's own space technology, the subjective spaceship syndrome becomes a viable proposition.[94] In the phenomenon's early years, the vast majority of craft-like forms were described in such terms as made them seem subject to Ford's ideas on streamlining. They all had seemingly non-functional, over-elaborate surface features, and were adorned with the kind of rocket-like protuberances that graced the American gas guzzlers of the 1950s. As car bodywork became more aerodynamically streamlined, UFOs underwent a comparable design change.[95] Hence the rather 'Victorian Science Fantasy Adamski Venusian Scout Ship' type UFO underwent a transformation in the moon-shot era of the 1960/70s, becoming altogether more slick and streamlined. This metamorphosis continued into the Eighties.[96] By then, the 'UFO role model' would seem to have been the concoctions of the movie industry's special-effects departments, as they tried to outdo each other in alien hardware in movies like *Star Wars*, and others of that ilk. Obligingly, UFOs became fitted with exotic features, such as piping, panels and retro rockets. I know imitation is supposed to be the sincerest form of flattery, but in this case, what's the point?[97] I can't understand why 'highly advanced' aliens would wish their craft to resemble the latest fads in 'primitive' terrestrial design logic. Can you?

Alien contacts?

The presumed 'pilots' of the flying saucers fared no better.[98] Once the unviability of their alleged solar origins was discovered from empirical data supplied by the various superpower space-probes, they – without explanation or apology – transferred their bases of operations to distant stars, far-flung galaxies and other even more unspecific distant locations. Their appearance changed, but not too radically at first. They became 'spacebrother' type aliens, but still retained a human-like appearance. Then, starting in the mid-Sixties, they really let their appearance go to pot.[99] They became dwarf-like, bulbous-headed horrors, with large, protruding, almond-shaped eyes, and rudimentary noses and mouths. Their complexions became corpse-like, with a distinct greyish cast. Perhaps they were returning to their roots, as it's clear that they now resembled any number of fictional aliens who had appeared on the covers of many of the pre-UFO age, pulp science-fiction magazines.[100] In this context, it is interesting to note that this type of alien, variously designated 'greys' or EBEs (Extraterrestrial Biological Entities), has become pre-eminent in America – the home of the pulp science-fiction magazine.

In keeping with our national temperament, British Ufonauts have not gone to such extreme metamorphic lengths.[101] For the most part, those reported by British percipients have remained reassuringly human looking. Their taste in clothes is also encouragingly eccentric, favouring skin-tight cat-suits paired with balaclava-like headgear. They are also noticeably more polite than their American counterparts. By comparison, the 'greys' appear to be rudely robotic, devoid of humour and personality. Despite these marked differences, both sets of spacefarers have something in common: that is their amateur attempts to expunge the memory of the encounter from the minds of their various percipients by post-hypnotic suggestion. Because of the failure on the part of these alleged entities to supress such memories, it is clear from the ongoing contactee/abductee material that the nature of contact has changed more than somewhat. In the good old days, Adamskian entities would treat their percipients to uplifting metaphysical monologues while transporting them – free of charge – on round-trips to the moon, Mars, Venus and Uranus. In the 1960s, as their appearance began to change for the worse, they became more distant. From the 1970s onwards, they really got the monk on, and sent their percipients to Coventry.[102] The most anyone can expect from them these days is to be ignored coldly, while being subjected to an embarrassingly emetic examination – anaesthetic not included.

This evolution in UFO entities, although ongoing, was never a truly lineal process.[103] Likewise, cultural factors do not always seem to dictate totally the format of these unnerving experiences. There has always been a wide variety of entity shapes extant. World-wide sightings of 'monsters', goblin-like humanoids, and giant or miniature anthropods surfaced in the past, and are still reported these days – albeit in smaller numbers. Very few 'monster' UFO incidents have occurred in Britain, which is puzzling, when you consider how rich our cultural folklore is with regard to mythical creatures.[104] Similarly, British percipients have had few documented visits from those clown princes of ufology – the MIB (the Men In Black).[105] Often oriental in looks, they are the bane of American ufology, due to their predilection for turning up and representing themselves as being from the Establishment, while attempting to put the frighteners on the hapless percipient. Their recorded behaviour is strange, to say the least, and – if they had been seen more regularly in Britain – would lead one to presume that they were from the Ministry of Funny Walks. Like UFOs, and other alleged UFO-related entities, no physical evidence has been produced to put their actual existence beyond doubt. Perhaps they are no longer cost-effective, as their numbers, even in America, have been in noticeable decline since the termination of Project Blue Book (an official USAAF UFO investigation body) in 1969. British witnesses still occasionally report visitations from alleged Men from the Ministry who, as their appearance and behaviour is always seemingly normal, must be accepted as bona fide human beings – even if their claimed identities are suspect.[106]

Subjective causes

From reviewing the foregoing, it seems that those aspects of the UFO enigma most suggestive of an extraterrestrial explanation exhibit strong subjective elements. Entity reports, like folk-tales, show marked cultural differences depending on their point of origin. Also, their content is too replete with anthropocentric cosmology – supported by an allegedly advanced technology that subtly reflects human aspirations in such matters – to be entirely convincing as an encounter with creatures from beyond the final frontier. Too much fiction and not enough science, I'd say. So, what instigates these errant experiences? Fabrication is the first thing that comes to mind – motivated by a desire for money, notoriety and possibly an adolescent urge to deride ufology. There are also people who are pathological liars, individuals driven by the need to tell tall tales. These are more to be pitied than castigated, as their motives are more psychological than pecuniary. But witness deception is far from being the only possible cause for UFO reports, that is, if you don't count those individuals who deceive even themselves in this regard.

Fantasy-prone personalities   One form of UFO experience most likely to have a subjective causation is the repeater phenomenon.[107] This relates to instances where a single individual claims to have experienced a constant stream of UFO incidents. There appear to be two classes of repeaters: those reporting low-strangeness, easily explained, incidents; and those claiming close-quarter observations of 'spaceships' and 'entities'. This latter group seems to include individuals with a history of paranormal experiences; everything from angels to astral travel is grist to their metaphysical mill. This class of witness could well be what is known as a fantasy-prone personality (FPP); that is, an individual who is prone to experiencing 'waking dreams'.[108] The fantasized surroundings featured in these occurrences are marked by their realistic vividness, and the illusory entities often encountered in these dreamscapes seem quite solid, and behave as if they had an independent existence.[109] Although most FPPs eventually come to realize that their experiences are lucid fantasies, there are those who have, or develop, a need to believe in the reality of these subjective experiences. They may, as a result, subconsciously use their 'visionary' ability either to reinforce belief systems impor-tant to them, or for ego inflation, or even as a catharsis. Other close-encounter witnesses, who live without vivid hallucinatory episodes intruding into their everyday lives, may well be 'dormant' FPPs, their unusual gift only becoming active when triggered by stressful situations. With this in mind, it is worth pointing out that some close-encounter witnesses report 'psychic' occurrences and black-outs before, and for sometime after, the onset of their more ufological experiences.

'One-off' Close Encounters   But what of 'one-off' close encounters, where a witness claims only a single UFO experience? It is possible that these also involve the subjective superimposition of a memorized UFO archetype on to a perception of the outside world. Many high-strangeness incidents occur in dark, low noise/activity environments: the ideal surroundings for inducing

sensory deprivation – and hallucinations; all that might be required is an individual in a receptive state of mind, and the presence of a suitably startling stimulus, for their psyche to turn towards thoughts of UFOs. Any of the phenomena outlined above would do the trick, as all of them are, by association, equated to the discoid archetype propagated by the media. The process involved in this transaction would be the long recognized one of how the human brain interprets visual stimuli in normal situations. The appearance of every object a human being sees in their lifetime is stored in the brain, for later comparison. When a previously seen object is seen again, the internal comparison assures a speedy recognition. In the subjective UFO experience, the unfamiliar visual stimuli are compared to a UFO image (possibly media generated, although there are other sources for UFO enculturation) dredged up from the perceiver's memory by reason of an inbuilt cultural expectation, and the memory of the subjective object is superimposed by the witness over the objective observation. But how could an hallucinatory experience result in the coherent narrative found in reports of alien contact? This again could have something to do with the way the human brain is 'wired'. Most of the dreams we recall, and consider to be a single fantasy, in actuality consist of random series, which an assimulator mechanism in the brain moulds into one, complete and logical, scenario. Could this process be responsible for creating a consistent, if somewhat weird, 'story line', from what was in acutality a mad whirl of unconnected hallucinatory images? Several high-strangeness reports contain references to observed anomalies affecting the sighting locale.[110] Is this an indication that the episode was entirely illusory, or that the witness's perception of reality was distorted by an unsuspected altered state of consciousness?

Anomalous amnesia   Also relevant are instances of 'missing time'.[111] A few UFO witnesses have claimed to have found themselves at locations far from where the incident was precipitated, with no memory of how they arrived there. Others report that they cannot account for significant portions of time subsequent to observing a UFO. A similar phenomenon often occurs with many percipient's recollections of close encounter/ abduction. Their memory of the event jumps from one happening to another without affording any clue as to how the sequence of remembered events is connected. This also often happens with recollections of dream impressions, in which context it is believed to be the result of the brain's inbuilt assimilator having difficulty in linking the dream sequence together. However, there is a better explanation for the missing time effect: it seems more probable that it owes its existence to what is known as traumatic amnesia. Apparently, the brain is capable of automatically editing input: I don't wish to know that, so kindly leave my brain. This capability is triggered by a number of things, particularly unpleasant events, sensory deprivation (boredom) or repetitive tasks. Throughout what is termed the fugue (day-dreaming) mental state, a person functions normally, but on autopilot as it were. They carry on walking, driving or whatever, but, due to the fugue, the ability to remember precise details of actions carried out while in the state is inhibited. You can remember what you were thinking about, but for the life of you, you can't remember what you were doing while you were thinking.[112] As it is possible that the FPP accepts their internal fantasy (thinking) as the real world, perhaps the effect is that while they cannot recall what they were actually doing, they recall as if real what they were thinking about. It has been demonstrated that the hypnotic trance is a highly fantasy-prone mental state. So, once again, caution must be applied to any UFO scenario derived by this method: as the results of Melvin Harris's investigation into the 'reincarnation evidence' on the Bloxham tapes unequivocally demonstrated.[113] Another good reason for caution, when confronted by ufological evidence obtained hypnotically, is the fact that Alvin Lawson and Dr W McCall produced equally evidential UFO material from hypnotized subjects *who had never ever had a UFO experience*.[114] So it begins to look very much like the final frontier is located somewhere a little bit closer to home than outer space.

All in the mind? It is time now to see if there are any biological factors which might support the contention that metaphysical manifestations, including those pertaining to UFOs, are more likely than not to be subjective.[115] To begin with, the majority of high-strangeness incidents only involve a single witness. Studies of witness psychology have also made some interesting discoveries.[116] The Anamnesis Protocol, conducted by Ken Phillips and Dr Alex Keul, seems to have discovered marked psychological differences between high-strangeness percipients and those who have never experienced such intrusion into their lives. Close-encounter witnesses have a greater ability to recall their dreams, have more psychic experiences, and are more cosmologically inclined than Mr or Mrs Average. It may be that some peripheral physical factor is being overlooked in all this testing: something as simple as Jenny

Randles suggested in *Mind Monsters*, that there might be a connection with blood sugar levels.[117] In this context, it is interesting to note that high-strangeness experiences normally occur at night – a time when blood sugar levels are at their lowest! Whatever the reasons, there is increasing indication that when it comes to solving the mystery of the UFOs, science will triumph over saucery in the end.

THE MUNDANE–SYNTHESISTIC HYPOTHESIS

After reviewing the major scientific concepts proposed, over the years, to account for UFOs, it appears that most of those examined have something to recommend them. Although many have at present only a theoretical basis, certain 'true UFO' reports so clearly display attributes theoretically attributed to the proposed scientific solutions that we are forced to consider that, at the very least, they are *potentially* viable as solutions to the mystery. In fact, they can, when taken in conjunction with each other, account for all the UFO phenomenon's documented attributes; so much so that it now becomes possible to propose the following: *'True UFO' reports can be explained by the implied interaction of diverse rare mundane stimuli.*

The ramifications of this proposal dispense with many of the insurmountable problems dogging ufological exegesis from its inception. If valid, it would explain why *no* clear patterns in UFO behaviour have ever emerged from comparative analyses of the documented reports. If a report of a riveted, plate-shaped, domed disc has a subjective cause, and another report, of a weaving, bobbing 'light', involves plasma vortex or ionization phenomena, it becomes all too clear why attempts directly to connect them have failed. The only thing connecting them could be the popular UFO mythos – which in itself is based in subjectivity. This twentieth-century folklore acts as both soul and guiding spirit to popular ufology. Without its services as a celestial seamstress, invisibly mending the glaring rips in the exotic tapestry of the UFO belief system, all that would exist would be a mere handful of sporadic reports, which would lack any apparent connection – as was the case with aerial anomaly reports occurring prior to 1947.[118]

The primary concern is to establish to what extent undetected misperception distorts the aparent number of 'true UFOs'. It is more than probable that, despite the intensive efforts of investigators, a good number of Identifiable Flying Object reports are erroneously accepted as 'inexplicable', due to the undetected element of witness misperception. In consideration of this factor, it is therefore assumed that half of any initial total of 'unknowns' is accountable in those terms. Hence, a base figure of 10 per cent unknowns, becomes 5 per cent, and so on, prior to reaching the stage detailed below.

Moving on to the genuine 'true UFO' population, a randomly selected sample of these reports, with an atypical strangeness population of 75 per cent low-strangeness incidents, and 25 per cent close-encounter incidents, could possibly be comprised as follows:

- 5 per cent of *low* strangeness and 10 per cent of *high* strangeness 'true UFO' reports are *undetected hoaxes*.
- 40 per cent of reports are observations of *anomalous mirages*; the majority being *low* strangeness incidents.
- 30 per cent of incidents, less than half of which are *high* strangeness reports, involve *ionization phenomena*.

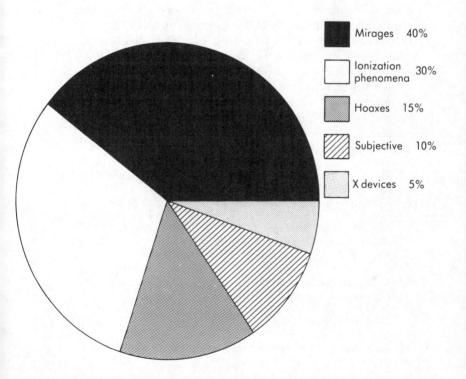

Figure 4 *The UFO phenomena: a theoretical model.*

- 5 per cent of reports, the majority being *low* strangeness incidents, relate to *unconventional aircraft*.
- 10 per cent of all UFO events, the vast majority being *high* strangeness incidents, are attributable to exotic *subjective phenomena*.

I have called this theoretical model of the UFO phenomenon the Mundane–Synthesistic Hypothesis, with synthesistic defined as *many separate factors cumulating into a single result*. The percentages quoted are approximations only, and are used only to indicate the general level which each effect plays in this concept of a completely naturalistic UFO phenomenon. We know that 85 per cent of UFO sightings are explicable. Of those remaining, many are almost certain to be attributable to exotic atmospheric, subjective and/or manufactured phenomena. Paradoxically, by adopting this strategy, the possibility of some UFO reports being the result of objective observation of really anomalous aerial apparitions is actually increased: the extraterrestrial hypothesis solution for one, as it is clear that the presently accepted 'base' number of unknowns is far too large for them *all* to have been spacecraft, and the reader is, therefore, left to his or her own deductions in the matter. It seems hardly likely that the Mundane–Synthesistic Hypothesis will be the last word in ufology. However, if it encourages others to seek scientific rather than science-fiction solutions to the UFO enigma, then the effort of compiling it will not have been wasted.

REFERENCES

1   Moore, R   'Characteristics of True UFOs', *BUFORA Bulletin*, 26 & 27
2   Hendry, A   *UFO Handbook* (Sphere, 1980): pp. 22–23
3   Figure quoted by BUFORA (British UFO Research Association)
4   Sieiger, B   *Project Blue Book* (Ballantine, 1976): pp. 23–36
5   BUFORA *UFO Investigation* (BUFORA, 1979): Appendix 11
6   *UFO Handbook* pp. 38–40
7   Randles, J   *UFO Study* (Hale, 1981): pp. 110–112
8   Campbell, S   'Astronomical UFOs', *BUFORA Bulletin*, 21: pp. 16–19
9   *UFO Handbook*: pp. 24–30
10   *UFO Handbook*: pp. 41–44
11   *UFO Handbook*: pp. 58–61
12   *UFO Investigation* (BUFORA, 1979): sections 7. H(2)–7. H(3)
13   *UFO Study*: pp. 119
14   Blackmore, S   *The Perception of UFOs. UFO/IFO* (Probe Press, 1982): pp. 12–13
15   *UFO Handbook*: pp. 153–154

16 Randles, J   *UFO Reality* (Hale, 1983): p. 26
17 BUFORA 'UFOs 1947–1987', *Fortean Tomes*, 1987: pp. 175
18 Harney, J   'The Plurality of Worlds', *Magonia*, Issue 6, 1981: p. 2
19 Shklovski, I S & Sagan, C   *Intelligent Life in the Universe* (Holden Day, 1966)
20 Turner, R   *Observers Manned Spaceflight* (Warne, 1978): pp. 168–180
21 Randles, J & Warrington, P   *UFOs: A British Viewpoint* (ABC Books, 1980) pp. 189–196
22 *The Star Wars Sourcebook* (West End Games Inc., 1987): pp. 6–7
23 Audouze, J & Israel, G   *The Cambridge Atlas of Astronomy* (Cambridge Press, 1988): pp. 274–275
24 Berry, A   *The Iron Sun* (Coronet, 1979)
25 Moore, W & Berlitz, C   *The Roswell Incident* (Granada, 1980)
26 Hopkins, B   *Intruders* (Sphere, 1988)
27 Smith, N   'British UFO Photographs', *UFO Times*, 3, BUFORA: pp. 3–8
28 Condon, Dr E U (Ed.)   *The Scientific Study of UFOs* (Bantam Books, 1969): pp. 598–653
29 *The Weather Book* (Mermaid Books, 1988): pp. 103–121
30 Corliss, W R   *Rare Halos, Mirages, Anomalous Rainbows* (Sourcebook Project, 1984): pp. 150–151
31 Campbell, S   'The Astro-Mirage Hypothesis', *Magonia*, 27 (Sept 1987)
32 Clarke, D & Oldroyd, G   *Spooklights: A British Survey* (Private, 1985)
33 Klass, P   *UFOs Explained* (Random House, 1974): pp. 63–71
34 British Astronomical Association Handbook
35 Delebecque, A   'Atmospheric Refractions at the Surface of Water', *Monthly Weather Review*, 1896, 24: p. 371
36 For example, Evans, H *Frontiers of Reality* (Guild Publishing, 1989): p. 51
37 Campbell, S   'UFO: Hoax or Mirage', *The British Journal of Photography*, 15 June 1989
38 Moore, R   'Characteristics of True UFOs', *BUFORA Bulletin*, 26 & 27
39 Campbell, S   'Mirage Over Edinburgh', *The Journal of Meterology*, November 1987, Vol. 12, No. 123
40 Corliss, W R   *Lightning, Auroras, Nocturnal Lights* (Sourcebook Project, 1983): pp. 54–91
41 Stenhoff, M   'Plasma Vortex Rings in the Lower Atmosphere', BUFORA 1976 Conference Proceedings: Table 1
42 *UFO Handbook*: pp. 247–248
43 *The Weather Book*: pp. 82–89
44 Meaden, G T   *The Circles Effect and its Mysteries* (Artetech Publications, 1989): pp. 53 & 74–80
45 ibid. pp. 93–98
46 ibid. pp. 82–83
47 Lockwood, C   'A Force to be Reckoned With', *The Unexplained*, No. 49: pp. 970–973
48 Figueiredo, J   'Manual of Psycho–Psychological Effects Attributable to UFO Phenomena', UFO Insight, Vol. 1, No. 5: p. 1–10
49 Corliss, W R   *Lightning, Auroras, Nocturnal Lights*: pp. 1–10 (Sourcebook Project, 1983): pp. 110–114

50 Persinger, M A & Lafreniere, G *Space–Time Transients and Unusual Events* (Nelson Hall, 1977)
51 Brady, Dr B T & Rockwell, G A 'The Laboratory Investigation of the Electrodynamics of Rock Fracture', *Nature*, May 1986
52 Devereux, P *Earthlights* (Turnstone, 1982)
53 Strand, E 'Project Hessdalen: Final Technical Report 1984' (Project Hessdalen, 1985)
54 Randles, J *The Pennine UFO Mystery* (Granada, 1983)
55 Devereux, P *Earthlights Revelation* (Blandford, 1990): pp. 59–86
56 Brady, Dr B T & Rockwell, G A *Nature*, May 1986
57 Devereux, P *Earthlights Revelation*: pp. 197–201
58 Klass, Phillip J *UFOs: Identified* (Random House, 1968)
59 'UFO Tracks Aircraft', *Yufos Quest*, Vol. 6, No. 4, Sept/Oct 1986: pp. 29–30
60 Campbell's 'Are UFOs an Atmospheric Phenomena?' *Journal of Transient Ariel Phenomena*, Vol. 2, No. 2, March 1980: pp. 34–35
61 Haines Dr, R *UFO Phenomena and the Behavioural Scientist* (Scarecrow Press, 1979): pp. 401
62 Corliss, W R *Lightning, Auroras, Nocturnal Lights* (Sourcebook Project, 1983): pp. 97
63 Randles, J & Fuller, P *Crop Circles: A Mystery Solved* (Hale, 1990): pp. 100–102
64 Campbell, S 'Jupiter and the Natural Theory of UFOs', *Journal of Transient Ariel Phenomena*, Vol. 3, No. 3: pp. 141–142
65 Story, R (Ed.) *The Encylopedia of UFOs* (New English Library, 1980): pp. 366–369
66 Campbell, S 'Close Encounter at Livingston', BUFORA 1982
67 Campbell, S 'UFO: Hoax or Mirage', *The British Journal of Photography*, 15 June 1989
68 Campbell, S 'Livingston: A New Hypothesis', *Journal of Transient Ariel Phenomena*, Vol. 4, No. 3: pp. 80–87
69 Randles, J 'Fire in the Sky', BUFORA 1989
70 Campbell, S 'Peter Day's UFO Movie', *The British Journal of Photography*, March 1991
71 Walter, W 'UFOs Over Germany', *BUFORA Bulletin*, No. 26 June 1988
72 Harbinson, W A 'The UFO Goes to War', *The Unexplained*, Vol. 4, Issue 38: pp. 746–749 (Orbis Publications, 1981)
73 Birdsall, M I *The Ultimate Solution. Twenty Twenty Vision* (Quest International, 1988): pp. 1–30
74 *Northern UFO News*, Sept/Oct 1986: pp. 2–3
75 Lear, J 'Grudge 13: The Missing Report', *UFO Brigantia* 36: pp. 11 & 20–26
76 Birdsall, G I 'Ufology: Into the Future?' *Quest*, Vol. 8, No. 1, 1988: pp. 2–15 (Quest International)
77 Birdsall, M I *The Ultimate Solution. Twenty Twenty Vision*: pp. 6–10
78 Sachs, M *The UFO Encyclopedia* (Corgi, 1981): pp. 108–109
79 Sachs, M *The UFO Encyclopedia*: p. 26
80 Birdsall, G I 'Ufology: Into the Future': pp. 8–9

81 The *Daily Mail*, 1 May 1986
82 Story, R (Ed.) *The Encyclopedia of UFOs* (New English Library, 1980): pp. 310–311
83 Davidson, L *Flying Saucers: An Analysis of the Air Force Project Blue Book Special Report No. 14* Blue Book Publishers, (White Plains, NY 1976)
84 Harbinson, W A 'Secret Weapons & Cyborgs', *The Unexplained*, Vol. 4, No. 40: pp. 790–793 (Orbis Publications, 1981)
85 Oberg, J *UFOs and Outer Space Mysteries* (The Donning Company, 1982): pp. 161–181
86 For example, Schuessler, J 'Blind Terror in Texas', *The Unexplained*, Vol. 9, Issue 107: pp. 2121–2146 (Orbis Publications, 1982)
87 Brookensmith, P 'UFOs: A Federal Case', *The Unexplained*, Vol. 5, Issue 56: pp. 1118–1120 (Orbis Publications, 1981)
88 Story, R (Ed.) *The Encyclopedia of UFOs*: pp. 45–51
89 Adamski, G & Leslie, D *Flying Saucers Have Landed* (T W Laurie, 1953)
90 Story, R (Ed.) *The Encyclopedia of UFOs*: pp. 45–50
91 Campbell, S 'The Birth of the UFO Myth', *Probe* Report, April 1983, Vol. 3, No. 4: pp. 5–9
92 For example, Cramp, L 'Did Scout Ship Land at Isle of Wight', *Flying Saucer Review*, Dec 1961, Vol. 7, No. 6: pp. 16–17; 'Heywood Saucer, 1972', *BUFORA Journal*, May/June 1978: p. 19; *BUFORA Journal*, Vol. 8, No. 2, April 1979: pp. 11–13; *UFO News Bulletin*, Vol. 2, No. 3, March–April 1980: p. 16; *BUFORA Bulletin*, No. 18, July 1985: pp. 2–3
93 *Yufos Journal*, Vol. 2, No. 2, May 1983: pp. 7 & 9
94 Story, R (Ed.) *The Encyclopedia of UFOs*: p. 338
95 BUFORA 'UFOs 1947–1987', *Fortean Tomes*, 1987: p. 73
96 Randles, J 'The UFO World 1986', BUFORA: p. 17
97 BUFORA *Phenomena* (Future, 1988): Plate 14, adjacent to p. 209
98 Story, R (Ed.) *The Encyclopedia of UFOs*: pp. 341–344, the Soccorro, New Mexico Incident
99 Fuller, John *The Interrupted Journey* (Corgi, 1981)
100 The Mekon from the DAN DARE comic strip appearing in *The Eagle* comic (*c.*1950s)
101 *The Janos People,* Johnson, F (Neville Spearman, 1982)
102 Hopkins, B *Intruders* (Sphere, 1988)
103 Bowen, C (Ed.) *The Humanoids* (Futura, 1977)
104 McEwan, G *Mystery Animals of Britain & Ireland* (Hale, 1987)
105 Evans, H 'Men in Black' articles appearing in *The Unexplained*, Vol. 3, Issue 26: pp. 510–513; Vol. 3, Issue 27: pp. 526–529; Vol. 3, Issue 29: pp. 578–580
106 Randles, J *UFO Study* (Hale, 1981): pp. 219–222
107 Randles, J & Whetnal, P *Alien Contacts* (Neville Spearman, 1980)
108 'All the World's a Stage', *The Unexplained*, Vol. 13, Issue 153: pp. 3050–3053
109 'Birmingham Witness Meets Spaceman', *Flying Saucer Review*, Mar–April 1958, Vol. 4, No. 2: pp. 5–6

110 Randles, J   *UFO Reality* (Hale, 1983): pp. 96–101
111 Randles, J & Warrington, P   *UFOs: A British Viewpoint* (ABC Books): pp. 155–163; such instances appearing throughout the experiences detailed
112 Evans, H   *Altered States of Consciousness* (Aquarian Press, 1989): pp. 77–80
113 Harris, M   *The Unexplained*, Vol. 12, Issue 135: pp. 2698–2790; Vol. 11, Issue 132: pp. 2626–2629; Vol. 12, Issue 135: pp. 2798–2800
114 Lawson, A   'The Abduction Experience: A Testable Hypothesis', *Magonia*, 10: pp. 3–18
115 Randles, J   *UFO Study* (Hale, 1981): pp. 198–202
116 BUFORA 'UFOs 1947–87', *Fortean Tomes*, 1987: pp. 230–237
117 Black, I   'A Mars a Day Helps you Work, Rest . . . and Meet Aliens!', *UFO Brigantia*, No. 41: pp. 11–12
118 Randles, J   *Mind Monsters* (Aquarian Press, 1990)

CHAPTER FIVE

A SECRET NEVER TO BE TOLD?

Roger Ford

Even before the explosion of flying saucers into the public forum, there had been a subculture devoted to the premiss that 'we are not alone'. Although most of these protoproponents of 'aliens in our midst' saw them in more occult terms as demons, gods, advanced souls et al., ET was not entirely neglected, and a number of manuscripts purported to be communications from other solar inhabitants. All that flying saucery did was to give added impetus to the beliefs of those who hungered for a *deus-ex-machina* solution to current human problems. So, from the sociological point of view, the idea of extraterrestrials is nothing really new and has demonstrably, in one form or another, been part of the weft and warp of Life As We Know It. That being the case, what, if anything, makes it different this time?

In the past, the aliens, of whatever variety, were always connected to a spiritual outlook: there was an element of unreality about them insofar as they could only be apprehended by those who were in some way worthy of the contact. With the advent of the Arnold report, things took on a more secular slant, and it seemed that just about anybody could expect to see flying saucers – worthy or not. In other words, a phenomenon long known to students of the various Arcana apparently made its bid to become part of objective reality, and reports surfaced that – taken at face value – strongly indicated that the earth was playing host to Something from Somewhere Else. Due no doubt to mankind's own burgeoning scientific aspirations, this 'elsewhere' was conceived of as being 'outer space'. The case was 'conclusively' proved over and over again as more and more evidential reports surfaced in the media of the day. No lesser person than Clyde Tombaugh, the discoverer of the planet Pluto, went on record with his own observation of a flying saucer, which should, considering his scientific standing at that time, have put the whole thing beyond any doubt.[1] But it did not, and his observation, made in the company of others as qualified as himself, was dismissed by the then foremost sceptic Donald Menzel, in a way that made it appear that Tombaugh was unable to tell his azimuth from his elevation. Although the ET hypothesis seemed the most economical for explaining the reports then surfacing, it was rejected outright, and in such terms that made it appear that a cover-up was in operation: this aspect of ufology has exercised the ingenuity of many highly qualified, and decidedly dedicated, proponents of the ET hypothesis ever since. The list of names of those who now accept that aliens from space are operating on earth is only exceeded by the number of letters after their names. So why, in the main, are their arguments not taken seriously, and they themselves become the butt of jokes in bad taste?

The problem, then as now, is the fact that nobody has yet produced a flying saucer for scientific study, which is not to say that such an object has not fallen into Establishment hands. In fact, it is maintained by Stanton Freidman, a nuclear physicist and a convinced and very convincing proponent of the ET hypothesis, that such alien hardware has been in the possession of the American authorities since 1947. So why don't they own up? Obtaining an answer to that question has employed the intellects of ufologists for well over 40 years.

Ufology, whether it intended to do so or not, has been instrumental in presenting human society with the same kind of information as upset the Cardinals at the time of Galileo. Those worthy upholders of the status quo refused to look through the telescope Galileo so obligingly made available to them in order to prove his point. They averred that they didn't need to because they already *knew* he was wrong. A similar attitude is now noticeable in the assertions of the present-day prelates of the scientific status quo. Certainly, if flying saucers are alien vehicles, our present consensus reality will become redundant: a prospect not taken lightly by those who have a vested interest in keeping things as they are. What good are degrees and diplomas in subjects that are no longer relevant? Hence the official animosity to ufology – especially in its ET paradigm. So, despite the currently indeterminate sociological risks involved, is there any evidence that UFOs have fallen into the hands of any of the major world governments? According to the 'crash retrievalists', there is. However, although the case that can be made is circumstantially strong, it has, as yet, made little impression, due to the expert debunking and outright stonewalling by the Establishment concerned. The burden of proof is with the ufologists who, due to the effort involved in their attempts to force an admission of cover-up from their Establishment antagonists, have ignored – or not recognized the potential for making their point – of a 'crash' that occurred well before ufology was a twinkle in the eye of the future.

It is a matter of public record that on 20 June 1908, at approximately 7 a.m. an object that eventually exploded with unprecedented violence in the air above the sparsely populated area in the central Siberian plateau known as the Tunguska, passed across the Himalayas, western China and Mongolia.[2] The first observation was made by travellers in the Gobi Desert, who watched in astonishment as the object traversed the sky as a well-defined point of light. At the time of this first observation, if we are to judge from documented reports, it would seem that the object was travelling well below the known speeds for incoming bolides, which vary between 51,500 and 148,000 km/hr (32,000 and 92,000 mph). In fact, its speed, as it passed over central Russia, is estimated to have been a comparatively leisurely 2,600 km/hr (1,600 mph). There are even indications that it was maintaining its altitude despite a noticeable deceleration in its forward momentum. The possibility that the object was in horizontal flight, at least by the time it was approaching its date with disaster over the Siberian taiga, is strongly argued by eyewitness testimony. According to this: 'An enormous "fiery object" had been seen over villages and towns throughout the Yenesei River Province, some described it as moving almost horizontally from the South.'[3]

From start to finish, the observed behaviour of the Tunguska object can be shown to be at odds with what could be expected of an incoming bolide. Therefore, although conventional science would feel less threatened by an inanimate explanation for it, on the lines of meteor, comet, small black hole or even contra-terrene matter, the recorded behaviour of the object makes 'intelligently guided device' the most probable explanation. In itself, the explosion of the object some eight km (five miles) up is enough to raise a forest of question marks on a par with the forest of trees flattened by the explosion. Firstly, inanimate objects do not explode: they either impact, burn up or disintegrate. Secondly, on the basis of eyewitness reports and the physical traces it left in its wake, the explosion was a nuclear one. But, atomic bombs in 1908? Professor Felix Zigel of the

Moscow Institute of Aviation, and a leading figure in modern Soviet studies of the 1908 Tunguska event, is adamant that no other conclusion is possible. He points out that there are just too many points of similarity with the effects generated by mankind's own nuclear endeavours for the Tunguska superblast to have been caused by anything else. One effect, in particular, would seem to be conclusive. It is clear from the evidence that the energy released by the exploding object was several per cent of the total energy output, and this ratio between the parameters is the hallmark of nuclear explosions.

However, if this fact is insufficient to persuade you that something decidedly different met its end in the cold Siberian skies, more convincing evidence supportive of the conclusion that an intelligently guided device was in difficulties as it overflew Russia can be deduced from the highly unusual behaviour of the object as it approached the point of explosion. For one thing, its speed was too low for it to have maintained altitude in almost horizontal flight in the way it reportedly did had it only been an inanimate intruder. The penultimate low speed argues for a correspondingly, anomalously low re-entry speed which, if it were only a meteoric body, would have resulted in it falling almost perpendicularly to earth, due to the action of gravity and atmospheric braking effect. Instead, it was seen to soar over the Asian mainland in a long sloping trajectory. Furthermore, it would seem from the documentation available that this strange object retained its integrity to the point of explosion. Unlike incandescent meteoric bodies, and even our own returning space junk, it did not give evidence of throwing off any smaller parts of itself as a result of ongoing and naturally generated disintegration due to uncontrolled re-entry. From this, it must be suspected that the object was in powered flight, and was being guided down rather than falling uncontrollably, and that the noise that accompanied its descent could have been generated by its power source in operation. This suspicion is accentuated by the fact that the object appears to have carried out a manoeuvre in the atmosphere, changing its direction of approach to the explosion site from south-east to south-west. Once again, Professor Zigel is adamant that all the extant evidence indicated that 'Before the blast the Tunguska body described in the atmosphere a tremendous arc of about 375 miles in extent (in azimuth).'[4]

Apparently the manoeuvre was initiated over a town called Keshma, and took the object off its original flight path towards the village of Preobrazhenka, where once again it changed direction in such a way that it would have crossed the original

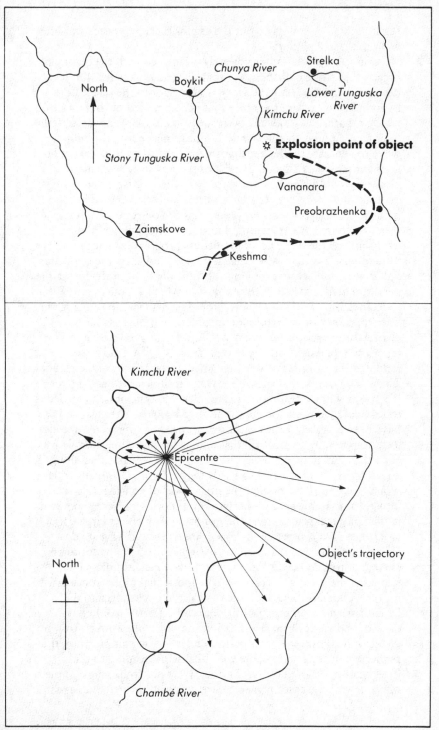

Figure 5 Maps showing the anomalous flight path and explosion pattern
of the Tunguska object.

flight path at right angles. But the explosion supervened, and up it went in a blaze of glory.

Turning now to another anomaly connected with the incoming object, that is the ballistic wave that allegedly preceded it in its descent. A massive ballistic wave is necessary to the scientific hypotheses to explain the noise that accompanied the object along its flight path. But if, as has been surmised, the object was actually in powered flight, then it would not have needed such a ballistic wave to generate the racket that startled the Russian peasants on its flight path – as anyone living close to any of today's major airports would be able to confirm. So is there or isn't there any evidence indicating the existence of this ballistic wave? The ballistic-wave hypothesis presumes that the object was moving at meteoric, certainly supersonic, speed up to the point of the explosion, as the noise accompanied its progress to that point. The difficulty here is that the evidence strongly indicates the opposite and that the object was moving subsonically – certainly during the penultimate phase before the explosion which vapourized it. What such an anomalously low speed would have meant in terms of the life expectancy of an inanimate intruder from outer space has already been argued, but what would the effect have been in regard to a massive ballistic wave? Arguably, it would have rendered the prospect of one being generated almost non-existent. There is no doubt that the object was subsonic as it passed over Russia, as witness testimony makes clear that the noise preceded the appearance of the object in the sky: a sequence that would have been reversed if the object was moving at supersonic speeds. Yet, despite this, science still insists that the preceding rumble was caused by a massive ballistic wave the object was pushing along ahead of itself as it rushed towards the ground. Necessarily, this would seem to presume that the object was of considerable size, or moving at extreme speed – perhaps even both – to have generated it. The physical traces argue the opposite. Any object large enough to survive such a supersonic descent intact should have made a considerable hole in the taiga, or in breaking up at an altitude of between three and eight km (two and five miles) should have peppered the area with craters as the individual pieces smashed into the Tunguska like a charge of celestial buckshot; and the ballistic wave – composed of incandescent gases – would have caused its own devastation ahead of the point of disintegration by virtue of it continuing for a period under its own momentum, thus rendering any epicentre somewhat diffuse. According to the investigations carried out at the site by Leonid Kulik, the complete opposite was the case. The epicentre was well defined and, even more strange, the major damage caused was behind and not ahead of the object's flight path. This can only mean that the massive ballistic wave, if ever it had existed in the first place, had disappeared in those final moments. From the data collected by successive expeditions to the area, it became clear that the destruction of the forest spread out fan-like behind the epicentre. This provoked Professor Zigel to speculate that this 'directional element' of the explosion argued for an object made up of 'two parts': an outer shell, and an interior containing something capable of exploding with nuclear violence. Perhaps even more significantly, the Kulik expeditions discovered that the epicentre was not even on the flight path of the object, but at some distance to one side. This one fact, when taken in conjunction with the other anomalies, can only serve to indicate the probability that the Tunguska object was stationary in the atmosphere when the explosion occurred. So, as inanimate intruders from outer space do not benefit from braking facilities which enable them to hover in the air while seeking a suitable place to impact, the probability is that the Tunguska object was in some way artificial – with all the ramifications that conclusion implies.[5]

If it is unlikely that the Tunguska object will be admitted to be an unnatural object which, for reasons that can never be known, came to grief over Siberia, how much more unlikely then the admission that the claims of modern ufological crash retrievalists will be ratified by orthodoxy? The difficulties in following this line of ufological endeavour are almost insurmountable. Not only is it categorically denied by sundry military and scientific Establishments that any ufological crash retrieval has ever occurred, but when an anomalous object is recovered by persons other than the usual authorities, it soon becomes clear that the find clarifies nothing, and only adds to the general confusion by the possibility of hoax entering into consideration – as was the case in the Scarborough sky crash affair of 1957.

This case exemplifies the twists and turns encountered when attempting to verify claims of alien intrusion. The story is that on the evening of 21 November 1957, three men were travelling by car across Silpho Moor in East Yorkshire when a disc, which they had all seen glowing in the sky, crashed to the ground near to their car. It is interesting to note in the account which appeared in *Flying Saucer Review* shortly afterwards that the car had mysteriously stalled only seconds before the object hit the ground. Electromagnetic effect, or faulty carburettor? In view of the denouement, it hardly matters. One of the occupants of the car got out and went to find the object. It had apparently come to ground a matter of some 35 m (40 yards) from where the car was standing. Coming upon it, he was able to ascertain that it was small, only 46 cm (18 in) in diameter, and saucer shaped. Having located the object, he went back to fetch his two companions to witness his find. As he did so, he passed a young couple who were hurriedly making their way towards the object. Allegedly, when he returned with his two friends to the site of the sky crash, the object and the couple were nowhere to be seen. Suitably annoyed, the trio left the moor and there the matter might have ended except that the saucer, or at least a similar saucer, was eventually recovered by offering a small reward in the local Press. The details of this amazing episode were confirmed first hand when I interviewed, in late 1989, one of the original protagonists, Mr P Longbottom. It was to him that the retrieved saucer was taken so that he could decipher some very strange markings on its surface and on a scroll which had been recovered from its interior.[6] He seemed completely convinced that the artefact brought to him was the same one seen to crash on Silpho Moor. But, it can be argued, in view of the loss of the original, and the financial gain involved in the recovery, there is no real guarantee that the object returned was the self-same one that was briefly glimpsed on the ground by one of the men who now sought Longbottom's help in interpreting the scroll. As far as I was able to ascertain, the saucer was not returned by the couple who were suspected of having abducted it from the moor. In some ways, these two are as big a mystery as the saucer itself, in so far as they turned up on the moor to carry out their dastardly deed and then were never heard from again. All the extant accounts, and my informant, Longbottom, agreed that the recovered saucer was shaped something like a child's spinning top, was 46 cm (18 in) in diameter, 23 cm (nine in) through its thickest part, weighed 16 kg (35 lb), and was composed of the most mundane of materials. It also seemed to have been made to such specifications as could have been duplicated, or even bettered, by terran manufacturing techniques. Not to put too fine a point on it, the thing looked a bit home made in more ways than one. Despite this, Mr Longbottom felt reasonably convinced that he had his hands on an alien artefact and insisted that if this was not so, why, at the time, were rumours rife of D–notices being served on the local Press to stop them reporting the incident? He even went so far as to claim that individuals akin to the American MIB (Men in Black) showed up for a brief period, and that poltergeist effects were experienced in the homes of the individuals who had found the saucer on Silpho Moor. These claims are quite ufologically orthodox, and have turned up in the testimony of percipients both before and after 1957. But what of the object itself? In itself, it was apparently unremarkable, and even my informant, some 30 or so years after the event, still had to admit that it could have been made on Earth by a sufficiently skilful metalworker. Apparently, when it was eventually opened up, there was discovered inside, not advanced alien automation, but copper tubing into which had been inserted a metal scroll, several pages in length, upon which had been incised words of cosmic wisdom. The outside of the saucer also had scratched upon it, in similar hieroglyphics, instructions on the disposition of the scroll. Mr Longbottom claimed that he had expended over one hundred hours in deciphering the hieroglyphics on both the outside of the saucer and the scroll it had contained. His results were, in many ways, hardly worth the effort, as the message, allegedly from an extraterrestrial called Ulo, contained nothing that was in any way evidential, and was merely a warning that the human race should mend its ways. In respect of this message, a writer with the pseudonym of Anthony Avendel put forward the most sensible opinion. He wrote: 'I accept this as a message, but I don't accept that it has come from another planet. I think it was devised as a method of presenting certain ideas to the public.'[7] In view of what then transpired, this seems fair comment. One of the investigating UFO groups had the object psychometrized (a mediumistic rather than scientific strategy), and by this means discovered that the object had been dropped from a Mercurian scout ship in transit to Yeovil. The investigation petered out and one group, with at least one member claiming alien contact, accepted the saucer as genuine; while another surmised that it was all a hoax by person or persons unknown. The saucer itself vanished, but Mr Longbottom told me that he felt that it still existed somewhere, and was possibly in the possession of the widow of the last known person to hold the saucer, but that her whereabouts were not known. In the end, it is hardly likely that the Silpho Moor affair was anything other than what it appeared to be at the time: some kind of hoax perpetrated by individuals who had let their atomic anxieties get the better of them and tried, in their own way, to do something about it. Yet, tantalizingly, even to this day, no one has come forward to claim responsibility for an episode that did much to detract from ufological credibility. The affair was tailor-made for Establishment science to step in and devastate ufology with a 'proper' investigation of the object – if indeed it was a hoax. The opportunity was ignored, and ufology was left to face the prospect that it had been taken for an interplanetary ride – metaphorically speaking of course. But by whom, and to what purpose?

The idea of deliberate disinformation being spread by Establishment sources to muddy ufological waters is held almost as an article of faith by those who pursue the crash-retrieval scenario. Some of the events surrounding the Silpho Moor affair could give rise to such speculations, but to understand why the idea of deliberate disinformation, especially in relation to retrieval of alien artefacts, has taken such a hold in some ufological quarters, the clock has to be turned back to the very beginnings of the UFO adventure – to the Maury Island 'hoax', which contained in embryo all the elements which later persuaded ufologists that deliberate attempts are being made to cover up some startling saucer secret.

To discuss, in isolation, the affair (which started with an alleged UFO sighting over Maury Island, in Puget Sound, Washington state) might be to miss the point entirely. For one thing, the year was 1947, and the sighting was dated three days before the one made by Kenneth Arnold of the objects he claimed to have seen over Mount Rainier in June of that year. It was also the year of the now much-disputed saucer crash at either Aztec or Roswell, or both, in New Mexico, also during June, which led to the Hangar 18 mythos, and the setting up of a covert council of experts under the title of Operation Majestic Twelve. The conduct of the accredited authorities in all the above left much to be desired, and even more to be explained, and led to the cover-up allegations which are, even today, gaining strength as more and more official documents are wrested from the grasp of a recalcitrant American Establishment by the application of the Freedom of Information Act. Of all the incidents which took place during that ufologically seminal year of 1947, the Maury Island 'hoax' best exemplifies the kind of difficulties encountered when trying to establish the truth about such events. It all started off with an uncomplicated, if dramatic, report by a coastguard (or harbour patrolman) named Harold Dahl. Allegedly, while in the vicinity of Maury Island, Harold Dahl saw a number of doughnut-shaped UFOs. The weather was deteriorating and Dahl had taken the boat close to Maury Island in anticipation of storm conditions. He was not alone on the boat because, in addition to the usual two crew members, he also had on board his son with his dog. According to the accounts given, notably in Harold Wilkins's *Flying Saucers on the Attack*, the UFOs descended from the overcast conditions almost directly over the boat. There were six of them. Five were orbiting the sixth, which appeared to be in difficulties. At that time, they were about 600 m (2,000 ft) above the waves. However, the one in apparent difficulties then descended to 150 m

(500 ft) above sea level, provoking Dahl into grounding his boat on Maury Island in anticipation of a crash. The other objects followed their companion down, but came to rest some 60 m (200 ft) above it. Having grounded the boat, it is alleged that Dahl began to photograph the objects, using the camera usually kept on board. Suddenly, one of the higher objects descended to the lower one and their hulls touched with 'a dull thud'. All the observers immediately dived for cover, expecting both objects to come crashing down. Instead, what appeared to be a 'little white metal' fell from the objects, to be followed instantly by a downfall of a much darker metal. This second shower was hot, as it is alleged steam rose from the sea as it fell into it. Some also fell on the beach of Maury Island, injuring Dahl's son and killing the dog. After this, the stricken object seemed to rally somewhat, and the group moved away until it was lost to sight over the sea. Dahl attempted to radio in to base, but he was unable to do so due to an inordinate amount of static present in the atmosphere. Dahl collected some of the remains of the 'metal' that had landed on the island and returned to base at Tacoma. Upon his return, he handed over the evidence, including the camera containing the photographs, to his superior, Fred Chrisman. Eventually, Chrisman returned to Maury Island, and apparently saw at least one of the objects, or one similar, for himself. By this time, Kenneth Arnold had achieved instant notoriety by reporting his sighting to the media and, presumably on the strength of it, was asked by the magazine publisher Ray Palmer to investigate the Maury Island affair.[8] Kenneth Arnold's involvement signalled the beginning of the 'high strangeness' period that ended in tragedy. For reasons best known to himself, Kenneth Arnold requested the assistance of Military Intelligence in his enquiries. This, in itself, is strange enough, given Establishment attitudes towards his patron, Ray Palmer. Even stranger, Military Intelligence apparently immediately, and massively, responded by sending in two officers and a plane-load of armed Marines to assist Arnold. Thinking about it, it is almost inconceivable that Military Intelligence should respond in this way to a request from a private individual, especially to a request for help to investigate something they claimed did not exist in the first place. What was it they expected to find? The party arrived at Tacoma airport on 31 July 1947. The plane was left under armed guard while the two officers sought out, and interviewed, Kenneth Arnold. Allegedly during this interview, behind closed doors in Arnold's hotel room, the officers showed Arnold photos and drawings of UFOs, one of which resembled one he had seen over the Cascades, about which only he at that time

knew. Clearly, if the story is taken at face value, it is obvious Military Intelligence knew far more about UFOs than should have been possible at that time – even if they were interested in them, which, it has always been claimed, they were not. In conducting their investigation, the two officers made certain to collect all evidence in the possession of others, but never set foot on Maury Island, apparently telling Arnold that they were under strict orders to go nowhere near the place – a strange investigation indeed!

While all this was going on, the bizarre element expanded with the arrival of a 'mystery phone caller'. This individual, never identified, was apparently able to keep the media up to date with what was happening. So much so that Arnold's bedroom was searched in a vain effort to locate the bugging device that was suspected to be hidden there. Nothing was found. The mystery caller capped all his previous efforts when he informed the *Tacoma Times* of the tragic plane crash that claimed the lives of the two officers and the Marines as they headed back to base with their ufological booty, some 12 hours before the official release of that information. Apparently he said:

> The C46 will be found. It crashed on the southwest side of Mount Rainier, where it was shot down because there were people in her who had information 'we' don't want to get out.[9]

The first question must be 'we' – 'we' who? But that isn't the worst of it. The plane was found, exactly as specified. But what sort of plane was it? The Report on the Scientific Study of Unidentified Flying Objects identifies it as a B25 bomber. But would Military Intelligence use such a vehicle, or is it more likely that a C46 marine transport would be used? And what about the downed marine transport that Arnold was allegedly searching for in this same area when he had his UFO sighting? Were military planes falling from the sky in droves during June 1947? Or is there some other explanation? The fact that the Arnold UFO scenario and the Maury Island UFO scenario both contain this plane crash element would seem to argue that there is. At this remove in time, it is difficult to draw a conclusion one way or the other. But what is clear is that someone somewhere was economical with the truth, and that implies – as has been maintained by ufologists for years – that some form of censorship, cover-up if you prefer, is operating when it comes to UFOs.

The 'official' explanation for the Maury Island affair was 'hoax'. If so, then who was hoaxing whom, and about what?

Almost certainly, something untoward occurred at Maury Island in 1947, but was it what everyone now believes it to have been. And if it was, why is the official explanation wanting in credibility? As the affair came to its end, the two major witnesses, Dahl and Chrisman, went missing, posted to parts unknown by the Coastguard Service. Yet, in the Report on the Scientific Study of Unidentified Flying Objects, published in 1969, it is confidently asserted that neither Dahl nor Chrisman were members of that service. So how could it post them into oblivion in 1947? It goes without saying that all the evidence collected by the two military security officers, including the Dahl photographs, went missing. But, apparently, so also did the 32 Marines, even though the wreckage of their plane was found – well, the wreckage of a plane was found. But, perhaps, there was more than one crash – or none at all?

During the investigation that followed the crash of the plane carrying the two officers, 32 Marines and the ufological evidence (before the wreckage was actually found on Mount Rainier), there came forward a highly qualified witness – the Sheriff of Kelso – who testified that he had seen the plane, with one engine ablaze, crash into the side of 'a hill'. Surely he could be expected to distinguish between Mount Rainer and a nondescript 'hill'. Even more strangely, it has been claimed, on the basis of this witness's testimony, that the plane took at least 11 minutes to fall to earth: enough time for a Mayday surely? Especially since, as a military plane, it could be expected to have radio facilities on board. Apparently the descent to disaster was so prolonged that two individuals had time to bail out, using the bomb doors. One of these individuals, an unnamed passenger, apparently claimed that he had no choice in the matter, as the pilot and crew had practically thrown him out, after strapping him into a parachute harness. Finally, despite two survivors, and a qualified witness on the ground, we are asked to believe the plane's location was not pinpointed, and a search had to be mounted. And that despite being seen to crash on an unspecified hillside, the wreckage was eventually located (precisely where the mystery phone caller said it would be) on the south-west face of Mount Rainier. It is probably fractionally easier to believe in flying saucers from space.

So what of the physical trace evidence, all of which did not vanish along with the 32 Marines at the time of the plane crash? The residue, left where it had fallen on the beach at Maury Island, was later officially pronounced to be 'smelter's slag'. Apart from the fact that there were no smelting works on Maury Island, which would have meant that the slag must have been dumped there secretively by the two witnesses, or by some unnamed commercial concern (there was 22 tons of the stuff), the slag itself was very peculiar for an industrial waste product. According to the information in Harold Wilkins's book, a portion of this slag was independently tested. The results of this testing showed it to be made up of four main constituents: calcium, iron, zinc and titanium. The calcium was found to be present in anomalously high proportion, and that it had not oxidized as is usual when it is heated in atmosphere. This strange slag also contained aluminium, manganese, copper, magnesium, silicon, nickel, lead, strontium and chromium, as well as traces of silver and tin. The manufacturing process that would leave such by-products has not yet been identified. In fact, when it comes to the Maury Island hoax, there is definitely very little that has been identified – especially the truth of the matter.

There is no doubt that the events of Maury Island set the pattern for much that was to follow later in ufology, especially when it came to the American Establishment's involvement. Typical of the effect that American entry into any UFO scenario seems to generate is what occurred regarding the Spitzbergen saucer.

Seemingly it was the late Frank Edwards who drew ufological attention to this strange case in 1966.[10] The story seemed simple enough, in that it referred to an object of unknown origins being found 'crashed' on Spitzbergen Island. Now Frank was a newshound, so, although the story was good copy, as taken from a report in the *Stuttgarter Tageblatt* of 5 September 1955, he checked for himself in 1964 by writing to a member of the Norwegian board of inquiry that had, allegedly, investigated the original incident. He writes that, after a time lapse of four months, he got this cryptic reply: 'I regret that it is impossible for me to respond to your questions at this time.' He promptly wrote back, asking when an answer might be forthcoming, but this time got no reply whatsoever. Now the Report on the Scientific Study of Unidentified Flying Objects insists that the case was a hoax perpetrated by a German journalist. But if that was so, why the strange reply to Frank Edwards's enquiry? By the time Frank wrote to the Norwegian investigator that solution was presumably known, so why was it impossible to give Frank a straight answer? As might be expected, there is a discrepancy between the information Frank Edwards gives and that given in the Condon report. The article referred to by Frank Edwards is alleged to have been predated by an article in a German newspaper, *Berliner Volksblatt*, which claimed the disc had 'Russian symbols' on it. It is further claimed that American Air Intelligence investigated at that time, discovering that the Norwegian government had no knowledge of the incident, and that subsequent ufological writers conveniently forgot the 'Russian symbols' when writing it up later. This seems insupportable, as in writing about the incident Frank Edwards drew particular attention to the *Stuttgarter Tageblatt* report which stated that: 'Some time ago a misunderstanding was caused by saying that this disc probably was of Soviet origin. It has – this we wish to state emphatically – not been built by any country on earth'. The source for this was given by Edwards as Colonel Gernod Darnbyl, Chairman of the Board of Inquiry, a member of which Frank Edwards was to subsequently quesion and get the strange reply given above. So, as is usual, the plot thickens, and we are left to decide who is hoaxing whom and about what. Edwards claims the original story appeared on the newswires *circa* 1952, during the well-known European 'flap'; the American Establishment say otherwise. Perhaps it is significant that the hoaxer seems never to have been unmasked in the Press, the story just disappearing from the newswires as the Americans got involved in the investigation.

It has ever been thus when 'crashed' UFOs, or fragments of them, have been claimed to have been recovered. Claim and counter-claim have muddied the ufological waters until sufficient time has passed for the public memory to fade, then the *coup de grâce* has been delivered by Establishment sources by merely implying that everybody else connected to whatever investigation was either lying or misinformed. Is it any wonder that American ufology is now almost paranoid in its pursuit of evidence to make good its claim that a 40-plus years' cover-up has been conducted regarding the ufological truth?

From the British viewpoint, it is difficult to imagine that such a cover-up could be successfully conducted over such a long period of time. Yet, when the Silpho Moor case was reinvestigated prior to a re-evaluation of it appearing in a British UFO journal, the investigator immediately found the phone acting up, in that when it was lifted from the cradle, no dialling tone was emitted but an open line was there. The dialling tone returned when the open line cleared with the kind of noise that one associated with a receiver being replaced. Even the investigator admitted that it could all have been coincidental – but what if it wasn't? And it is that 'what if' that has kept the possibility of a cosmic cover-up a perennial possibility in ufology, and any number of highly qualified, and decidely dedicated, ufologists have spent lifetimes trying to unmask the 'secret' that they felt would never be told without their investigative involvement.

REFERENCES

1 Michel, Aime   *The Truth About Flying Saucers* (Corgi, 1958)
2 Atkins, Thomas & Baxter, John   *The Fire Came By* (MacDonald & Jane's, 1976)
3 ibid.
4 ibid.
5 Barclay, David   'The Siberian Spaceship Disaster', *The Unknown*, August 1985
6 'Return to Silpho Moor', *The UFO Debate*, April 1990
7 ibid.
8 Wilkins, Harold   *Flying Saucers on the Attack* (Ace Books, 1967)
9 ibid.
10 Edwards, Frank   *Flying Saucers Serious Business* (Mayflower Dell, 1967)

CHAPTER SIX

SPACESHIPS THAT PASS IN THE NIGHT

Therese M Barclay

The problems facing the serious ufologist are the same today as they have always been – Who do you believe? Which do you accept? The protestations of the percipients, or the equally decisive denials of the debunkers? To some extent, the sceptics can be ignored as, in most cases, they are merely giving an opinion about what they feel is, or is not, possible. And the lessons of the past 40 or so years clearly indicate that the parameters which any form of scepticism takes as its corner-stones are likely to be dispensed with in inverse ratio to their seeming improbability. Scepticism, of whatever sort, always argues retrogressively; that is to say, its 'common-sense' arguments derive from past cosmologies, when anyone who has watched the way the world is going can only be certain that the future will be nothing like the past. The dichotomy grows wider, and faster, the closer the twenty-first century approaches. The flying saucers are real. But it might be that they are real in a way our present-day cosmologies can't conceive. What might be happening is that witnesses are describing a twenty-first century reality in terms of present-day parameters. If this is so, then it is no use approaching Establishment bodies for an explanation. Even if the explanation were known, or suspected, the issue would be ignored in the way the cardinals ignored Galileo's telescope – and for the very same reason. It might be best then, when addressing the problem, to accept what the percipient is saying without trying for any conclusions, without making the attempt to fit the data into the presently extant cultural consensus; to attempt instead, by listening to the witness, to find some way to confront the actual phenomena for oneself, and leave it at that.

In pursuit of this strategy, the best witness is the one who avoids media exposure, and only discusses their experience with you after demanding reassurances of anonymity. Why? Because such a witness is probably the least likely one to be either perpetrating a hoax or attention seeking in other ways, and so greater credence can be placed in what they say. Most times, these individuals approach you with a view to getting some explanation for the untoward event that has disturbed the even tenor of their days. Almost without exception, before their own sighting, they were sceptical of the claims of others. Now they find themselves tarred with the same brush. It is always a salutory experience. If you are honest, the most reassurance that you can give them is that they are not alone, as their experience is paralleled by others on a world-wide, and ongoing, basis. Certainly, you will come across the sincere witnesses who have probably misperceived mundane phenomena: plane lights, satellites and sundry other everyday stimuli which they have mistaken for anomalous aeroforms. But even here the best you can tell them is that it is probable that they are mistaken. For without being with them at the time of their sighting, you cannot categorically rule out the alien option – as this, previously unpublished, example will indicate.

During 1989, while investigating a witness who had claimed to be a 'repeater', but who was suspected of having misperceived much that had been reported as UFOs, the investigator was contacted one night by this witness in a high state of excitement, claiming that flotillas of UFOs were passing overhead.[1] The investigator, although it was well after midnight, immediately went to the site with the avowed intention of demonstrating to the person that they were mistaken. Upon his arrival, the witness immediately pointed out balls of light that were passing across the sky, from east to west. On that night, the sky was made up of fast-moving clouds, which allowed only brief glimpses of the lights as they passed overhead. The clouds were passing west to east, and the investigator immediately knew the explanation: the cloud movement was providing the optical illusion that the stars were moving. But how to prove it to the witness? The method decided on was to use the wall of the house as a fixed reference, and by standing close to it, line it up with a star so that the illusion would be destroyed, as the point of light would remain in the same place as the clouds moved across it. Simple. Casually, the investigator took up position to test the strategy before calling the witness to do likewise. A star was carefully lined up so that it was at the apex of the guttering at the corner of the house. Certainly, the star remained stationary, but the investigator was astonished to see

balls of light, singly and in echelons of up to five, passing swiftly
through the sky. After that, the investigator took up several
positions, using fixed points of reference, to make absolutely sure
that optical illusion was ruled out. The clincher came when the sky
suddenly cleared of cloud altogether, and a number of lights
passed across the now-open skies. The only other explanation that
could possibly be invoked was military aircraft, but the lights had
moved across the sky in such numbers, and for such a protracted
length of time, that some noise should have been heard. But the
procession had been in total silence. By the time it had ended, the
witness had managed to drag several of the neighbours from their
homes, and all were agreed that it was the lights that had been
moving. The military plane explanation was taken under
advisement, but at least two of the neighbours said that a similar
sighting had taken place two or three years earlier, and at that
time no explanation had been forthcoming. Investigations this
time were equally fruitless, and so the matter remains
indeterminate. But only because it involves meandering nocturnal
lights. The next case to be discussed admits to no such ambiguity.

The witness contacted us in early 1987, and in due course told
us of an experience that she, and her husband, had undergone in
July 1986.[2] At that time, she and her husband were returning to
their home in Bradford by car. As it was coming up to rush-hour,
it was decided to circumnavigate the suburbs rather than risk
being caught up in the usual city-centre traffic jam, even though
this would add distance to the journey. A route was chosen that
would take them past a supermarket where they intended to make
a purchase. As the car was travelling along the ring road, at the
point where it intersects with one of the major exit roads, the
witness was surprised to see, hanging low over the intersection, a
large lenticular aeroform which seemed to her 'to be in the centre
of the road, as though it was observing the traffic.' According to
the witness, the object then followed them home. Throughout the
remainder of the journey, she tried to call the attention of others
to what she was watching, but failed – either because it was not
visible to others or, perhaps, they did not want to admit to seeing
it. On arrival at their home, the object took up station over the
cottage. It remained there for a considerable period as the witness
kept going outside to see if it was still there. But, by the following
morning, it had departed.

This witness was aware of flying saucers, as occasionally
detailed in the Press, and she was also cognizant of the fact that
those who reported them usually were held up to ridicule, which is
why the sighting was not reported in the usual way: we only got to

know of it because her sister lived next door to us. The witness herself, and her husband, were reluctant to discuss the matter until they were absolutely certain that their experience would not become media fodder, and that in discussing the case in the literature they would not be identified. Interestingly, it was learned during the many conversations we had that her family had a history of psychism, but that this was the first time she had seen a flying saucer, because that is what she maintained it was: that is to say, an unidentifiable, lenticular object which, close up, 'seemed to have like a mauvish grey haze around it.'

By the time the witness had reached her home, she had become convinced that, whatever it was, it was under intelligent direction and, because of one particular manoeuvre, knew where she lived in advance. Apparently, when the car pulled up, the object was directly in front of it, at just above street-lamp level – so close at this point that the 'mauvish haze' was visible. The car could not be driven up to the witness's home because it was the end one in a block of three cottages that shared a communal yard. Although at that point there should have been no way of telling which of the cottages the witness would eventually enter, the object moved over to the correct cottage. As the witness described it: '. . . just shot . . . right quick . . . and hovered straight above our cottage, and hovered there as if it knew that was our cottage . . .'

When such an account is given, there are only two choices: either it is true or it is false. On this particular occasion, we chose to believe the witness, mainly because her sincerity was so apparent. No claims to cosmic selection were made. Her own ideas about what had been seen were admitted as being 'tentative'. And, all in all, the impression was gained that she would have preferred it if the entire episode had never occurred. This witness is still known to us some five years after the event, and she is now what she was then, a normal northern housewife, preferring bingo to ufology any day of the week.

The alien-spaceship type of UFO has been consistently reported by individuals with some social standing, such as military and civilian pilots, customs officers, police personnel, astronomers, rocket engineers, etc. In fact, the kind of individual whose testimony regarding any other event that they had witnessed would be taken very seriously indeed. The difficulty is that, persuasive though their evidence might be, much of it is not conclusive to third parties, and this results in any professional percipient daring enough to make their experience known becoming the target for all those persons in ufology who have a particular axe to grind.

Any number of times, when investigating reports, such individuals have insisted on anonymity for this very reason. Quite typical of the kind of report received under those conditions is the following one, originally submitted by a senior customs official, and later confirmed by an astronomer.

During the latter half of 1989, there was something of a minor 'flap' in the Aire Valley.[3] The whole thing was apparently triggered by an object that overflew the area at low level in the early hours of Saturday 15 July 1989. This object, described by those who saw it as being brilliantly lit and as large as the full moon, traversed the county of Yorkshire. At approximately 2.20 a.m., a customs officer was going home after having finished his shift of duty at Yeadon Airport, West Yorkshire. As he was travelling in his car in the vicinity of Horsforth, the object crossed his field of view. It was moving in a roughly north-east–south-west trajectory and moving slowly enough for the officer to pull over, get out of his car, and watch till it was lost to sight behind the tree-covered contours of the surrounding terrain. He described the object as being very low in the sky and having the apparent size of the full moon – a comparison he was able to confirm for himself, as the real moon was also in the sky at that time. He was able to ascertain the direction the object was travelling in because he knew that the road he was on pointed almost due west, and the object crossed his field of vision at an angle to it. His immediate concern was that he was watching a conventional plane coming down in flames, so low did it appear in the sky. However, after getting out of his car, he could see that it was maintaining its altitude, and so could not have been an ordinary plane in difficulties. So what was it?

Subsequent investigations were, in the end, only able to determine what it was not. After a carefully worded appeal in the local Press, a number of individuals came forward with complementary reports. However, the most evidential was the one given by an astronomer who had been out skywatching that night at his home, high up on one of the many steep hillsides which characterize that part of Yorkshire. According to his testimony, it seemed probable that the object came into his view just as it was going out of the view of the customs officer. The astronomer had the object in sight for at least seven seconds: a period of time, he was quick to point out, that was anomalous in terms of the usual meteoric observations, which usually last only fractions of a second. He, too, remarked upon the apparent low altitude of the object, because of which he had initially thought that it must crash into the hills on the side of the valley furthest from his observation-point. As it successfully negotiated this hazard, it suddenly flashed bright-coloured lights, or 'colour changes' according to the witness. Then it became a 'dark object', inside of which he could see something like a fire burning. It presented an aspect similar to a jet plane on afterburner seen from the rear. And in this mode it diminished in the distance until he lost it to sight. Despite his own observation of its anomalous meteoric behaviour, this astronomer tentatively identified the intruder as a slow meteor. Ignoring his own observation of its low altitude, he surmised that it might have been something at the fringes of the atmosphere which had bounced off back into space. To present such a striking naked-eye sighting, he admitted that such an object must, of necessity, have been as large as a building. The violent colour changes, he attributed to it being 'quenched in the atmosphere.' Although it seemed to the investigator that this witness was stretching meteoric parameters to accommodate his astronomical interpretation, his tentative identification of a bolide had some merit, due to his expertise.

Assuming that it had been a high-altitude event (the apparent low altitude being caused by some kind of misperception), the object, travelling as it did across the country, should have been visible over a large area. Consequently, the investigator contacted an astronomical association based in Todmorden. According to the spokesperson, the membership had been out and about on the night in question. Because viewing conditions had been almost ideal, at least 50 members had availed themselves of the opportunity to view the heavens. But not one of them had reported seeing anything remotely like the object seen to cross the sky over the periphery of the Leeds–Bradford conurbation. The conclusion must be that the object was as low in the sky as the observers first supposed and was, therefore, below the viewing horizon of the Todmorden Astronomical Association's members. Todmorden is only a matter of a few miles west of the point where the object was observed, which would have necessarily put it at very low altitude for it to be below the Todmorden horizon. This, in itself, clearly indicates that we are not dealing with a bolide of some description, but rather with an anomalous aeroform that meets all the requirements of a UFO. In many ways this report is typical of the kind that have for the true believers kept alive the reality of probable alien intrusion. The original witness, the customs officer, after weeks of analysing his own experience for himself, reluctantly came to this same conclusion, on the grounds that anything that large and that low in the sky could only maintain its altitude in the way it did if it was being driven – a valid point, given his undeniable expertise in aircraft behaviour.

Yet, from the same data, sceptics would be quick to point out that all that was seen was a light, and on this basis begin to dismiss the evidence as misperception compounded by hysteria. Not having been there at the time, they would probably imply that the object was neither as large nor as bright as the witnesses insisted it was, and would seize upon the slow meteor explanation tentatively put forward by the astronomer, even though it takes little account of the sequence of events as witnessed by the astronomer himself, and the fact that the Todmorden group saw nothing – something they would inevitably have done had the sighting been generated by an inanimate celestial object. So, as with many other evidential sightings, especially as it recedes into the past, the battle lines would have been drawn, positions become entrenched, and winning the argument become more important than clarifying the event that the argument was all about. It is this crusading aspect of ufology that has kept it going in circles for well over 40 years, while the phenomenon has gone on its way, untroubled by either the sanction or acceptance of the contending parties. All the proponents of the various paradigms seem to feel that if their particular paradigm is correct, which to them it is, all the others must be wrong. However, none of them seem to have taken this to its logical conclusion by grasping the fact that, while not all of them can be right, all of them could be totally wrong.

As might be expected, the various official bodies contacted in regard to the above episode expressed a consuming disinterest, and so the matter was not resolved. However, in soliciting other witnesses via the local Press, we were brought into contact with a woman whom we shall call by the pseudonym Elizabeth. This particular witness, a normal no-nonsense northern type, claimed to have had an experience with a ball-of-light type of phenomenon earlier in that same year. According to Elizabeth, late on the night of 18 January 1989, she had been walking her dog in the fields adjacent to her home in Rawdon, West Yorkshire, when she had seen what can only be described as a nocturnal meandering light.[4] These nightly excursions with the dog were part of her normal daily routine, but this was the first time she had seen anything like the object she described. Apparently, she had been on her way back home, walking down the field, trying to find the dog which had disappeared into the undergrowth at the edge, presumably in pursuit of something small and furry. In looking around, she noticed, coming up from behind her, a large 'ball of light'. She insisted it was much larger than even the brightest star in the sky. It was travelling in a roughly east–west direction, and although the nearby airport had been closed to traffic from 10 p.m., she immediately suspected aircraft light. She stood and listened for engine noise, but the silence of the night remained undisturbed as the light moved in leisurely fashion across her field of vision. As it began to draw away, it seemed to her that it paused in the sky and, for reasons she could not define, she felt that it was watching her. Unnerved, she looked down to find her dog, and was surprised to see it at her side also, apparently, staring at the light, which once again was moving off into the distance. She herself admitted to some confusion as to the exact sequence of events, and although there were tantalizing hints of some kind of time loss, there was no way of proving it, as the witness admitted that she had not checked the time when she got home. Perhaps disappointingly, this witness then reported several other nocturnal encounters with lights in the sky, including a sighting of a huge 'dark red disc' which, she was quite adamant, performed a brief touchdown directly in front of the air traffic control tower at Yeadon Airport, which the view from her bedroom window overlooks. Needless to say, no confirmation, or denial for that matter, was forthcoming from the airport allegedly involved, which inevitably seemed to indicate that the witness was now mentally and emotionally predisposed to seeing UFOs, and was probably mispercieving mundane objects. But what of her first encounter? Could the scenario be clarified? In this attempt, we were fairly lucky, as Elizabeth was dissatisfied with her own recollection of the event and was amenable to a suggestion of hypnotic regression to clarify the matter.

So a session was arranged with a reputable medical hypnotist. It was presumed by all concerned that all that was required was an enhancement of memories already consciously, if a bit confusedly, recalled. However, towards the end of the session, almost inadvertently, the hypnotist asked the witness to clarify a point which had been passed over at the start. Immediately, Elizabeth began to describe a large, almost classic flying saucer. Apparently, at the point where the light had seemed to pause in the sky before continuing on its way, there was a segment that had been consciously forgotten. Instead of just moving away, the light had approached at speed, eventually resolving into a large battleship-grey flying saucer with three large riding lights underneath, and a bank of smaller lights delineating the circumference. It came to rest in the air, about 60 m (200 ft) away from her. Elizabeth was standing on a slope which led down to a small lake of water, known locally as The Dam, and it was over this that the object was hovering, its lights reflecting in the water. Before she had time to take all this in, the object fired lights at her. These lights emanated from the extreme edge of the object, and were stroboscopic in their intensity. During this period, the witness indicated that she was unable to move or to cry out, gripped by an unaccountable paralysis. The light barrage ended, and the object then withdrew. When the regression session ended, these bizarre memories were accessible to the conscious witness. But although she said they seemed real to her, she was reluctant to accept them as such and attempted to rationalize them into something more acceptable, one suggestion being that it had been a helicopter of some kind; but even then, she could not explain the total absence of sound that had prevailed during the entire episode. Eventually, she came to accept the experience as real and, perhaps in over-compensation for her original scepticism, entered into an almost contactee-type scenario of the true believer kind, which rendered any further testimony from her slightly suspect, and the hypnotic regression was not followed up as originally intended.

Enquiries in the area brought forward no further witnesses to this particular event, even though several other anecdotal sightings were uncovered in the process. As might be expected, the local airport could not (would not?) offer any help, other than to confirm that the facility was closed down each night at 10 p.m. in accordance with an agreement not to keep people in the area awake all hours with unacceptable levels of aircraft noise. For a brief period, the investigation seemed to be getting somewhere when Elizabeth claimed that she had been contacted by the American base at Menwith Hill about the matter. However, promised revelations were never forthcoming, except for a photograph – sent anonymously – which allegedly shows the dome of a saucer on the ground in the area in question. So, the affair eventually petered out without real conclusion, which seems about par for the course.

The trouble is, of course, that most times the investigator is called in after the event – sometimes well after the event – but is, nevertheless, expected to produce an understandable result. Typical of this is the report that was given to me by a woman living in the same block of flats as myself. According to her testimony, the event took place in the summer of 1979.[5] At that time, the witness worked at a local light-engineering works that boasted excellent recreational facilities. Seemingly, my neighbour, along with two friends from the same company, was returning to the industrial complex with the intention of availing herself of these facilities. It was early evening, approximately 7 p.m., and quite light. The three were walking towards Dockfield Road, when they became aware of a red object in the sky which seemed to be pacing them. Once again, it was initially conjectured by the witnesses that the object was probably a helicopter, and they proceeded on their way. Eventually, with the object now directly over them, they came to an old iron bridge that spanned a canal. As they started over the bridge, they became aware that an object, similar to the red one, but much lower, was coming towards them, apparently following the line of the canal. The approaches to the industrial estate at the end of Dockfield Road can be extremely deserted, and the three women now panicked. Because it was nearer to their works than to return to the main road, they opted to make a dash for it. As they speedily set out, the first object was seen to take up position behind and in line with the other. This manoeuvre completed, both objects began to flash bright green lights at the three witnesses, presumably lending wings to their heels. Breathless, and with the objects still in tow, they arrived at the gatehouse of the factory. Their excited shouts brought the gateman out to investigate. They pointed out the lights to him. He took one look, confirmed that he could see them, then retreated swiftly into the gatehouse, declaring that 'it was more than his job's worth' to stand gawping at funny lights when there was work to be done. The lights were now at a very low level and close enough for their lens-like shape to be seen clearly. At this point, the witnesses could also see that the brilliant green flashes were coming from the extreme edges of the objects. As it seemed to the witnesses that the objects were manoeuvring to place themselves directly over them, they too retreated into the gatehouse to await developments. When, after an indeterminate period (perhaps something of the order of five minutes, although it no doubt felt longer to them), nothing further alarming happened, they ventured outside, expecting to see the objects directly over the gatehouse, but instead found they were gone. Having had enough entertainment for one night, they summoned a taxi and then went home.

Even after having spoken at length with all the main witnesses, the matter remains a mystery. Yet again one is forced to conclude that something untoward occurred, without being able satisfactorily to prove it beyond reasonable doubt. The indeterminacy of the case is not helped by the possibility of a further mystery being contained within it. It seems that as the witnesses crossed the old iron bridge, and while they were watching the approach of the second object, they remembered the sky as being quite bright. Yet when they reached the gatehouse, the stars were showing in a rapidly darkening sky. The distance from the bridge to the gatehouse could be covered in ten minutes, even at a gentle stroll. At the pace they were moving it should have taken much less. So, tantalizingly, a possible time anomaly seems to be indicated. They had not taken particular note of the time when they had set out. They surmised that it had been around 7 to 7.15 p.m, which would have put them on the iron bridge by approximately 7.45. Due to all the excitement, they had not thought to check the clock in the gatehouse upon their arrival. The witness who was my immediate neighbour feels that it was certainly well after 10 p.m. when she finally arrived home in the taxi. That would mean that the overall period would be in the order of two and a half hours, which seems overlong for the scenario described. The distance to the works social club can be walked, there and back, quite comfortably from the flats in which we both reside in just less than an hour. So, if the estimate of the actual time elapsed during the experience is even nearly correct, there is the possibility of a time anomaly – even allowing for the admitted skywatching that went on as events progressed. It is unlikely that the matter will be resolved satisfactorily, and not merely because individuals caught in these events lose all sense of proportion, and fail to properly observe, and so remember accurately, what occurred – as the next case to be discussed will demonstrate.

On Thursday 19 April 1990, a man with his two young sons watched an object cross the sky over their home in the Odsal Top area of Bradford.[6] It was a protracted sighting, and because of the clearness of the sky, and the low altitude of the object, they were left in no doubt that they had observed something quite outside the usual air traffic that crosses Bradford's skies to and from Yeadon Airport. Fortunately, the percipients did not panic, and after carefully watching the object until it disappeared into the distance, went back into their home and made separate sketches of what they had seen before discussing the event among themselves. It was the father who eventually made contact with us and, after extracting the usual promises of anonymity in the event of publication, gave the details of his and his sons' most unusual sighting.

On the day in question, the father had been working all day, improving the interior of the family home. By 8.15 p.m. he was ready to call it a day, and was encouraged in this decision by the sound of an ice-cream van's jangling theme somewhere in the vicinity. In company with his two sons, Steven, aged 10, and David, aged 7, he jumped into his car and set out to find the ice-cream van. The car had only just cleared the drive when the

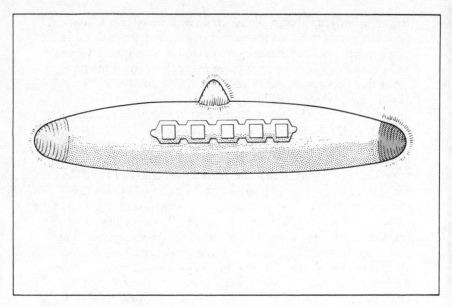

Figure 6 Diagram of an object seen over Bradford, England, on 19 April 1990.

youngest son pointed out something he could see in the sky. The sight was sufficiently arresting for the father to pull over immediately to the kerb so that they all could get out and take a better look. In their testimony, they describe a cigar-shaped object of metallic appearance, low in the sky and coming directly towards them. It had brilliant lights front and rear, with a large 'domed' light over the centre. It passed right over them, and was low enough for them to make out that it had what appeared to be a row of windows directly beneath the central light. They could also clearly see that it had neither wings nor tail assembly. No noise that they were aware of accompanied it in its flight over-head. When asked to estimate its size, they compared it to a tennis ball at arm's length, or perhaps a cigarette packet held similarly. This estimate is subjective. However, it does indicate that the object loomed quite unusually large in their field of view. In trying to describe the lights, they said they were red and green, with a flashing amber one in the centre, and joked that it was probably an interstellar traffic-light that had come adrift. Even so, they were at pains to stress that their description of the lights was only approximate, as these had a tone and intensity that set them well apart from their earthly equivalents. The boys, in particular, said that there was something about these lights that they could not find words to describe. The percipients gave us the sketches they had made, and we set out to discover if the object had been viewed by anyone else. Our efforts met with failure. The local media ignored our report, and the material we had submitted with it was 'lost'. It has, in fact, now returned to us, some two years after submission, without comment, so make of that what you will; especially since the father of the two boys discovered that a work colleague had also seen the object over Halifax earlier in the same day. Efforts to make this particular witness stand up and be counted were rebuffed, as the person in question 'did not want to become a laughing-stock.' Even so, we were able to discover that the object had been seen over Shelf (a town near Halifax) at approximately 8.00 p.m., some 15 to 30 minutes before it was spotted by the witness at Odsal Top. Allegedly, it was very low, and brought what traffic there was to a halt, while drivers and passengers watched it shine down a brilliant beam of light. Our witness said that his colleague had heard it suggested that what had been seen was a helicopter, to which his reply was that if it had been a helicopter, 'Then it was the biggest damn helicopter I've ever seen'. Although further enquiries unearthed more unsubstantiated rumours about this event, nothing that would constitute the kind of proof that the sceptical would accept was located. So this sighting joins the myriad others waiting for the day when flying saucers land to be accepted as genuine.

This kind of thing seems par for the ufological course. Time and again, evidential reports have been given by credible witnesses, only to be disbelieved, not only by the sceptics, but by most of the ufological fraternity as well. It seems that everyone always assumes that if only a smidgen more information had been forthcoming, the event would have been identified as misperception of something mundane. All you have to do is report a UFO, or even show a photograph of one, to discover immediately that even those who publicly present themselves as ufologists disbelieve your evidence as a matter of course. And if you persist, you soon come to realize that you have been relegated, in their view, to the level of superstitious fool. Is it any wonder then that many witnesses will never come forward for fear of ridicule, leaving the field wide open to those who report things for reasons other than truth or altruism. The reason why this situation pertains, and has been self-perpetuating since the dawn of modern ufology, seems to be connected to the fact that many ufologists have never had even a peripherally ufological experience, and therefore cannot conceive how such things can be. The assumption is made that the witness is in some way mistaken. They have a point when it comes to high-altitude lights in the sky, but when ordinary people report extraordinary airborne vehicles, any scepticism is merely supercilious patronage by someone who overestimates their own intellectual powers. At this point in time, no one has categorically disproved the existence of flying saucers, or even rendered unviable the proposition that they come from somewhere out in space. The fact remains that these things continue to infest the atmosphere and, more than occasionally, someone inadvertently bumps into one – as I seemingly did on the evening of Wednesday 11 April 1990.

That evening I was on Ilkley Moor with a colleague.[7] We had earlier been to visit the author/investigator Nigel Mortimer who, at that time, lived in Addingham, near Ilkley, to ask him to look into a very interesting report concerning 'burnt circles' which had appeared on the moor. On the return journey it was decided to go up on to the moor to take a look for ourselves and to take some shots with a camera which I had recently purchased. We arrived at a site on the moor at about 8.15 p.m. and, leaving the car, prepared to take photographs. As we did so, we noticed in the sky a row of three bright lights, at an elevation of about 50°. Despite the time of evening, the sky was still bright and cloudless, and no stars were visible. Initially thinking the lights were probably on a plane making an approach to Yeadon Airport (a common sight over the moor), we looked for burnt circles to photograph. It is likely, being unfamiliar with the area, we had gone on to the moor at the wrong place, because, some ten to fifteen minutes later, no circles had been found, and we returned to where we had parked the car. We were surprised to see the three lights, unchanged in aspect, still hanging in the air exactly where we had left them when setting out on our search. Puzzled, we listened carefully for the characteristic sound of a helicopter, but despite the stillness all around us, no such sound could be heard. Almost jocularly, my companion pointed out that the lights were apparently hovering directly over the spot where an alleged abduction had taken place some years earlier, and so shouldn't we take a photograph 'just in case'. A series of shots were attempted but the camera jammed and only one was achieved. Now the camera jamming had nothing whatsoever to do with any alien presence: it was my unfamiliarity with the mechanism which was the sole cause of the wind-on lever getting stuck. We both turned our attention to the process of unjamming it, and after addressing the recalcitrant camera in such terms as are not to be found in any Alien to English dictionary, succeeded in freeing the film. On turning back to continue photographing the object, we discovered that it had gone. It had not overflown us while our attention had been on the camera. Or, at least if it had, it had done so silently. Our field of view was quite unrestricted, so that if it had departed in any other direction, assuming it was a conventional aircraft of some kind, it should still have been visible to us somewhere in the sky. But the sky was clear, and slipping into that particularly vibrant violet that characterizes nightfall on the moor. Disappointed, and not a little frustrated at our inability to identify what we had seen, we called it a day and went home.

In due time, the film which contained the one shot I had been able to take of the object was developed, and another surprise was awaiting me. The image on the developed print bore no real resemblance to the object that I had thought I was photographing. Instead of the three bright lights I had expected, the image on the film showed an object carrying several diffuse lights. The object itself, though tantalizingly elliptical, was too indistinct for any real determination to be made, even when enlarged. This in itself is puzzling, as the photograph was taken through the same telephoto lens that had satisfactorily resolved other distant images of wildfowl that were on the same roll of film. So, while it is quite inappropriate to claim the photograph is that of a flying saucer, it can be claimed that it certainly is one of a UFO.

Of course, efforts were made to resolve the puzzle, but Yeadon Airport advised that they had nothing airborne in the vicinity at the time, and that only left the possibility of military aircraft. Undeniably these do frequent the airspace over the moor, but no reply has yet been forthcoming from this direction. So, as with many of the people who give their reports to us, we are left to accept even our own testimony at face value, or consider ourselves fantasy prone or worse. And this is the essential dilemma of ufological investigation. What is true, and what is not? Whom do you believe, the percipient or the lack of corroborative evidence produced by the investigator? It has been going on for over 40 years; so much so, that ufological investigation has become almost as predictably circular as the alleged flying saucers that such investigation was set up to enquire into in the first place.

It seems to me that this situation will not improve until a complete reversal of attitude towards the problem is taken on board by those who set out to 'prove' or 'disprove' the existence of a phenomenon to be studied. The cases quoted in this chapter are, in their way, a microcosm of what awaits UFO investigators on a global basis. As far as I am concerned, the matter is now settled in favour of the existence of anomalous aeroforms in our atmosphere. The enquiry is not a scientific one, as the phenomenon is incapable of replication by the efforts of the investigator, as is required by 'the scientific method'. Rather, the pursuit of the enigmatic UFO is akin to a police enquiry, an exercise in detection and deduction. The circumstantial evidence is now such as to put beyond reasonable doubt the main thesis that intelligently guided vehicles of a kind not attributable to the efforts of human technology are abroad in the world. To maintain otherwise is to accuse a host of credible witnesses of being unable to know and describe what they have seen. Such an attitude is demeaning to your fellow man, and can only be subscribed to by those whose intellectual arrogance is only outmatched by their lack of maturity. Witnesses deserve to be believed; even more so when they describe actual aeroforms, and not merely anomalous 'lights' in the sky. Witnesses do not talk about their experiences to be considered either fools or charlatans: usually, the experience has traumatized them, and they are seeking an explanation which will help them put it into context of the social consensus they subscribe to. Many, because of the inexpertise of the investigator, eventually move into one or other of the belief systems that support those who have had these experiences. Consequently, modern ufology is something like a crusade between opposing factions, rather than the impartial investigation it ought to be. While this situation pertains, the flying saucers will remain a mystery. It is time to believe the witnesses and, instead of endlessly 'analysing' their reports, seek instead to confront the phenomenon first hand. It is not quite so difficult as some might think – just a little inconvenient at times. During March 1989, a ufological colleague, well known for his somewhat cavalier approach to the study, was contacted by phone in the dead of night by a witness who was at that time under investigation by him.[8] This particular witness was seemingly prone to seeing flying saucers at the drop of a hat, and would probably have been dismissed long since by the more serious minded of the ufological fraternity. However, my colleague was ever ready to follow any lead, and so he answered the phone, and did what the caller asked him to do: that was, go outside and look at a flying saucer. The witness's house was ideally placed to afford extensive views over the area, and the person insisted that a flying saucer was heading towards my colleague's home. Taking the phone outside with him (something he was able to do because the cord was of such length that it allowed the phone to be taken into any room on the ground floor), he looked for the UFO. He immediately located a light source in the sky which, if it continued in its observed trajectory, would pass directly overhead. Once overhead, he could clearly see an object that was sharply triangular, with white lights at each corner and a dull red one centrally placed. The object was so low that the street-lights reflected along its fuselage. For approximately 40 minutes, the witness remaining on the line throughout, the object was watched while it performed a series of lackadaisical manoeuvres in the night sky. Eventually, it departed to the south. It was silent during the whole time it was in view. So, what was it? Neither my colleague nor myself would care to hazard a guess at this time. As he said:

> It does not really matter what it was. All that matters is that it *was,* proving beyond a shadow of a doubt that there are still things that are not dreamt of in any philosophy presently extant.

I tend to agree with him as, in my view, the future of ufology lies in the acceptance of these strange visitors as part and parcel of the panorama of life on earth. Indeed why should they be expected to accommodate any of our parochial cosmologies? In the end, it might turn out that it is we who will have to accommodate theirs.

REFERENCES

1   Author's private case file
2   'Close Encounter (Fact or Fiction)', *UFO Debate*, Issue 1, February 1990
3   ibid.
4   'Aire Valley Saucers?' *UFO Debate*, Issue 2, April 1990
5   'Shipley Saucer Scare', *UFO Debate*, Issue 4, August 1990
6   'Yorkshire's UFO Tourist Trade', *UFO Debate*, Issue 3, June 1990
7   ibid.
8   Author's private case file

CHAPTER SEVEN

ALL IN THE EYE OF THE BEHOLDER?

Joseph Dormer B.Sc.

One of the most tantalizing characteristics of UFOs, from the investigator's point of view, is their tendency to suddenly disappear in mid-air, and from radar screens. Ghosts too, as every psychic researcher knows, have this capability. A superficial similarity between two completely different phenomena? Perhaps not, as analyses of reports on both kinds of phenomena reveal other correlations between them that are impossible to dismiss as coincidence. Consider the following account, given to me by a teacher in Rochdale, England, who, not wishing to commit social suicide, requested anonymity:

> It was late November and I had just got home from college. It was already dusk and, as my mother prepared to pull the curtains, she drew my attention to something she could see in the darkening sky. I looked out through the window and saw this extraordinary craft just hanging there, low in the sky, motionless and completely silent. It was huge. I mean it must have been about 100 feet long. It was cylindrically shaped, but rounded at the ends. There were port holes along its entire length, and I could see figures in silver space suits moving about inside. I couldn't believe what I was seeing. I wanted to cry out, but couldn't . . . I mean I literally could not speak or move. Neither of us could. It was as if we were paralysed. We just stood there, watching this thing as it began to glide slowly

across the sky. Then suddenly it was gone. It did not just move off at tremendous speed, I'm certain of that – it just vanished into thin air. And another strange thing was that we seemed to be watching it for only a few minutes or so, yet when I looked at my watch afterwards, I found that a whole hour had gone by.

The files of ufologists everywhere are bulging with cases just like this one. Anyone familiar with even a handful of them will instantly recognize the same features: the silence of the craft, its sudden disappearance, the feeling of paralysis in the witness, the missing time and, despite the absurdity of it all, the presence of multiple witnesses. While aliens appear in a variety of different forms, these underlying patterns remain the same. Few UFO researchers are apparently aware, however, that these same patterns are to be found in reports of ghosts. Witnesses to UFO disappearances often describe the disappearance in terms of the

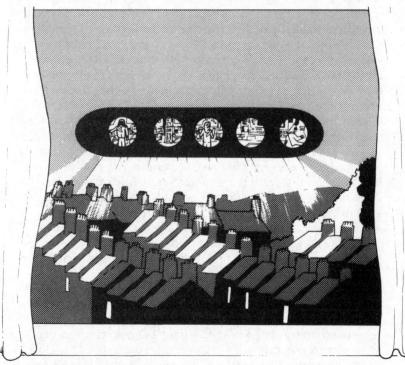

Figure 7 Sketch of a sighting of a UFO over Rochdale, England, from a description by a witness.

object leaving 'faster than the eye could follow'. But this is just a rationalization on their part, an attempt to make the unbelievable, believable. Most witnesses just say something like: 'It just vanished . . . suddenly it wasn't there anymore.' Ghosts, too, seem to be able to perform this vanishing trick with equal ease. Witnesses use a variety of images to try to convey the suddenness with which the ghost vanished: 'It vanished like a bubble bursting' reads one report; while another describes the ghostly figure disappearing 'suddenly, like pricking a balloon with a pin'; and yet another states that the ghost vanished 'as suddenly as a light goes out'. Anyone familiar with the UFO documentation must now suspect that these two kinds of 'appearances' are interrelated. This suspicion can only be enhanced when it is realized that both phenomena share the ability to generate silence. It is not just a matter of the apparition being silent: as often as not, witnesses remark on a complete absence of sound; any normal background noises, including bird-song, are seemingly suppressed as if by magic. As reported in *Northern UFO News* in October 1990, a witness, in describing a ufological incident, remarks that 'the birds stopped singing'. In the same issue, another witness states how 'the nearby A6 road was oddly silent during the sighting'; yet another remembers that while the incident was taking place, there was 'no sound at all'. Occasionally, it has to be admitted, UFO percipients recall hearing buzzing, humming or whining noises at the onset of their experience, but these might turn out to be the exceptions that prove the rule, important clues to which I shall return later. Ghosts, too, are generally silent. In one account, the witness writes that 'there was no sound of footsteps as it walked, despite the hard surface'; and another, that 'there was no sound of breath, though it seemed to be breathing heavily'. Sometimes it is precisely this lack of sound that leads the witness to realize that things are not quite right. As with the witness who said 'an eerie feeling began to steal over me . . . it began to dawn on me that there had been something definitely odd about the occurrence – the scene had been quite noiseless.' One cannot help but remark that there is something quite odd about ufology's silence on this similarity. And it does not end there.

Paralysis and the inability to speak afflict both ghost and UFO percipients. When one witness tried to speak to the ghost, she was surprised to find that 'no noise came from my voice and no response from legs or body'. Similarly, UFO reports reveal this same witness effect. Persons unfortunate enough to get too close to an apparently alien craft and its crew, especially if the crew consists of those most aggressive of UFO occupants, the 'greys' or EBEs (Extraterrestrial Biological Entities), have frequently been zapped by beams of light and, apparently as a result, have found themselves unable to speak or move. Some, perhaps as the consequence of some inbuilt psychological defence system, put the condition down to fear or fascination: 'I was spellbound' they say, or 'I was paralysed with fright'. The main reason why we must suspect that these assumptions by witnesses are subjective is because the same effects ensue even when the percipient is quite unafraid.

A further correlation between the appearances of ghosts and that of UFO entities is that they both seem to converse with their percipients by telepathy. In the case of ufology, this mental ability is one of the reasons why percipients think they have been talking to spacemen: the entities telepathically told them so! This, along with the other information they divulge, including the propulsion system of their various ships, and their reasons for coming to earth – often, apparently, to advise us altruistically of impending doom and disaster – is all conveyed telepathically. As the percipient John Avely put it, 'They didn't speak in my [language] . . . didn't use words . . . I thought what they were saying . . .' Spectres, too, as if the experience of death has deprived them of any language they spoke while in the body, also resort to telepathic, non-verbal communication to get their point across – usually doom and disaster like the ufonauts, but perhaps not quite so eschatologically apocalyptic. One subject, who claimed to have carried on a post-mortem conversation with her grandfather, said the dialogue, at least on the grandfather's side was carried out 'not in words . . . he communicated in thought . . . His lips could have moved slightly, but there were no spoken words, I'm sure of that.' The question must be why do deceased humans seem to share an ability with aliens from another planet? Or are aliens ghosts playing charades?

Missing time also features strongly in accounts of UFO encounters. A whole subschool of ufological thought revolves around what this could mean in ET terms. However, it should be noted (before ufologists of this persuasion convince themselves that they have found something new and wonderful) that time loss also features in accounts of interactions with other forms of apparitional anomalies, as the following account, published for the first time, will demonstrate:

> One evening towards the end of 1972 I was playing, with my friend Debbie, on a railway embankment near to my home. It was a pleasant

evening and the sun was setting. We sat for a while on the grass, and as we sat we saw a train approaching, so we moved back to watch it pass. It moved very slowly, and the odd thing was that I don't remember it making any noise. It was a steam train, billowing smoke and I think it was green in colour. Neither my friend nor I thought anything about the incident, and after we watched the train chuff into the distance we decided to head back.

On returning home, we found that our parents were furious. We thought that we had been out for about thirty minutes . . . we had actually been missing for a couple of hours. When I recounted our adventures to my father I was severely punished for telling lies. As he explained, trains had not run there for years, and it was impossible for them to do so, as there were no tracks. Even though it was so long ago, and I was only a child at the time, I can still recall seeing the train vividly.

As a ufologist I cannot help wondering what happened to the children during that apparently missing segment of time. What would they have recalled under hypnosis I wonder? Abduction aboard a train? Perhaps, but the question would then be – by whom? But the real question is: how can more than one person share the same bizarre experience if it is merely subjective?

Despite the absurdities endemic in much of what has been reported about them, both apparitions of the dear departed and observations of alien craft and their occupants have frequently had more than one witness. Incidents of this nature, when seen simultaneously by a number of witnesses, are called, at least in ufology, multiple-witness events, and are supposed to be extremely indicative of the objective reality of flying saucers. In which case, ghosts must be equally objectively real, as C N M Tyrell, of the Society for Psychical Research, has documented no less that 130 cases of apparitions being seen by more than one witness. Reports of large numbers of people seeing the same anomalous apparition are rare, though Celia Green, of the Oxford Institute of Psychical Research, has on her files cases involving as many as eight witnesses. It is much the same in ufology. While there are many multiple-witness sightings of lights in the sky (LITS), percipient numbers dwindle as the 'strangeness' content of any particular encounter escalates. Why this should be so is still a matter of debate, but could it have anything to do with whatever is manifesting itself?

Investigators into psychic phenomena of all varieties, including UFOs, have often testified to the irritating elusiveness of the phenomena, and the uncanny way in which their attempts to record the phenomena seem to be thwarted. Cameras jam for no reason, instruments inexplicably malfunction, and the anomalous activity, whatever it happens to be, ceases just at the point beyond which recording instruments could be brought to bear, only to resume again when such equipment is dismantled. It seems almost as if some cosmic censor is deliberately inhibiting progress in certain areas of research. The UFO phenomenon, on this occasion, can lay claim to a unique form of censorship in the persons of the mysterious Men in Black (MIB), who try to browbeat witnesses into silence. They often pose as Establishment employees, like Air Force or Ministry of Defence officials, but it is clear from their recorded bizarre looks and behaviour that they are nothing of the sort, but just another aspect of the overall UFO mystery.

The foregoing is not supposed to be an exhaustive exposition of the correlations which exist between ghosts and UFOs, indeed between all forms of paranormal apparitions, but it is hopefully sufficient to indicate that some kind of link does exist between traditional ghosts and today's technological phantasms. Those who have had UFO encounters might now protest that there was nothing remotely ghost-like in whatever they came into contact with. The craft was real, solid, metallic. The aliens grabbed them with an all-too-physical force. However, it must now be pointed out that ghosts, too, contrary to public belief about them, can seem as objectively real as anything else in the material world. 'I'd like to stress,' writes one witness to a ghostly encounter, 'that in no way was I conscious that he [the ghost] was a ghost'. Another, even though she realized at the time that what she was viewing was the ghost of her grandfather, insists 'he looked so real I eventually stretched out my hand to touch him'. Both statements enhance the possibility of a link between these apparently disparate phenomena.

Often, it is only after the experience has ended that the witness learns, to their astonishment, that the person they have seen, supposedly still in the flesh, had died some time previously – or was many miles away from the location where they were seen by the witness. And yes, before you ask, to complicate the issue even further, there are reports of ghosts of the living. At the point of realization, the witness comes to believe that what they have seen is not of this world. Tyrell lists the following among the standards to which genuine ghosts must conform:

1. It must appear solid and three dimensional;
2. It must react as we ourselves do to physical objects or obstructions.

After analysing many hundreds of cases, Celia Green has reached the conclusion that, whatever else they may be, ghosts are hallucinatory. And most modern parapsychologists would agree with her – which isn't the same as saying she is correct. However, in view of her conclusion about ghosts, must we now consider UFOs to be hallucinatory? The dream-like absurdities and paradoxes endemic in close-encounter reports would seem to cry out for such an interpretation. Nowhere is this inbuilt absurdity more evident than in the bewildering variety of UFO occupants that have been reported over the past 40 years. Is it even remotely conceivable that our skies are teeming with, not just a plethora of UFO types, but also with their equally varied pilots? Tin-can men, goblins, jelly men and humanoids of every imaginable shape, hue and size have allegedly been seen: from the cold, clinical 'greys' encountered in the USA, through the aggressive dwarfs of South America, to the tall British blond-haired 'space brother', and, quite recently, Russian 'giants'. All of these entities so amusingly reflect the national spirit/*Zeitgeist* of the country in which their appearances predominate. Can it be merely coincidence that they, and their machines, have accurately mirrored our cultural expectations in the area of space travel. Time was when the alien visitors came from Mars, Venus, Jupiter's moon Ganymede, Uranus, Neptune and the dark side of the moon, or so they told their percipients – telepathically of course. But that was before the space programme of the superpowers had demonstrated beyond doubt that the solar system was devoid of Life As We Know It. Unabashed at this set-back, the aliens relocated to Zeta-Reticuli, Sirius, Orion, the Pleiades: you name it, as long as it is far enough away, that's where they are from, so they would have us believe. As this enforced removal was occurring, so too did their spaceships change. The dials and levers, so overwhelmingly obvious in the Flash Gordon Fifties, were gradually replaced by lasers, computer consoles and ion-drive propulsion systems. It all makes one suppose that if the UFO phenomenon had been around in the days of the Industrial Revolution, the spaceships would have been steam-driven – perhaps they were, if the testimony relating to the phantom train mentioned earlier has any validity. The whole charade is an affront to common sense. Absurd beyond belief. But why should ordinary, otherwise perfectly credible persons tell such impossible tales? In most cases, there is not a scrap of evidence to indicate that they are hoaxing, or have any motivation to do so. On the contrary, there is every reason to believe that they are telling the truth, and recounting an experience which was real, at least to them. So what is going on? The answer surely, must be that they are hallucinating. They are not over-imagining, fantasizing, day-dreaming or confabulating: they are undergoing an experience which is indistinguishable from reality.

On 6 July 1989, the Fylde Coast UFO Investigation Group (FUFOIG) in England received a telephone call from a witness (name and address on file) who wished to report the sighting of a UFO over the sea and central promenade at Blackpool. The major interest in this report was that the witness said the UFO was being pursued by a Tornado aircraft.

At 11.10 p.m. the previous evening, the witness – who is a taxi-driver in Blackpool – was driving down Grasmere Road, towards Central Drive, when he saw, through the open window of his cab, a brightly glowing, red/orange ball-shaped object in the sky over the sea. He had barely been watching it for more than a couple of seconds when it moved 'faster than the eye could see' to another part of the sky. There it hovered for a further period of seconds before repeating the manoeuvre. Then it just disappeared. Within no more than five seconds of the object's disappearance, an RAF Tornado, flying very low (at approximately 150 m/500 ft) and very fast, with its wings swept right back, shot across the sky from over the sea, in the direction of the UFO's last known position. According to the witness:

> It had no lights on at all, which is unusual because it was dusk, though not completely dark. And there was another odd thing. The noise from the Tornado should have been deafening, yet there was no noise at all.

As it swept across the sky, the witness saw smoke in front of the aircraft and also behind it, with a dull flash in the middle which he believes could only have been an air-to-air missile being fired at the UFO. After the Tornado had disappeared out of sight, the witness noticed some persons pointing up at the sky.

The whole incident is absurd. A Tornado firing a missile at a UFO over a built-up area? Even the witness seems to acknowledge, at least on one level, that it makes no sense at all. Yet he knows what he saw with his own eyes. 'I can even tell you what kind of Tornado it was,' he told me at a subsequent interview. 'It was a F3.' So, yet again, we have a case of an ordinary individual reporting something which was not an normal everyday observation. In fact, what he reported seems impossible. So what is going on? The clue, I believe, is in the Tornado's unaccountable silence. As argued, the absence of sound is a common feature, not only of UFO reports, but of all kinds of apparitional phenomena. Seemingly the Cosmic Conjuror always weaves a web of silence around his audience whenever he is up to his tricks! It is also an interesting confirmation of the previously posited correlation between all forms of anomalous phenomena that the glowing object seen by the Blackpool taxi-driver not only disappeared, suddenly, in mid-air, but seems to have performed this act twice – each time reappearing in another part of the sky before finally vanishing for ever. In his written report, the witness says that the object moved *at a fantastic speed, faster than the eye could see*! and it is clear that he means just that. He did not see it move. To his eyes it simply disappeared from one part of the sky to reappear in another. This would suggest at least three hallucinatory phases, even before the appearance of the Tornado. This temporal discontinuity also appears in dreams, and has featured in other apparitional experiences.

We can now begin to understand why the patterns running through UFO and ghost reports should take the form that they do. Certainly, the silence and the telepathic communication are no longer puzzling when we realize that it is the primary visual, non-verbal, unconscious mind that is putting on the show. But what of the physiological effects? Surely it is because the subject is in a state of trance, or enchantment, and not because he is afraid or awestruck, or has been zapped by a trigger-happy alien with a paralysis gun, that he is unable to move or speak. And the sudden disappearance of the UFO or ghost? Surely this occurs the moment the spell is broken and the subject returns to normal consciousness. And he cannot always recall all of his experience for the same reason that he cannot always recall all of his dreams.

Proponents of the old Extraterrestrial hypothesis (ETH) will, of course, insist upon a different interpretation which they will urge us all to consider with an open mind. If a witness cannot account for a couple of hours, it is because the aliens have erased the experience from his memory. They communicate telepathically because – obviously – they can't speak our language. As for the background silence – you might think this would fox them, but no – one ET hypothesizer recently suggested to me that the aliens might well have some kind of anti-sound device with which they can silence all background noise! Certainly, let us keep an open mind by all means, but not so open that our brains fall out. Such tortuous, *ad hoc* reasoning is often symptomatic of a compelling desire to cling to the ETH at all costs. But it can sometimes be due to a simple inability to realize how real 'hallucinatory' experiences can be. Just how 'real' can be dramatically demonstrated by an incident which happened to C G Jung, described in his autobiography, *Dreams, Memories and Reflections*, as one of the most curious experiences in his life. As Jung's life was filled with curious events, we may judge from his emphasis just how great an impression this particular experience made upon him.

It was 1936 and, during a brief stay in Ravenna, Italy, Jung and a female acquaintance (*sic*) paid a visit to the Baptistry of the Orthodox. On entering it, Jung was surprised to find a strange blue light permeating the place:

> The wonder of this light, without any visible source, did not trouble me . . . [though] . . . I was somewhat amazed because, in place of the windows I remembered having seen on my first visit, there were four great mosaics of incredible beauty which it seems I had entirely forgotten.

Jung then goes on to describe the mosaics in great detail, of all of which he 'retained the most distinct memory . . . and to this day can see every detail before my eyes.' Jung and his friend stood before the mosaics, discussing them for a full 20 minutes before leaving for nearby Alinari, where they hoped to be able to buy photographs of them. They could not find any. When they returned home, Jung asked a friend who was going to Ravenna if he would try to obtain photographs of the mosaics. The friend could not find any photographs either, and he discovered the reason why there weren't any: the mosaics did not exist! The point being that if even a psychologist of Jung's stature was unable to tell the difference between hallucination, which the mosaics must have been, and objective reality, then what chance does an ordinary person have when faced with an experience of the same nature? Yet it is almost impossible to convince anyone who has had such an experience that it was an hallucination.

Such witnesses 'know' that what they have seen so clearly with their own eyes was perfectly 'real', sometimes, in some strange way, even more 'real' than anything else they have ever experienced. Above all, they know they are not mad, and, surely, it is only madmen who have hallucinations? Therefore, what they saw was real. QED. That perfectly ordinary and sane individuals can hallucinate, perhaps for the first and only time in their lives, is extraordinary enough, but that such hallucinations can be shared seems weird beyond belief. Yet this is exactly what seems to be happening in multiple-witness cases. However rare they may be – and they may be rarer than we think – they do sometimes occur, both within and outside the parameters of the UFO phenomenon. To what extent subjects who are collectively hallucinating see the same thing is difficult to determine. Through discussing the Ravenna incident with the friend who had shared his experience with the mosaics, and who had 'long refused to believe that what she had seen with her own eyes had not existed', Jung was able to ascertain that at least the principle features of their joint hallucination had been identical. Celia Green, on the other hand, has found that although reports from different subjects greatly resemble each other, they frequently reveal discrepancies. But since even witnesses to, say, a road accident, cannot always agree on the details, we can only reserve judgement. Through analysing many hundreds of written accounts of ghosts, Celia Green has also made the very interesting discovery that not only is the apparitional figure hallucinated, *but so too is the whole environment.* A candle, which was burning brightly while the ghost was present, is seen afterwards never to have been lit. A window that was open is in fact shut. In all other respects the substitute environment is identical to the 'real' one. An experience such as this, when the witness's whole field of perception is hallucinated, is known as metachoric. Because of its obvious internal absurdity, it, therefore, becomes probable that the Blackpool Tornado/UFO event was a metachoric hallucination. This would explain why the event was reported by no one else, even though the percipient saw several persons pointing up to the sky. Those other witnesses must have been part and parcel of the substitute environment in which the entire episode occurred. If the 'true UFO' experience is a metachoric hallucination, then some light may be shed on cases where all kinds of distortions to the environment are noted. The lack of naturally generated background noise, the absence of traffic on a normally busy road, parts of the landscape that 'disappear' after the experience, and sometimes what seem to be strangely symbolic features could all be attributed to the metachoric hallucination. Consider the following case as one example of the kind that overflow the archives of ufology.

In the small hours of 7 October 1975, two men set out for a drive to a lake not far from their trailer home in Maine, USA. On the way, the car turns off, of its own volition according to the driver, down a back road. Continuing their journey, the men both notice how unusually silent the night has suddenly become, and that the only sign of life is a group of cows in a field, shaking their heads oddly from side to side. A little further along this road, they notice a light in the sky. As they approach, they can see that it is a huge cylindrical craft surrounded by multicoloured lights. In panic, the driver floors the accelerator and the chase is on, the object in hot pursuit. Suddenly, a brilliant beam of light hits the car and the next thing the men remember is coming to a mile or so down the road, sitting in the car with the engine off. Glancing at each other, they both notice that the other's eyes are glowing bright orange (an odd feature that we shall come across again). Deciding to forget their original plans, they head for home. On the way, the car engine stalls and the radio goes dead. Two disc-shaped objects now appear in the sky, performing fantastic aerial manoeuvres before falling, in the familiar dead-leaf fashion, into a nearby pond. A strange mist envelopes the car. During all this time, no other vehicle goes by, even though the road could normally be expected to be busy. When the fog begins to lift, they watch two ducks go by, then two geese, then two ducks again: everything in twos. Even the cows are getting up in twos. Eventually, the men try the engine again, and this time it starts. Once again, they head for home, but the nightmare isn't over . . . yet. Following this experience, the two men suffer from a number of symptoms. Their eyes burn, their throats are parched, and they have difficulty in breathing. Two days later, a stranger knocks at the door of their trailer and, when they go to see what he wants, they are immediately warned by him not to speak of their experience to anyone. And this, the reader is assured, is one of the more sensible saucer scenarios that ufologists have been called upon to investigate over the years.

Seriously though, what can be made of a case like this one? The car driving itself, the absence of sound, the animals going two by two, and the glowing eyes of the witnesses, all point to the experience being a metachoric hallucination. A joint metachoric hallucination? How are we to understand the sharing of such an experience, and what about the physical effects? It is as if the witnesses were standing with one foot in the real world and the other in the silent, timeless world of dreams. At this point, I should perhaps make clear that, in considering metachoric hallucination as a possible paradigm, I am not necessarily denying that some UFOs might possess a degree of reality independent of the percipients' minds, perhaps of any mind. You may object, of course, that I am now using words to make them mean what I want them to mean. For me the problem is this: if a sheep goes miaow and catches mice – is it still a sheep? Well, I would hold that it is, albeit a pretty funny one. In this context, it can be said that an hallucination that can be shared is also a pretty funny one

– funny peculiar, and not funny Ha, Ha. So until more is known about that particular 'animal', it is probably best to stick with a word we are familiar with, rather than attempt to coin a new one. But whatever terminology we eventually decide on to describe them, it seems abundantly clear that UFOs and their occupants are not 'real' in the same way as this book you are now reading is 'real'. The latter can be captured convincingly on film, whereas UFOs cannot: that is why there are no extant photographs of alien craft that have not been devalued as evidence by thorough investigation and analysis. There are, of course, plenty of LITS photos that are still categorized as 'unexplained', but although they have stood up to all the tests, they are still inconclusive for the good reason that, while it can be proved that a photograph is a fake, it is impossible to demonstrate beyond a shadow of a doubt that any particular photograph is genuine.

It is the same with those peripherally paranormal people – the fairies. These alleged ethereal inhabitants of lonely dells and misty forest glades, who once filled us with the same numinous sense of awe and wonder that UFOs do today, came in an almost infinite variety of forms: there were nymphs, sylphs, leprechauns, goblins, pixies, undines, kelpies and selkies. Yet the only photographic evidence that we have of their actual existence are those allegedly taken in Cottingley, West Yorkshire, by two children. The photographs depict the kind of gossamer-winged fairies that were common in Victorian children's picture-books – no wonder, seeing as how that is where they came from, as the perpetrators confessed half a century later. Like 'true UFOs', 'real fairies' seem a little camera-shy. Not surprisingly, this is not the only characteristic that the little folk share with the aliens. Jacques Vallee, writing in *Passport to Magonia*, demonstrated that the same motifs, or archetypal cultural threads, run through both fairy and UFO lore. And a close examination of traditional accounts of fairy encounters leaves little doubt that the psychological state of the witness can find its exact counterpart in today's percipients of interplanetary encounters. If ghosts, UFOs and fairies share the same patterns, what then of other fabulous beings, like angels, demons, dragons, lake monsters, black dogs, and the gods and goddesses of the ancient and not so ancient world? And if 'visions' of UFOs and, by the same token, of all the above-named manifestations are but hallucinations, albeit of a specialized variety, then what of visions of the Blessed Virgin Mary, St Paul's vision on the road to Damascus, and all the other visions attested to by saints and sinners alike? Perhaps the endless fable and genealogy of *all* human mythology is part and parcel of one single and underlying phenomenon. The ramifications in this idea are disturbing, to say the least. If angels and aliens are interchangeable, and all the gods and goddesses no different from all the other mythological beings, then it has to be suspected that the origin of all the world's religions, both major and minor, might be explicable in terms of such encounters. It might well be that to solve the UFO mystery will be to solve *all* mysteries – for ever – and then we will be left to go home in the dark alone. Given the nature of the human animal, such a secret, were it true, would be well worth covering up.

The trouble with many of these manifestations is the paucity and low quality of the data. We cannot enter a time-machine and travel back through the centuries, report form in hand, to question witnesses. Nevertheless, the patterns which are discernible at this remove in time do tend to confirm those that have been noticed in modern reports. The Cosmic Conjuror, it seems, once performed the same tricks with fairies and angels as are apparently done today with ghosts, UFOs and big hairy monsters (BHMs).

The yeti, sasquatch, bigfoot, or big hairy monsters (BHMs) as they are known collectively, are sighted almost all over the world, though none has ever been captured, not even on film – if we ignore a few dubious photographs of probable jokers in hairy jumpsuits. No skeletal remains, not even a single bone, have ever been found, which in itself is sufficient to indicate that BHMs probably only exist in that same twilight zone that is home to ghosts, fairies, UFOs et al. The number of BHMs that have been seen in concert with UFOs is further evidence of a hidden link between the two phenomena. In August 1972, for instance, a brightly glowing light was seen in the nocturnal skies above a cornfield in Rochdale, Indiana. Shortly afterwards, a big, hairy ape-like creature was seen going into the field. A smell 'like dead animals or garbage' permeated the air. The creature, which was seen on several occasions by persons living in the area, had another strange attribute: when it ran through undergrowth, *no sound could be heard*. BHMs are not always silent, however. The Tibetan yeti continues to shatter the night with its blood-chilling cry. Nevertheless, the absence of sound where it should normally be expected to occur is the hallmark of the BHM, as is the case with other mythical beings. They may be seen *and* heard, though rarely at the same time. This may reflect the mind's inability to co-ordinate visual with auditory hallucinations, or even to cope with more than one sense at a time. It is often difficult to decide whether a case should go in the BHM or UFO file. On 25 October 1973, farmer Stephen Pulaski saw a large red ball of light coming down over a field outside Uniontown, Pennsylvania. More than a dozen relatives and neighbours witnessed it. When Stephen and a neighbour's two children went to investigate, they came upon two ape-like creatures, over two metres (seven feet) tall, and covered in long grey hair. The creature's eyes glowed an eerie yellow/green (c.f. the Maine case above). Stephen and one of the children now began to complain of burning eyes. Investigators, who soon arrived on the scene, also began to suffer physical symptoms. They complained of light-headedness and had difficulty in breathing. The smell of sulphur filled the air. BHMs with BO have been variously described as smelling 'like garbage', 'like someone who hasn't taken a bath for a year', or – most often – 'like sulphur'. This peculiar sulphurous smell is also frequently reported in UFO sightings. In medieval times, such nasty niffs were associated with demons, and the Devil himself would allegedly often announce his presence with a particularly obnoxious sulphurous smell. Interestingly, the Devil was sometimes said to take the form of a black dog: a creature, still allegedly sighted in many countries, including Britain, which is associated with an unpleasant sulphurous smell. Its eyes are reputed to glow like red-hot coals; its movements are made in sinister silence; and it often disappears suddenly in mid-air.

We can now begin to appreciate how all these apparently unconnected phenomena are interrelated. Further, they often overlap to such an extent that no clear dividing line can be drawn between them. There are UFOs that appear with BHMs; UFO occupants that look like goblins or trolls. There are UFOs associated with the appearance of lake and sea monsters – for example, the bright orange and green ball of fire that was seen off Pendennis Point, near Falmouth, England, shortly before Morgawr, the Cornish sea monster, was sighted. And when PC Alan Godfrey was abducted aboard a UFO in Todmorden, England, he was surprised to find among the other seeming spacefarers – a big black dog. And one of my favourite examples of bizarre ufology: the UFO that landed in a *cemetery* in Savannah, Georgia, on 9 September 1973, and out tumbled ten black dogs. If, as all these connecting features seem to indicate, UFOs, ghosts, fairies, black dogs, lake monsters, BHMs and BVMs – to name but a selection – are all part of a single underlying phenomenon, then in looking to the stars for a solution to the UFO mystery, we are missing what is probably right under our very noses: we should be looking within ourselves as UFOs, their occupants and the whole panoply of the paranormal may be nothing more than close encounters with the contents of our own psyche – or rather, with its age-old cultural archetypes which now and then surface, like sea monsters, just for a moment or two, before plummeting back to the depths of the collective unconscious. Yet, if we accept that the UFO experience is hallucinatory, we are immediately confronted by a truly baffling paradox: what kind of an hallucination is it that can interfere with cars, burn grass, leave physical ground traces, and cause radiation burns in percipients? It is not that we don't yet know the answer. According to the present consensus reality – *there is no answer!* So, ufologists are now in a situation analagous to the one physicists found themselves in at the turn of the century, when they discovered that the behaviour of light was paradoxical in terms of its observed properties: sometimes it seemed to behave like a wave and at other times like a particle. It could not be both – could it? Common sense must surely indicate that something can't be two mutually exclusive things at the same time, but that's what it turned out to be. The discovery spelled the doom of the universe as a great machine, and catapulted us all into the bizarre world of quantum theory, which, if I understand it aright, holds that the universe can be any damn thing it wants to be, and it is under no compulsion to accommodate human common sense in the matter. Perhaps, like light, the phenomenon we are presently trying to understand is also dual in nature, which we presently perceive in terms of mutually exclusive properties. Logically, they can't be – otherwise there would be no phenomena to puzzle us. New wave ufologists are trying to reconcile the seemingly irreconcilable by proposing the existence of a family of exotic, previously unknown atmospheric phenomena (UAP) with such bizarre parameters that they can explain everything – from lights in the sky to close encounters and abduction by aliens – with physical effects. But can they?

The theory was first systematically formulated by a Canadian psychologist (that's interesting: why not a seismologist?) named Michael Persinger who, with Gyslaine Lafreniere, carried out a large-scale computer study which showed that most UFO sightings occur on, or in close proximity to, geological fault areas. These are areas in which tectonic/seismic activity is omnipresent due to fracture or folding in the earth's crust. Geological stresses build up over a period of time and are then released in an earthquake. The whole process begins over again almost immediately. In approaching the problem in this way, Persinger and Lafreniere were replicating the work done by the French researcher, Ferdinand Lagrange, in 1968. He had used the 1954 'UFO Wave' sightings as his data, and got the same results. Where Persinger and Lafreniere differed was in their interpretation. They contended that, as pressure is built up in the rocks in the fault, transduction of mechanical energy to electrical energy (the reverse of the process that gave the waiting world the quartz watch) creates columns of ionized air over the fault line which can sometimes glow through incandescence – the piezo-electrical effect. These glowing ionized forms, which Persinger called 'transients', could move along in the air for short periods above the fault line generating them, possibly giving rise to many lights in the sky-type reports. In Britain, Paul Devereux carried out a similar study, which also showed a definite correlation between areas of geological faulting and what he calls 'earthlights'. There would seem to be certain 'window areas', above the faults, where anyone can experience strange light phenomena if they are prepared to wait around long enough. There is a wealth of photographic evidence now extant to make this point almost conclusively. Devereux also proposes that there is strong evidence, based not only on the testimony of others, but also on his own experiences, that earthlights display intelligent behaviour: either they have a rudimentary intelligence of their own, or they are able to react to the thoughts of the observer. A most outrageous idea, so I will do no more than mention it here, and point out that if it is true the implications are astonishing.

But how can earthlights and/or transients account for those reports that contain mention of structured craft and alien occupants? And what of the other physical effects noted in many UFO reports? Persinger, who is an expert on the effects of electromagnetism on the brain, predicts exactly what would happen when a person came into close proximity with one of these exotic light forms. First, they would experience any one of a number of physical symptoms: tingling sensations, hair standing on end, eyes watering or burning, nausea, feelings of fear, oppression or tranquillity. Anything sound familiar? All these effects have, at one time or another, been reported by UFO witnesses. Then, at close proximity, Persinger postulates the light form could induce hallucination in the percipient by electromagnetically stimulating the temporal lobe cortex. This is the area in the brain which projects a sense of meaningfulness on to the world, and it is also connected with religio/mystical experience. Thus, by short circuiting the brain's natural bio-electricity, this unknown atmospheric phenomenon could account not only for LITS, but could competently explain the whole gamut of UFO/paranormal experience. It is a bold theory. Yet evidence is being increasingly found that indicates that Persinger and his colleagues could be on the right track. Further evidence indicates that there may be a whole family of naturally generated exotic light forms that could cause these same effects.

In recent years, atmospheric physicist Dr Terence Meaden has been trying to explain the puzzling formation of circles of varying complexity that have been appearing in cornfields in England. He has proposed the existence of a previously unknown form of whirlwind – the ionized plasma vortex. These he sees as occurring in the lee of isolated hills or escarpments when meteorological conditions are favourable to their formation. There is also some evidence that indicates that the proximity of geological faulting is a factor in the formation of the Meaden Vortex, and that the same meteorological conditions which favour the formation of vortices might also be the trigger for the formation of Persinger's transients. While ET enthusiasts everywhere were agog with the interplanetary possibilities of corn circles, supporters of Dr Meaden's interpretation were at pains to denounce any connection whatsoever with UFOs. In the event they were wrong. To everyone's surprise, especially Dr Meaden's, the plasma vortex turned out to have a great deal to do with the alien phenomenon, spectacularly explaining even some of the most baffling cases. The evidence is very compelling when we look at some of the effects of the plasma vortex; effects which are not only predicted by Dr Meaden's theory, but, to a large extent, borne out by eyewitness accounts from those who have seen vortices and described them as such, forming around the time and in the area where crop circles have subsequently been discovered (c.f. those predicted by Persinger for his transients). These include a tingling sensation, skin prickling, bristles standing out, vehicles and windows vibrating, trees shaking violently, buzzing, humming and whistling noises, compass-needle distortion, sulphurous smell, engine failure (diesels exempted), light failure, radio static, skin burns and circular marks on the ground – in fact, the entire ufological shooting match. Seriously though, the correlation is too exact to be ignored by ufologists – ET hypothesizers exempted! What is most damning of nuts and bolts ufology in Dr Meaden's theories is that they were never conceived as an *ad hoc* attempt to explain away UFOs in terms of a hitherto-unknown atmospheric phenomenon. Dr Meaden was UFO illiterate and, even now, as he told me recently, he is only just beginning to familiarize himself with the data. So he can't be blamed for deliberately shooting the saucers down. It was only when others, more familiar with the UFO documentation than himself, applied his theory to the UFO data that it was realized just how much it could explain. Cases which had given even the sceptics explanatory headaches now disappeared like Disprin dissolved in water.

Take the case of PC Alan Godfrey. Those who would dismiss this event as inexplicable can now be shown to be on shaky ground. The details of this case are now too well known to need repeating here fully. Suffice it to say that on 29 November 1980, PC Godfrey encountered an almost classic flying saucer in Burnley Road, Todmorden, England. It resembled a rotating, top-shaped object with portholes. But now comes the interesting part: he noticed that nearby trees were shaking, although the night was calm, and that his police car radio was rendered inoperative by an inordinate amount of static. His next memory was of being seated in the car several yards down the road, with the craft gone and with no idea of how he had got there. He later returned to the site with a colleague, and they discovered a circular 'swirled' pattern on the wet road. Under hypnosis, PC Godfrey recalled being 'taken aboard' the craft and being subjected to an examination of sorts. His abductors were a humanoid called Joseph, dwarfs, robots and a large black dog. PC Godfrey's experience took place during a mini-flap (lasting five days) in that area. There surfaced over the period many LITS reports, so can it only be a coincidence that the Craven Fault runs virtually underneath the affected area? And to cap it all, the incident occurred during the passage of a clearing weather frontal system. In short, all the conditions were in place for the formation of plasma vortices or earthlights – or perhaps both at the same time, considering the topography of the area in which the events occurred. If you re-read the previously mentioned list of UAP properties, you will certainly find exactly those described by PC Godfrey. It is also possible that his aliens were created by his own subconscious as the emanations from the earthlight, or plasma vortex, scrambled his psyche. To explain it in this way in no way denigrates the witness's original testimony; on the contrary, it shows just how accurately he conveyed the details of his bizarre experience to the investigators. Can many other UFO experiences be interpreted in this way, and with the same ease? It is beginning to look that way, as case after case vanishes in a puff of atmospheric logic when touched by Meaden's magic wand – sorry wind.

However, at the present state of knowledge, few would suggest that exotic atmospheric phenomena are responsible for each and every UFO report ever made. There may yet be discovered other ways in which hallucinations can be induced by electromagnetically stimulating the temporal lobe cortex. The process might even occur spontaneously, as with epilepsy. Whatever the actual *modus operandi*, in virtually all cases where there is evidence of physical effects, as well as an unknown percentage of the rest, some form of UAP is likely to be the agent. And the synchronous proximity of many ancient sites and dwellings to geological fault lines leads to the inevitable speculation that our pre-scientific ancestors were well aware of what we are only now becoming able tentatively to contemplate: that these 'window areas' look out on to the landscapes of the mind.

We have now reached a position in our understanding of the phenomenon where it is no longer tenable to hold that UFOs are not susceptible to the scientific mind. As Jacques Vallee has correctly pointed out, there is no such thing as an unscientific subject, only the approach is scientific or otherwise. And the approach of science has always been to formulate a hypothesis, then test it to destruction. If it survives, then some reliance can be placed on its propositions: Persinger has done just that. While the flying saucer faithful awaited the landing of extraterrestrials on the White House lawn, Persinger dragged them into his laboratory and made them perform to order. *Persinger has replicated the UFO experience under laboratory conditions!* What he did was to construct a helmet filled with electrical circuitry designed to emit a magnetic field to stimulate the temporal lobe cortex. Volunteers who wore this helmet were given the suggestion that they could see a strange light in the sky, and asked to say what happened next. All described abduction experiences that were indistinguishable from the real thing – if there is a real thing. Perhaps Persinger's magnetically induced experiences *are* the real thing. The conclusion that seems inescapable is that if these aliens had not already been present in the psyches of the volunteers, they could not have hallucinated them in the way described. Perhaps the alien archetype is part and parcel of our mental baggage (HG has a lot to answer for!) and this is why UFOs can cast such a spell of fascination over us.

It is inevitable here that a parallel must be drawn with the process of religious conversions. The UFO experience is extremely convincing to those who have undergone it. Ask any abductee and they will – if they are honest – confess to total belief in ETH (peripheral details differ with each individual but that doesn't matter). The ancient world, without the benefit of science fiction (there has to be science before you can write science fiction), had a mythological consensus that saw advanced non-humans in terms of gods, angels, demons etc. It seems reasonable, therefore, to suppose that any pre-scientific abductee/contactee would interpret their experiences in a religious rather than a technological context. This, I venture to suggest, is how religion came into being in the first place, and still holds considerable sway as, inevitably, some encounters are interpreted in a religious context – as the affair at Fatima, in 1917, clearly indicates. Even more evidential is how technological phenomena, UFOs, have actually generated a kind of quasi-religion in some quarters. It is the aliens that inhabit the unexplored inner space of our minds, and not the aliens tearing about in outer space who are the source of our wonder and fascination with UFOs. It is they who seduce our reason and lead us into blind belief; they are the price we pay for being what we are.

Yet how did these bogies of the mind begin? Even more pertinent, how do new archetypes come to be formed within the collective unconscious? Through some natural psychological and sociological need? Or was it the act of some divine or external intelligence? Not to put too fine a point on it, are we genetically programmed to be potty? Is unconscious insanity a necessary adjunct to conscious creativity? Let's go back to that first sensational saucer story of 24 June 1947. Too bad they were not really saucer shaped: the truth of the matter is that the objects Kenneth Arnold claimed to have seen were crescent shaped, but the popular media never were ones to let facts get in the way of a good story. All Arnold did was to compare the objects' apparent motion to 'a saucer skipped over water'. But the pen is mightier than the truth, and the resulting story gave birth to the flying saucer. The realization that the first flying saucers were not, after all, flying saucers was probably the first nail in ETs' coffin (which I can't resist saying is also probably saucer shaped, but you will have to await the late edition to find out). Persinger's electromagnetic initiative is probably the hole in which it will finally be interred. And the headstone? Probably a cromlech raised over an earth fault. Does all this mean that ufology is dead? Some are already saying this; so successful has the electromagnetic/UAP model been in explaining the previously inexplicable that its proponents, with some justification, triumphantly proclaim from every available podium that the game is over. The riddle is solved. But in their haste to tell us it is all wrapped up, perhaps they have forgotten mankind's penchant for hereafters. So, is there life after death for ET?

Few can deny that, with the UAP hypothesis and Persinger's helmet, a giant step has been taken in what appears to be the right direction. More real progress has been made with this paradigm than was made by all the rest that have excercised ufological ingenuity over the past four decades. But – and there is always a *but* – there remain certain puzzling aspects of the phenomenon, pieces of the jigsaw that still need a little forcing to make them fit. Can we be so certain that the alien beings apparently lurking in the darkness just below the threshold of everyday consciousness are *purely* the product of science fiction and the sensational Press? There is no doubt that the up and coming generation are swamped in the stuff, but what of the past? Remember, some of the early alien-encounter reports came from remote rural areas. These reports were filed by isolated rural folk, many of whom were unable to read a newspaper, too poor to own a TV, and who had, consequently, never even heard of UFOs. Early abduction cases suffer from the same problem – the percipients' UFO illiteracy. Antonio Villas Boas, a Brazilian farmer, was working in his fields one night (it's cooler then), when down came a UFO; out jumped four humanoid beings and dragged him on board. If he had known what was waiting for him, perhaps he would not have been so initially reluctant: he was seduced by a siren from the stars – and if ETH is true, please god I should be so lucky. The report of his adventures, in what we must now suspect was an interplanetary brothel (well, there were red lights all over it according to the witness), was not published until 1964, in *Flying Saucer Review*. The delay was experimental, in that the story was withheld for a period to see if any others like it turned up. They didn't. More's the pity, some might say. Abduction did continue, but more in the mould of what occurred to Barney and Betty Hill on a lonely road in New Hampshire. Still, apart from the sexual content of the Villas Boas Case, the two abductions had many points in common, even though, due to the delay in publishing, the Hills had never heard of Villas Boas. It is difficult to see how these aspects of the phenomenon can be explained without having to rewrite the psychology textbooks. Answers may have to be found outside the framework of conventional science. In particular, we may find ourselves having to lend an ear to the ideas of Rupert Sheldrake.

Like many biologists, Rupert Sheldrake was disconcerted by the way rats, for instance, which have learned how to solve a puzzle (like escaping from a maze), seemed to be able to transmit this information to other rats – even those on the other side of the Atlantic. Apparently, once a few rat geniuses have solved any particular puzzle, other rats immediately improve in performance. In order to explain this transfer of information, as well as overcome other problems in the life sciences, Rupert Sheldrake suggested that each individual has a morphogenic field, which exists independently of the brain and acts as a template for that individual's behaviour. This, in turn, is part of a greater species morphogenic field. When a group of rats anywhere learn how to solve a puzzle, their morphogenic fields register the solution, which modify the information in the species morphogenic field. From then on, rats everywhere will have an increased chance of solving that particular puzzle for themselves. The theory has been dismissed as mystical nonsense by many of Sheldrake's contemporaries, as well as by the editor of *Nature* magazine, who once asked if Sheldrake's book was fit for burning. Yet the theory has stood up well under experiments, some quite ingenious, designed to test its validity. Something akin to Sheldrake's morphogenic fields might have to be posited if we are ever to explain how new archetypes are formed, and then transmitted throughout the globe. An extension of this theory could well explain the mechanics of the collective hallucination.

Throughout, I have tried to show that the origin of UFOs, and their alien occupants, probably lies within us. Further evidence for this may lie in the strange but apparently meaningless coincidences with which ufology abounds: the mini-wave of sightings at Bettyhill in 1979; mysterious UFO-related events surrounding the death of Adamski (not the contactee but someone else with the same name); an encounter with aliens from Janus which coincided with the publication of Arthur Koestler's book *Janus*, in which he put forward a psychological interpretation of UFOs. I suppose it could just be that the aliens are having a little joke at our expense. But it seems more likely that it is the collective unconscious operating behind the whole charade. For the unconscious mind 'thinks' – if that is the right word – by association; it deals in analogies, metaphors and synchronicity: a process that we all can see working in our dreams every night. This must surely also occur at the deeper, non-verbal, collective level. No other explanation, I believe, can better account for those seemingly meaningless coincidences – unless we dismiss them all as pure chance. But what is pure chance anyway? In a cause-and-effect universe, which we believe ours to be, can it exist at all? But now we are stepping into the realms of wilder speculation, and must tread carefully. Nevertheless, it is in this direction that I believe future research must go. Ufologists everywhere are beginning to come up with similar ideas. Perhaps we are all tuned to the same morphogenic field – who knows? But it is clear that, at last, we seem to be zeroing in on the phenomenon that has entertained and exasperated generations of investigators. If the phenomenon continues to run true to form, there are, no doubt, surprises waiting in the wings of time. It might be that, in the end, the solution will be such that we will find ourselves face to face with something truly unexpected. And if that happens, I'm sure I don't know what it will turn out to be.

BIBLIOGRAPHY

Bord, J & C   *Alien Animals* (Grafton, 1980)

Clarke, D & Roberts, A   *Phantoms of the Sky* (Robert Hind, 1990)

Devereux, P   *Earthlights Revelation* (Blandford, 1990)

Flying Saucer Review, Vol. 20, No. 1 (1974); Vol. 22, No. 2

Green, C & McCreery, C   *Apparitions* (Hamish Hamilton, 1975)

Jung, C G   *Memories, Dreams, Reflections* (Collins & Routledge, 1963)

Meaden, G T   *The Circles Effect and its Mysteries* (Artetch Publishing, 1989)

Northern UFO News (October, 1990)

Persinger, M & Lafreniere, G   *Space–Time Transients and Unusual Events* (Nelson Hall, 1977)

Randles, J & Fuller, P   *Crop Circles: A Mystery Solved* (Hale, 1990)

Vallee, J   *Passport to Magonia* (Neville Spearman, 1970)

CHAPTER EIGHT

ABDUCTION: AN ALIEN EXPERIENCE?

Charlotte A O'Conner

A few days before the earthquake that struck Bakersfield, California, on 22 August 1952, Mr Cecil Michael saw a 'flying saucer'. The eventual result was that he was abducted by its strange occupants and transported by them to a planet called Hell. At the outset, the scenario would have satisfied even the most pernickety ET hypothesizer, but by the time the experience had ended, the parameters had expanded to include segmentally vanishing aliens, telepathic conversations, out-of-the-body experience (OOBE), a meeting with the Devil himself, and rescue from Hell by Jesus Christ. Demonstrably, from his own account of what he underwent, it is clear that the percipient found it to be a jumble of the pseudo-scientific and the sacrilegious which made very little sense to him. At the end, he could only say of his untoward experience: 'Perhaps men of great knowledge and wisdom . . . can decipher the true advanced meaning of it.'[1]

Unfortunately, some 40 years on, nobody – least of all men of great knowledge and wisdom – has succeeded in deciphering the meaning of the abduction experience. Perhaps they can hardly be blamed as this one aspect of overall ufology outdoes all the rest when it comes to confusion and cosmological codswallop. Unless, as some are prone to do (and can you blame them), you dismiss the entire ufological documentation that relates to abductions as the product of a peculiar kind of paranoia, there is no getting away from the possibility that something strange has apparently been taking liberties with sundry members of the human race for some considerable time.

Providing you do not insist on spacemen, the abduction

experience is really nothing new: throughout the ages there have been reports of individuals being 'taken' by non-human entities. All that now seems to have happened is that the format of abduction has been updated to accommodate the new scientific superstitions that have replaced the old magical ones. Unfortunately, accepting this premiss does not bring us any closer to understanding what kind of experience 'abduction' really is.

Over the years, the content of aberrant abductee adventures has posed insurmountable problems for those ufologists who attempted some kind of investigation. A major difficulty was that no two abductees seemed to share the same abductors. It was not just a matter of the alien hardware being different, the entities themselves were completely different in size, shape and, on occasion, in claimed point of origin. The conclusion that had to be drawn, if you were a proponent of ETH, was that either the earth was a major source of exobiological and exosociological input for every alien community in the universe – or something else was happening. The interpretive difficulties presented to ufologists in this area are exemplified by the abduction of PC Alan Godfrey in the Burnley Road, Todmorden, England, in the early hours of the morning of 29 November 1980.[2] Initially, the constable recalled seeing the object, and apparently had it in view long enough for him to make a sketch of it. Then, inexplicably, he found himself, still in his police vehicle, some distance beyond the point where he had seen the 'saucer'. Nonplussed, he returned to his police station. If that had been the end of it, then all it would have amounted to would have been yet another well-attested case of close encounter. But some weeks later, while being interviewed by ufological investigators, PC Godfrey suddenly began to recall other details. These consciously recalled details expanded the original incident into something more sinister.[3] His flashback memories contained the recollection of 'a voice' warning him that he was seeing something he shouldn't. Strange really, when you consider that, under hypnosis, he remembered being abducted aboard the very object the voice told him he should not be seeing in the first place. The internal incongruities of his story grew worse when he came to describe the beings who had abducted him. The leader was a somewhat biblically bedecked being called Yoseph (Joseph). Also on board the saucer were a number of dwarfs, and a large black dog. To say that their presence was paradoxical, in terms of the more overtly technological trappings noted by the constable, is perhaps to understate the matter. Firstly, one must surely wonder why an alien spaceship should have such a kosher captain. And what of the dwarfs and the dog? Despite the abductive orthodoxy of the 'medical examination' the constable remembered being subjected to under hypnosis, it seems unlikely that spacenapping is a sufficient explanation for the experience Alan Godfrey underwent. To further undermine any attempt at explanation, Alan Godfrey eventually had what seemed to be memories of mutually exclusive scenarios from the inception of the experience. So what really happened to him? As yet, there is no real explanation for the events as they were attested to by the witness. The best conclusion that can be reached seems to be that Godfrey did have an experience, but *what kind* of experience is another matter.

An element that seems common to abduction experiences is the paradoxical juxtaposition of technological and psychical elements within the overall adventure. In the case of Alan Godfrey, it just happened to be a figure from local folklore – a black dog. Godfrey admitted that the presence of this dog 'disturbed him': no wonder when you realize that this creature is allegedly the Devil in disguise. Certainly scientific ufology would have liked to relegate Godfrey and the Semitic spacefarer to the realms of phantasmagoria, but that would not have explained the physical trace evidence (the inexplicable damage done to the PC's, no doubt regulation, boots) or the other physical synchronicities that surrounded this encounter: the fact that Godfrey admitted being 'strangely drawn' to the object, which he initially thought was a public bus; also the fact that he was in that area looking for some cows which had gone mysteriously missing and which, just as mysteriously, returned after the incident. They were found in a field directly adjacent to the farm from which they had gone missing: the very same field that PC Godfrey remembers going into at the onset of his experience – if memory serves him correctly that is. Cownapping is a ufological accomplishment that has been reported in other areas, notably during the Welsh flap of 1974–77.[4]

The psychism inherent in abduction events that seemingly have a material genesis – that is the percipient at least seems to be waylaid by an alien craft and their material body is abducted – is bad enough; but what interpretive contortions can explain those events where the witness claims that only their 'spiritual body' (soul?) was abducted? Can this be taken as confirmation of OOBE experience, and the probability of life after death? Logically one might think so, but there is the problem of the aliens who are equally real (or unreal) in both types of abduction. One witness of my acquaintance, whom I shall call Charlie, claimed that he had been 'spiritually' taken from his bed to a star system at the 'far side of the universe'.[5] Nothing would shake his conviction that, despite the non-material genesis of his adventure, it was a real event. The reason he was so sure was that there was no break in consciousness: he was 'awake' from the moment he was snatched spiritually from his bed until he was similarly returned to it, and – once again in the body – sat up and lit a cigarette.[5]

Jerome Clarke reported on an incident that occurred in 1969 where elements of material abduction were intermingled with those of the spiritual variety. The incident initially developed as a variation on the lonely road at night variety. A couple returning from a holiday encountered a UFO just south of Salt Lake City, Utah.[6] It was midnight as the object approached. There was a car-chase sequence, during which the car seemed not to be under the control of the driver because it would not go faster than 90 km/hr (55 mph) with the gas pedal pushed to the floor. Then the couple pulled into a roadside rest area, and parked up facing what they thought was a parked and lighted camper. (The UFO, by the way, was still visible to them at this time, hovering a few metres away.) Their intention was to go across to the camper to find someone to confirm for them that they weren't going crazy. But 'something' peered out of the camper's window, and the sight of it was so unsettling that the plan was shelved. Then the couple underwent a period of sheer terror as 'entities' approached the car they were sitting in. Unable to stand it any longer, the wife drove the car away from the spot. Yet again, the car refused to go above 90 km/hr (55 mph). The couple travelled for a considerable distance, taking turns at driving. All the while, the UFO stayed in touch. Came the dawn, and they were relieved to see the UFO fall further behind, until it finally flew away over the desert. The couple's relief was short-lived, however, as further down the road they came across the camper they thought they had left, still parked up, in the rest area. How it had got there before them, they had no idea, but in daylight it looked just like an ordinary Ford camper. They decided to overtake it, and the passenger, who at that time was the wife, would look in as they passed to see who was driving it. It must have seemed like a good idea at the time, but, as their car overtook the camper, the wife could see who was driving, and she wished she couldn't: the driver and passenger were headless. Shades of Sleepy Hollow! The conscious recollections of the witnesses were weird enough, but the investigator, suspecting that there might be more to it, eventually persuaded the percipients to undergo regression hypnosis. It was during this hypnotic investigation that it came to light that the wife, at least, had experienced the main abduction via OOBE. She had described it as like 'a shadow of herself going up into the air'. So perhaps, in the face of this testimony, it can be suspected that abduction experiences, even those with apparent alien hardware in the scenario recalled, have at base a purely hypnogogic reality.

This conclusion can find some support in the documented experience that overtook a percipient of a UFO one week after the original sighting. On the morning of the eighth day after the UFO sighting, the percipient awoke and went downstairs, to be greeted by her husband with the words: 'I hope you aren't going to go walk about tonight like you did last night.'[7] Seemingly, her husband had found her outside the house, in a kind of trance from which he could not awaken her. He guided her back and into bed, where she then remained until morning. The only words she addressed to her husband while she was in the trance-like state were a query as to whether she had her clothes on. But, even then she gave no evidence of hearing his confirmation in the affirmative, as she repeated the question several times. This witness was startled by the fact that she had no recollection of the night's events. Her conscious recall ended just prior to going to bed, at a point where she had found the back door open during her check to see if the house was secure for the night. According to her husband, he had found his wife standing outside their home, staring blankly into the sky in the direction of where the previous week's UFO had last been seen. Neither witness ventured an opinion in the matter, and the wife refused any attempt at clarification by regression hypnosis. The investigators, with only the conscious recall of the witness to draw upon, speculated that the woman might well have been undergoing an abduction experience, which had – by the time the husband found her – reached the point of medical examination, hence the wife's anxiety about her clothing; the inference being that abduction events are internal phantasmagorias. But even then, this explanation leaves untouched the question of how such mental events are precipitated, and from where they derive their strange and disturbing content.

Presuming, for a moment, that abduction is something inflicted on witnesses by themselves, we have to explain the overall similarities between events reported by different witnesses at different locations who knew nothing of each other's experiences. Also there is the matter of why, despite the dissimilarities of the hardware and the entities involved, witnesses always seem to want to interpret their experiences in a spacenapping format. Certainly, a psychological explanation could be invoked that would probably explain those abductions where only one percipient was the victim. We all carry around in our subconscious the baggage of enculturation that includes the popular scientific consensus of our day – without realizing it, unless, of course, you happen to be a fan of the scientific fiction of the times, beginning with Wells and ending (for the moment) with Spielberg, which has conditioned our expectations of life on other worlds. Since the turn of the century, the dissemination of popular science, and science fiction, has made sure that no one can go through childhood without coming into contact with it. The present generation, especially in the developed countries, is supersaturated with it. Films, TV, comics, video games – all present aspects of alienness to the uncritical minds of pre-adolescents. Therefore, it could be argued as psychologically unsurprising if, at some future time, these resurfaced as an adult abduction scenario. In support of this, it can be pointed out that present-day abduction scenarios contain aliens the likes of which were common on the covers of pulp science-fiction magazines half a century or more ago. In many ways, there is no need to invoke Jungian archetypes to explain the physiognomy of the various entities who have allegedly abducted individuals on a world-wide basis. One need only turn to the pages of *Thrilling Wonder Stories, Amazing* or similar magazines published during the early part of this century to find an abundance of aliens that fit the descriptions given by modern abductees. But, as Jung said of his archetype hypothesis: 'Unfortunately however, there are good reasons why the UFOs cannot be disposed of in this simple manner.'[8] Not only the UFOs, but their presumed pilots, as well, refuse to be categorized as being merely products of the febrile human imagination.

The aspect of abduction experiences that seems to argue conclusively against them being solely a product of an individual's imagination is the fact that on more than one occasion multiple witnesses were involved. The classic case, which could even be seen as the template for all future abductions, was the one involving Barney and Betty Hill. Yet again the genesis of the experience was in the car on lonely road format.[9] But it gradually escalated to the point where Barney and Betty allegedly saw an alien spacecraft and were taken aboard by its occupants. From the extensive documentation of the event, it would seem that Barney and Betty shared an identical experience. However, there are some crucial differences in what they experienced, which might indicate that this was not necessarily the case. The main protagonist was definitely Betty: it was her version that came to dominate the joint testimony, because she seemingly kept her eyes open, while Barney did not. It would seem from this that Barney's testimony was only confirmatory to the extent that he agreed that something had happened to them on that lonely New Hampshire road. But it was from Betty's testimony that most of the details were drawn. Is it possible, if the trauma is severe enough, for one person to draw another, at least peripherally, into the hallucination they are having? Crowd psychology would indicate that the answer could be yes: for example, the Martian invasion of the United States, courtesy of Orson Welles. Apparently, the panic generated by Welles's radio programme was such that several individuals claimed to have actually seen the Martian machines striding across the country. Similarly at Fatima, in 1917, at the culmination of a highly emotional series of visions by three uneducated peasant children, many people in the crowd were persuaded that they had seen the sun dance in the sky.[10] That it did no such thing is confirmed by the fact that none of the world's astronomical observatories noticed anything untoward in the behaviour of our parent star. So, obviously, something else took place at Fatima: possibly a kind of mass hysteria, generated, conditioned and guided by the religious fervour that was displayed by the visionaries. It is difficult to say, but either there is a mundane psychological explanation for what occurs in abduction events, or we must face the ineluctable possibility that we are the subject of cosmic kidnapping.

A possible clue to why the abduction scenario has turned out the way it has might be contained in the somewhat similar phenomenon of contactee-ism that became all the rage during the early days of ufology. George Adamski set the pattern, and while most of his claims have now been discredited, there is just an outside chance that he did actually get his start from a bona fide abduction experience, which he then embroidered into the tales of interplanetary derring-do with which he entertained a generation of true believers. Many others followed his lead. But while their aliens were different from his, they apparently shared the same concerns. Those early aliens never seemed to tire of warning humanity of the dangers of atomic fission. The purport of most of the contactee messages seems to have been that the 'spacebrothers will save us' in the event of atomic war. In the climate of the times, it was probably very reassuring to some. It can then, perhaps, be seen as synchronous that the decline of the contactee syndrome coincided with the Cuban missile crisis. How close we came will never properly be known, but it was close enough to scare the pants off everyone, and to make clear that *nobody,* except ourselves, was going to save us from the results of our own follies – least of all a bunch of pansy aliens with names like the latest acrylic fibres. These days the 'warning' aspect of abduction remains but the concomitant implication that the aliens will save us from atomic, ecological or any other self-inflicted danger is seemingly missing. I wonder why?

There are those still in ufology who would stoutly maintain that human beings, despite their many other shortcomings, cannot deceive themselves with self-generated hallucinations; even less could they deceive others. Therefore, the aliens are real, and it is only our perception of them that is faulty. Perhaps, because they are so highly advanced, there is a communication problem. But nobody is going to tell them that percipients cannot tell when something is real or not; especially when it comes to intercourse with aliens – sexual intercourse that is. First published in *Flying Saucer Review* in 1964, the case of Antonio Villas Boas was deemed 'The Most Amazing Case Of All'. The story goes that, while working in his fields late at night, this Brazilian farmer was abducted aboard a flying saucer, there to be sexually molested by a 'spacewoman'.[11] The case, given the seal of approval by Dr Olavo Fontes, was seen in many quarters as proof positive that aliens were conducting experiments to produce viable offspring from a union between themselves and human subjects. Prior to this, such experiments had allegedly only involved human females, and the supposition now was that the aliens, having failed in that area because they were unable to be present during pregnancy and birth, had decided to change tack, and make sure that any offspring would be under their care from the word go. Villas Boas, with the usual male chauvinism, tried to offload the blame entirely by implying that he wasn't in control of himself. However, it is clear from his testimony that he was not all that reluctant to co-operate, as the act of coitus was engaged in more than once. Olavo Fontes discovered physical traces when examining Villas Boas that seemed to indicate the validity of the experience he recounted, but it was also admitted that 'the very content of his story is in itself the biggest argument against its veracity'. Why should that be? Must a man be called a liar because he claims to have 'humped a hallucination'? Because, if we reject the ETH implications, and still accept that Villas Boas was 'telling the truth as he knew it', that is the only option left. Can't be done? Don't you believe it!

In 1982, the BBC screened a dramatized documentary, 'The Story of Ruth'. It concerned the strange malady of Ruth, a married American living in London, who eventually sought the services of a psychiatrist to help her come to terms with what was troubling her. The symptoms that drove Ruth to the psychiatrist were such that they threatened to destroy, not just her marriage, but Ruth herself. The major reason that Ruth was in such emotional dire straits was that she was hallucinating an apparition of her father which seemed to be as real as any living person. This was not a case of post-mortem return, as her father was alive and well back in the USA. The point of this case, at least for ufology and the abduction experience, is the fact that the paternal doppelganger hallucinated by Ruth behaved in all respects as if her father were really there. The phantasmagoric image blocked out light and objects in the way normal bodies do when interposed between them and the viewer. And it led Ruth a dog's life. Fortunately for her, Dr Schatzman was a psychiatrist in a million. Not only did he not diagnose her 'psychotic', he helped her to learn how to control her capability for producing mental clones. From being a patient Ruth became a co-worker on her own case and, in the end, instead of being frightened by her capacity, used it for entertainment. But the incident that has ramifications in the area of shared-abduction scenarios happened while she was in America visiting her father: she created a doppelganger of her husband – which was *also* seen by her father. Apparently, on two previous occasions, when her husband was away from home, Ruth had created his doppelganger and made love to it. Both experiences, she admitted, were sexually very satisfying.[12] Just like the real thing. Now tell me where reality ends and phantasmagoria takes over? If this sort of thing is a naturally occurring human capacity, it might explain not only Villas Boas's enjoyable abduction, but also all those succubae and incubi that allegedly harassed the hell out of celibate medieval monks.

Now it begins to appear that, instead of looking for aliens in the woodpile, we should instead take a closer look at ourselves, to discover the alien within. All UFO-encounter stories, not just those that include abduction and/or contact have a definite whiff of morbid psychology about them. Those who have become involved, investigators and percipients alike, seem convinced that these scientific apparitions are trying to tell us something: it is just that nobody is quite sure what it might be. Throughout, there is a general air of impending doom, and time and again contactees have been involved by the aliens in nonsensical initiatives to save the world from sundry prophesied disasters, most of which, had they happened, would have made any and all remedial strategies redundant.

Through his association with Uri Geller (another contactee claimant), Dr Andrija Puharich was drawn into an attempt to avert atomic war by an interdimensional group, calling itself The Nine.[13] Apparently, they had chosen Geller in childhood, and programmed him to avert the impending catastrophe.[13] It was all a very exciting, in a Blovatskian sort of way, as The Nine, sitting in a spaceship called Spectra some 53,069 light ages (light ages?) away, indulged in a series of mediumistic apport of various objects to prove their existence. All in all, it seemed pretty poor stuff, especially as the group even claimed to control the universe. They also promised a mass landing of UFOs on the earth . . . soon (which in ufonaut-speak means never). In the end, even Puharich seemed to feel that the space spooks were nothing if not a bunch of cosmic comedians. Too bad he didn't keep that in mind when, after the Geller phenomenon waned, he got caught up in another contactee scenario. This time the communicators were The Management. But the plot was almost the same, it was a mediumistic type of contact, and – yet again a mass landing of UFOs was promised.[14] As the only connection between the two cosmodramas seems to be Puharich himself, perhaps it can be surmised that it was he, and not Geller, who hallucinated it all, after the fashion of Ruth with her father. I would consider that it is undeniable that Geller was at his psychic best while he was with Puharich.

From the foregoing, it has to be considered as possible that all ufological incidents, from outright abduction to more physically inclined scenarios, might derive from the depths of the human psyche. In fact if there is such a thin line between what is real and what is not, we have to consider the possibility that the distinctions we daily make in this regard are redundant.[15] The difficulty, as always with ufology, is that hypotheses can be piled upon hypotheses depending on just how much, or how little, of the documentation you are prepared to countenance as genuine. There always has been a problem with hoaxes in ufology. It was bad enough in the days when the saucers seemed content to stay in the skies, but the situation is infinitely worse when it comes to abductee claims. Typical of the kind of confusion that can arise in any ufological enquiry is that which followed the claim of abduction that emanated from Ilkley Moor, England, around 1987. Without appearing to make a determination either way, it is instructive to consider the reception this case initially got when it first surfaced into the ufological limelight.

The case first came to the attention of British ufology at large when the witness contacted Jenny Randles approximately two days after his Ilkley Moor experience. It was all a bit cloak and dagger, as the witness apparently only gave a box number, and by the time Jenny Randles had run him to earth, he had already involved another UFO group. This group had come to the immediate conclusion that the object involved was a spacecraft. Fairly unsubstantiated accusations were bandied about in the fanzines that the investigators were not being as forthcoming as they should have been with the information available, and that the longer the investigation went on, the more the story told by the witness was enhanced by additional details. The implication was that it was all a hoax, in which the investigators were possibly involved.[16] Sometimes a ufologist's lot is not a happy one, because there is no way of defending yourself against this kind of charge. Whatever stand is taken by the accused only serves to involve them further in recriminatory debate to the detriment of the case under investigation. It is more likely that flying saucers are spaceships than that the ufologists involved in this investigation were party to a hoax. In some ways it is even unlikely that the event was a hoax at all. As an abduction, the scenario was nothing if not orthodox. The witness claimed that as he was crossing Ilkley Moor, in the vicinity of a group of buildings known as White Wells, he was accosted by a green-looking, four-foot humanoid. Initially, the witness claimed only to have seen the entity and the UFO, and to have a photograph of said entity as proof of his experience. As entity photographs go, this one was a beauty. The entity was clearly visible, as was a strange blueish object which allegedly was a box-like protrusion on the UFO which, in the photograph, is masked by the local topography. Objections were immediately raised against this photo on the grounds that the camera, the type of film, and the time of day it was claimed the photo was taken, were not consonant with the result allegedly obtained. As the investigation went ahead, the witness allowed himself to be regressed hypnotically, and from this came the main elements of the abduction.

When he first saw the alien, the witness now remembered being 'unable to move'. Under hypnosis, he said: 'Oh! I can't move . . . I'm stuck, and everything's gone fuzzy. I'm floating along in the air.'[17] This remark in itself is highly enlightening as, rather than indicating that the witness was bodily levitated into the saucer, it seems more likely to have been the onset of an OOBE. Once aboard the spaceship, which was parked in a nearby depression, the witness was apparently whisked off into orbit, where he was shown a kind of disaster movie which included scenes of starving millions and effluent flowing into a river. Some of the material he was allegedly shown he refused to reveal to the investigators: an entity-imposed secrecy which connects his experience with all manner of other 'visions', including those of Alan Godfrey and the children of Fatima. It is also interesting that he claims to have heard a humming sound, which increased in volume when the spaceship took off. Apart from the fact that this noise has been heard at other points on the moor, there is the matter of the apparitions at Fatima which also involved a humming noise while the vision was in progress. In fact, strange humming sounds are seemingly a necessary adjunct to many visionary episodes. As the abduction ended, the witness was released and, turning back, had time for just one shot of the entity. So the photograph, if the estimated time loss was correct, was taken much later in the day than was originally supposed, and the objections to it are therefore negated. I have seen this photograph, and was quite impressed by it. If it is indeed a fake, as some have implied, then the photographer should immediately offer his services to Spielberg. For me, the most tantalizing thing about it was not the rather troll-like entity, but the blue box which is a little to one side and above where the entity is standing. This particular feature has been explained as a reflective outcrop of rock, and there is no doubt that there is a rock in the wall of the depression which almost fits the bill. But there is something else about that blue box that would seem to indicate that more than just the rock was responsible for it. Looked at closely, it can be seen to contain the image of a cherubic face which is looking directly at the entity. Quite synchronous really when you know that the entity has been compared to a demon. Even this demonic entity would seem to be no stranger to the moor if local folklore is to be believed. There are any number of green men reports that have emanated from this area in recent years, but perhaps the most evidential one concerns the buildings at White Wells. At one time, this was a spa of sorts where people came to take the waters. One morning in 1878, Mr William Butterfield, the caretaker, went to open the healing baths for public use.[18] It was something he did day in and day out, but on this particular day he found he could not get in. The key, which usually turned without trouble, seemed to melt into the lock, making it unable to spring the mechanism. As soon as it was removed from the lock, it returned to normal. Eventually, Mr Butterfield gained entrance by other means, and found to his dismay that the baths were occupied by a number of green goblin-like entities. He also noticed that the air was filled by a strange buzzing sound. With his arrival, the entities apparently decamped back on to the moor. So it's not surprising that this manifestation is now reported in a UFO-abduction context. For the moment, the case of the Ilkley Moor abduction remains as much a mystery as ever. The investigators admit that if it is a hoax, then it is a very clever one, and leave the matter of belief or disbelief to individual preference.[19]

We now seem to have wandered far from the original concept of abductions as some kind of spacenapping by alien or aliens unknown. Such a departure is only possible if the American documentation of this strange facet of ufology is ignored. For some reason, American entities seemed a tad less benign than British ones, even from the earliest ufological times. A case in point is that of the 'Hopkinsville Goblins' of 1955. On 22 August 1955, the Sutton family, who had a farm just outside Hopkinsville, Kentucky, were apparently besieged in their home by a group of goblinesque entities with elephantine ears, huge eyes, slit-like mouths, and extremely long arms which ended in claw-like appendages.[20] The entities' attitude was interpreted as hostile by the Suttons, and when one got too close, a charge of buckshot was directed at it. Obviously hit, the entity tumbled backwards, then to the surprise of the marksman, jumped up and carried on as if nothing had happened. Although other kinds of entities have been reported from alleged abductions in America, there is, as with other reports from that nation, a preponderance of the small humanoid variety of entity involved. Beginning way back, and escalating into modern times, this kind of UFO occupant has dominated the American scene. Initially, these entities, while not exactly friendly, were not overtly hostile, but the picture is gradually changing as more and more reports surface alleging that surgical implantation of strange devices into abductees is being carried out by this type of entity. In tandem with this surgical technique, it also alleged that these same ufonauts are engaged in a programme to breed hybrid children.[21] According to Budd Hopkins, at least one of his witnesses remembers being impregnated at age 13, by a 'strange, grey skinned, large eyed figure who inserted a thin tubelike instrument into her.' The foetus produced by this artificial insemination was apparently aborted, but, Hopkins points out, at her first examination, the gynaecologist found that, despite her pregnancy, her hymen was still intact. As for his other witnesses, according to Hopkins they all recall an almost identical abduction, and later being shown a baby that was only partly human. These various witnesses are allegedly unaware of each other's existence, so that would seem to rule out collusion on their part. The inference is that some kind of clandestine exobiological or genetic experimentation is going on. But if so – to what eventual purpose? The temptation is to ignore this type of report as not being a valid part of serious scientific ufology, which is still concerned in defining exactly what kind of phenomenon UFOs really are. The trouble is that abduction cannot be subtracted from the ufological puzzle, as it is intimately connected to all the rest, and in many ways supplies a *raison d'être* for the appearance of allegedly extraterrestrial vehicles in our atmosphere. And, in any case, their content would seem to invalidate any scientific effort to identify the phenomenon as the product of mundane, but misperceived, causes.

Perhaps not so strange a precedent for the present abduction scene – especially the American one, involving as it does the despicable 'greys' – can be found in a particular paranoia that overtook the science-fiction world in 1945. In that year, a story called 'I Remember Lemuria' was published in *Amazing Stories*.[22] It concerned the carryings-on of a race of dreadful dwarfs who lived beneath the earth. As a science-fiction adventure, it was quite typical of the genre of the day, and really should not have caused the commotion that it did. It triggered what *Life* magazine was pleased to call: 'The Most Celebrated Mystery to Rock The Science Fiction World'. Seemingly, as soon as the edition hit the news-stands, people began writing in to *Amazing Stories* to say that they had met the villains of the piece in the flesh. How could that be possible when the villains were fictional? Or were they? The resultant row was fuelled by the same sort of claims that now appear in UFO guise. Perhaps somewhere in the human psyche there lurk all the archetypes we fear, waiting only for the correct stimuli to bring them to life. In 1945, it was the Richard S Shaver stories. In later years, it was the UFO stories. Not quite. The power of the Shaver stories to disturb the imagination rested on the claim that they were a fictionalized account of something factual. They contained, in embryo, all the elements of today's ufology, including the alleged hardware and the tendency to abduction for sexual purposes. In more ways that one, it could be maintained with some justification that ufology is the Shaver mystery made manifest, especially since the editor responsible for the publication and the publicizing of the Shaver 'mystery' was also to be responsible for the publication and the publicizing of the flying saucer 'mystery'. Perhaps without quite knowing how he did it, but cognizant of the human race's capacity to objectify its psychological terrors (as with the broadcast of Orson Welles's interpretation of H G Wells's *War of the Worlds*, which had people panicking and seeing Martians on the march), Ray Palmer contrived to give the world nightmares. In essence, he provided a new technological skeleton on which could be hung all the pre-scientific folklore of the past. It is not surprising then, that ufology has gradually drawn all other mysteries to itself. Or hadn't you noticed that all mankind's mythologies have now been interpreted in a ufological context? Consult the literature – I am sure you will be surprised.

So, where does that leave us, in terms of abduction as an alien experience? Really, in this area, we are all living in a dream – and an American dream at that. In the past, the probable manifestation of this 'cultural consensus dream' was the religious vision, and the sighting of figures from folklore, such as Shuck the black dog, and trolls, like those seen by the caretaker of White Wells. All these images are the archetypes of the Jungian 'collective unconscious', and no matter how they were originally formed, they are now part and parcel of our racial heritage. They are extremely resilient, and can change their guise at the drop of a hat to accommodate any prevailing cultural requirement. At all times and in all climes, persons have reported encounters with whatever deific archetypes were then prevalent. These various encounters served to confirm, or bolster, the prevailing consensus. The Christian consensus provides a good example in the BVM who, over the centuries, appeared to Catholics from Guadalupe to Garabandal. In the main, her visits tended to confirm and uphold that Catholic consensus subscribed to by the masses. In this context, it is interesting to note that in her latest visit to Medjugorje, in Yugoslavia, she began to reflect – much to the discomfort of the old guard – the growing grass-roots ecumenism in the Church of Rome.[23] What these archetypes seem to represent is *us* talking to ourselves. By means of them we process and ratify our changing cultural experience, and in this way we eventually become what we dream we are. They help us to face our fears and, in time, to exorcise them. It is no coincidence that they are reflective of reality, for they are the means by which we cajole, instruct, comfort and in many other ways propel our race to its inevitable destiny. On the one hand, they personify our finest aspirations; while on the other hand, they exemplify the anxieties those aspirations engender. We are the ape who would be God, and by means of our cultural dreams we keep before us the prizes and the penalties incumbent in such an undertaking.

As the twentieth century progressed, the world became secularized to a remarkable degree and mankind stood in danger of being deprived of his spiritual dream. So, to be understood anew, the collective unconscious had to come up with a new archetype, a veritable *deus ex machina*. The template for the sudden influx of flying saucers and their occupants was already in place in the human psyche. Hugo Gernsback, and others like him, had seen to that. Ray Palmer provided the means of expression and so, probably with a sigh of resignation, the old gods donned spacesuits and yielded to the inevitable. They became a dream fit for the space age. That a process something like this was in operation in the creation of ufology is evinced by the fact that the perceived entities, and their hardware, evolved exactly in keeping with the public perception of how such things should look. Initially, the entities had strong, physical affinities with the kind of advanced human adept beloved of theosophy and the magical societies of the turn of the century, and even Jesus turned up under his cosmic name – Sananda.[24] The conveyances looked like illustrations for a Jules Verne novel, but gradually they came to resemble the creations of the science fictioneers of the Forties and Fifties. Ongoing enculturation made sure that the aliens looked alien, but in such a way as was understandable in human terms. However, if their manifestations are a cultural condition, why are they seen by some and not by others? It is my contention, borne out by my own experiences, that everybody at some stage in their lives, has a conscious 'cultural dream' experience. Depending on the 'tunnel reality' they subscribe to, its content could include entities as widely varied as the Ghost of Christmas Past to Monka from Mars. The clue that it is a segment of the cultural dream will be that, besides being relevant in a personal way, it will contain elements applicable to the human race as a whole. For example, in September 1978 a woman living in close proximity to the most famous fish and chip shop in all the world – Harry Ramsden's, in Rawdon, England – saw a vision of the BVM.[25] Her description of a petite young woman, dressed in a shiny white gown and wearing a crown of unusual brilliance, was sufficient identification, as it correlated exactly with all the other descriptions given by percipients of this manifestation. The witness, a Roman Catholic, found the vision personally reassuring, as the changes her Church had undergone in terms of its liturgy since the 1970s had 'destabilized' her faith. But the vision also concerned the state of the world, and this BVM vouchsafed to this witness that The End Of The World Was Nigh, and that flying saucers would be intimately connected with its demise. The reason why only a few individuals seem to retain the memory of these events is, I presume, the same reason why persons do not remember those dreams that come during sleep.

This racial dream hypothesis will not meet with instant acceptance in ufological quarters, I am sure. However, it would seem to offer an acceptable *modus operandi* for investigation. However, to pursue it properly, investigators will have to forget their fixation with the proving or disproving of ufological events in materialistic terms, and to look instead at the psychology of the witnesses in terms of the consensus reality of the day and age in which they live. The real clue is in the subjectivity of the phenomenon that not only reflects any particular percipient's 'tunnel reality', but at the same time accommodates societies' communal expectations. To approach ufology from this aspect is not to devalue it in any way; quite the contrary in fact: anyone who thinks that dreams are unimportant when compared to the cut and thrust of daily living is sadly mistaken. People can live quite comfortably without many of the essentials of modern living; but deprive them of their dreams, and they go mad – or worse. Seemingly, the controlled confusion of our dreams is what keeps us functional in the real world. Perhaps a similar precondition is set against the well-being of society as a whole. To preserve our sanity in a mad, mad, mad world, we might need the cultural craziness that the UFO phenomenon so obligingly supplies. Perhaps it cuts even deeper than that.

This twentieth century, especially since the half-way mark, has witnessed a remarkable erosion of public confidence in those organizations that once were thought capable of creating a better world. The vast mass of persons, especially in the developed nations, have turned their backs – whether they publicly admit it or not – on organized religion as irrelevant, on science as destructive, and on politics as self-serving, leaving a vacuum to be filled. Perhaps the collective unconscious is preparing the way for the UFO phenomenon to fill that gap as the 'old gods' re-establish their prerogatives in different guise. As Whitley Strieber has pertinently pointed out: 'The only thing now needed to make the UFO Myth a new religion of remarkable scope and force is a single undeniable sighting.'[26] According to the documentation, there already has been any number of these, so what is stopping it? Not a lot. All that is missing is the human race's realization of the truth about UFOs:

> We have found a strange footprint on the shores of the unknown. We have devised profound theories, one after another, to account for its origin. At last we have succeeded in reconstructing the creature that made the footprint. And Lo! . . . It's our own![27]

REFERENCES

1 Michael, C   *Round-trip to Hell in a Flying Saucer* (Roofhopper Enterprises, 1971)
2 Rimmer, J   *The Evidence for Alien Abductions* (Aquarian Press, 1984)
3 Randles, J   *The Pennine UFO Mystery* (Granada, 1983)
4 Pugh & Holiday   *The Dyfed Enigma* (Coronet, 1981)
5 Author's personal file
6 Scott Rogo, D (Ed.)   *UFO Abductions* (Signet, 1980)
7 Barclay, D & T M   'Close Encounter: Fact or Fiction?' *The UFO Debate*, No. 1, Feb 1990
8 Jung, C G   *Flying Saucers: A Modern Myth of Things Seen in the Sky* (Routledge & Keegan Paul, 1987)
9 Fuller, J   *The Interrupted Journey* (Souvenir, 1980)
10 O'Sullivan, Fr P   *Our Lady of Fatima* (Brown and Nolan, 1943; o.p.)
11 Scott Rogo, D (Ed.)   *UFO Abductions* (Signet, 1980)
12 Christie-Murray, D   'Stalked by a Nightmare', *The Unexplained*, Vol. 10, Issue 110
13 Wilson, C   'The World of Uri Geller', *The Unexplained*, Vol. 3, Issue 32
14 Holroyd, S   *Briefing for the Landing on Planet Earth* (W H Allen, 1977)
15 Stieger, B   *Gods of Aquarius* (Granada, 1980)
16 Editorial by Paul Bennet, *Earth* magazine, Issue No. 11, August 1988
17 Hough, P   'Alien Abduction on Ilkley Moor – A Scientific Enquiry', *UFO Universe* 1988
18 Barclay, T M   'Fortean Interlude', *The UFO Debate*, Issue No. 5, October 1990
19 Hough & Randles   *Looking for the Aliens* (Blandford, 1991)
20 Lorenzen, C & J   *Flying Saucer Occupants* (Signet, 1967)
21 Hopkins, B   *Intruders* (Sphere, 1988)
22 Ford, R   'The Man who Invented the Flying Saucers', *The Skeptic*, Vol. 4, Issue 6
23 Craig, M   *Spark from Heaven* (Hodder & Stoughton, 1988)
24 Brownell, W S (compiler)   *UFOs: Key to Earth's Destiny* (Legion of Light Publications, 1980)
25 Barclay, D   'The BVM in West Yorkshire', *The UFO Debate*, Issue 4, August 1990
26 Vallee, J   *Dimensions* (Souvenir, 1988)
27 Wilson, R A   *Cosmic Trigger: Final Secret of the Illuminati* (Abacus, 1979)

CHAPTER NINE

TOWARDS A FULL EXPLANATION

David Barclay

Having read this far, the reader is now – hopefully – aware of the complexity of the subject under study. It is not, and never really was, a simple matter of determining whether the Martians had landed, or not. Nor can the subject be approached as a matter of personal belief, or otherwise. It is counter-productive to the study to adopt any intransigent viewpoint regarding it, whether of true belief or even truer disbelief. Yet the way the subject is presently addressed practically forces value-judgements of this nature upon any prospective investigator. Ally this with the fact that many come to the study bringing their preconceptions with them and you have the recipe for ufology as it presently stands: a loosely interconnected series of belief systems from which anyone can choose on the basis of personal preference alone.

Of these various belief systems, scepticism is perhaps the most counter-productive, and least defensible. Still to maintain, in the face of the mountains of documented evidence to the contrary, that ufology is 'all sound and fury signifying nothing' is an act of faith rather than an intellectual conclusion. Those who subscribe to this view make the unwarranted assumption that their inability to see beyond the ephemeral parameters imposed on consensus reality by present-day enculturation somehow endows them with an infallible 'scientific scepticism' that can define for ever the limits of what can, or cannot, be. At another level, such 'scepticism' can be seen to be an expression of the kind of conservatism that is resistant to change: a fear reaction that seeks to cling to the seemingly safe certainties of the past. Fortunately, such attitudes have never, in the end, prevailed, otherwise we would all still be living in caves. Our universe, even as we presently perceive it, is so obviously a place where anything can happen, that it should be considered the height of intellectual folly to say with certainty – no matter how apparently well informed by the parochial prejudices of the present – that anything is inherently impossible. There is no law which says that the universe must only produce phenomena which are understandable in human terms. This is especially true of the UFO phenomenon, which gives every indication of being completely alien to anything the human race has so far encountered. And, at the present time, there is no way of knowing the limits of its 'alienness'. So, unless you are prepared to imply that your fellow men are mostly credulous fools, unable to discern between Venus, floaters in the eye, weather balloons, etc. and material constructions apparently not the product of any earthly technology, then you must restrain your scepticism until such times as the existence, or otherwise, of UFOs has been empirically demonstrated, either by experience, or, if such is possible, replication. Any genuine sceptic should be able to argue from the data as convincingly for the existence of UFOs as for their non-existence, because all scepticism should really be about is the non-acceptance of unproven absolutes, and not the 'disproving' of ideas and possibilities which make persons feel uncomfortable because they conflict with their internal ego-supportive cosmologies. So, let us have no more scepticism, at least not of the ufological kind, which is mostly based on social and intellectual prejudice, and which is little more than a belief system in itself.

Although it is necessary, it is difficult to be critical of those individuals who are convinced, beyond any shadow of doubt, that UFOs exist in terms of the consensus that interprets the data as spaceships in the sky. The major reason why this paradigm has such an enduring hold on the public imagination is simply because the majority of reports, especially from the seminal days of the 1940s and 1950s, seemingly describe objects which leave very little room for interpretation of them as anything else. For those persons making these reports, the matter is understandably beyond argument, otherwise they would have to consider themselves as suitable cases for treatment, which, as even a cursory glance at the documentation will unequivocally demonstrate, they most certainly are not. Although, in ufological speculation, much is made of percipients' alleged attachment to 'misperception', and the media's predeliction for sensationalism, it was John A Keel who pointed out that, in fact, the opposite was more probably nearer the truth.[1] When properly listened to, witnesses usually give an accurate description of what was seen; it is just that they sometimes tend to intersperse their narrative with speculations about the meaning of the incident. Similarly, the media usually report reasonably accurately, but they too spice up their stories with the prognostications of whatever ufological pundits they can persuade to open their mouths and put their feet in it. I have been 'quoted' on occasion, and after the first shock at how ridiculous I was made to appear, I realized that every word printed had been spoken by me at some point during the interview. It wasn't the paper's fault I sounded silly: it was mine; I just hadn't known how to be interviewed. So now I choose my words with more care. The first thing I make sure they know is that I am not an expert; that, in fact, there are no ufological experts at all: just a number of interested individuals who have spent greater, or lesser, time mulling it all over. Even the people who have made enormous contributions to the genre have not really told anyone what UFOs are – only what they are not.

In some ways, it is a pity that the study got side-tracked into thinking of its brief in terms of UFOs (Unidentified Flying Objects), instead of remaining with flying saucers, no matter how intellectually embarrassing they found that name. UFOs can indeed be anything from earthlights to misperceived communications satellites. However, flying saucers can only be one thing, something that deeply disturbs the percipient because it gives every evidence of being outrageously alien. For instance, one day while gardening, I heard a voice tell me that if I cared to look behind me I would see a flying saucer. I was startled because, although I did not recognize the voice, it addressed me by name. Fortunately, there was someone with me at the time, so I asked them to take a look and tell me if they saw anything in the sky behind me. It was immediately apparent from their expression that they did. So I turned round to look. There in the sky, almost directly overhead, was a large, featureless, cigar-shaped object that looked as if it were made of brushed aluminium. It was at quite low altitude, and in no particular hurry. While we both were watching, a plane crossed the sky above the object, and this too was low; low enough for detail to be made out. The plane went one way, the object another, and the plane moved the faster of the two. So what was the object? Even worse, who had called my attention to it? My companion had heard nothing, and there was nobody else about. The neighbours were out, and the part of the garden I was in was secluded, so I can only presume that it was whoever was on board that object and that, as well as encountering an anomalous object, I had also experienced that other mysterious phenomenon – telepathy. The incident brought home to me the fine pickle percipients find themselves in when trying to make similar scenarios sound sensible to third parties. On this occasion I was the percipient, and I wasn't entirely convinced by the episode. For my part I was, and still am, more fascinated by the possibility of telepathy, than the probability that there are things flying over our heads that have nothing to do with human technology.

In many ways, I see the ufological fascination with the possible hardware that generates reports (i.e., spaceships, earthlights, mirages, UAPs, etc.) as something of an Achilles heel, as it has distracted many competent ufologists from a contemplation of the real mystery of ufology: the alleged casual conversations with allegedly superior entities, not necessarily from outer space. From the very beginning, the UFO phenomenon had a disturbing interface with what is known as 'the paranormal'. But even though Kenneth Arnold himself allegedly alluded to this strange non-material aspect of ufological manifestations, it was somehow ignored, either deliberately or inadvertently, by those who initially set themselves the task of determining the solution to the mystery.[2] Consequently, ufology has languished in the hands of persons who saw it all in terms of kind of neo-Victorian 'hard science' and 'empirical proofs'. Because of this somewhat inflexible, dated 'scientific' attitude on the part of ufologists (both pro and con), ufological exegesis became, and has largely remained, a straight choice between misperception of known – or extremely rare, therefore presently unknown – natural phenomena and man-made objects and the minions of Ming the Merciless or madness. Because the dichotomy became seemingly irreconcilable, the legend of the cosmic cover-up developed, and much argumentative energy has been expended in attempts to force the Establishment to admit to something that it was quite clear from the beginning it had no intention of doing – come what may. Ufology thereby became, not so much a debate regarding the phenomenon, as a crusade to 'prove' the validity of a limited number of preconceived 'truths'.

Despite this unproductive confrontation with authority, the documentation does argue strongly, almost conclusively, for some form of non-human intrusion on this planet. Even if the only reports extant were of the anomalous-aeroform variety, there are still enough of them to arouse the suspicion that 'where there's foo, there's fire'. Once it is realized that there is an equal number of reports of alien lifeforms associated with ufological manifestations, then the luxury of ego jousting – no matter how emotionally seductive – has to be laid aside, as it is imperative that a solution be found, just in case the manifesting intelligence is not so altruistic as some proponents of the extraterrestrial hypothesis like to think it is. To speculate from the data that

> the UFO Phenomenon can be fitted to the hypothesis that they represent the prenatal care of the Earthman by a linked superbeing, in prep- aration for the forthcoming linkage of the human species and the birth of another linked super- being[3]

is being incredibly naïve by assuming that 'somebody up there loves us'. I mean to say . . . do we, the alleged 'superbeings' of anthropoidal evolution, anxiously oversee and nurture the evolutionary development of our simian cousins so that, some day, we can joyously welcome them into the human family? Like hell we do. So when it comes to assessing the allegedly altruistic intentions of any possible entities, it is as well to remember that, in nature, there is no such thing as interspecies altruism. In fact, altruism is not a naturally occurring phenomenon at all, but only one of the many inventions of the human mind. In any case, at the moment we only have the word of sundry 'entities' regarding their alleged benevolence towards us. There is, however, one other aspect that should force caution upon those inclined to the 'spacebrothers will save us' scenario. For some reason, it has always been assumed that because the posited 'alien intelligence' has apparently chosen to interact with us, it can be assumed that it has thereby conferred upon us equality with itself. Not necessarily so since, as already mentioned above, our own interactions with the many other lifeforms on this planet demonstrate the opposite. Our race interacts, in all kinds of ways, with the other species on this planet. We seek them out, we train them, we have them in our homes, and generally force ourselves upon them in other sundry ways. But, whatever such attentions might indicate to the animals, we do not see it as conferring upon them equality with us, and never will. The UFO mystery must be resolved before we make the mistake of assuming a non-existent parity with the possible lifeform that masks its activities behind it. For all we know, it might not even consider us intelligent, but merely a precocious predator who got lucky, and is thereby a suitable subject for its exosociological and exobiological experimentation. Perhaps that lifeform is right. And this is the trouble with ufology as it is presently practised: too many unwarranted anthropocentric assumptions masquerading as indisputable inferences.

To be serious, the present paradigms for the interpretation of ufological data are extremely limited in their imaginativeness. Each one can only make its point by ignoring the part of the data that argues against it. Even those more open-minded than the rest feel that the UFO phenomenon cannot be everything that is indicated in the documentation. But what if it is? What if it is everything that is indicated by the data, because it is not anything indicated by the data, but something else with the capability of convincingly personifying anything it chooses in pursuit of ends so alien that the human mind would have the same success in understanding them as do the experimental monkeys in understanding what is behind the experiences they undergo in laboratories world-wide? To take the analogy further. What if the alleged 'superiority' of the UFO intelligence is based, not in some form of humanly understandable and, therefore, potentially replicable technology, but in genetically endowed potentials; the kind of genetic potentials that make the scientist everlastingly superior to the monkey in his laboratory? The kind of genetic potentials that would make the 'reality' the UFO phenomenon occupies for ever closed to us as, for the same genetic reason, the 'reality' we occupy is forever closed to our simian cousins. Distressing as this might seem to some, it is time we found out for certain because, at the very least, it might stop the UFO phenomenon monkeying about with us, as it seemingly has done these past 40 or so years.

To assess properly the import of ufological intrusions, it's first necessary to call attention to something that, although it has been touched upon any number of times in the literature, nobody has yet taken to its logical conclusion. The issue has been ducked. And can you wonder? It is something that will change our perception of reality, and our place in it, more radically than the theory of evolution ever did, if ever it is demonstrated as fact. What might *it* be? It is the undeniable interface ufology has with theology. The inherent ramifications of this cosmological correlation are such that one can well understand why Establishments would wish to keep a lid on it, and prefer instead to endure the contumely associated with the lesser evil of being accused of concealing the 'truth' about the extraterrestrial nature of UFOs. The religious aspect of ufology has been noticed before, and has been commented upon by writers of the calibre of Desmond Leslie, Brinsley le Poer Trench (Lord Clancarty), R L Dione and, latterly, Whitley Streiber. All of these, and many of their equally erudite ufological colleagues, have been forced into the admission that it is clear from the data that the UFO phenomenon seems to have clear links with many of mankind's mythic beliefs. This overtly 'religious' element in UFO manifestations is not something that has been forced from the data by mere human interpretation, but has, on many occasions, been introduced into the UFO scenario by the manifesting entities. Perhaps the most evidential modern encounter in this regard is that undergone by Betty Andreasson in January 1967. Overtly ufological in its genesis, the event was investigated by a staunch proponent of the extraterrestrial hypothesis, Raymond Fowler, who was eventually forced by the data he obtained from the main percipient to admit, in regard to the religious content of Betty's experience, that 'We dare not dismiss it, because it may provide the focal point, the very reason, for the abduction.'[4]

A similar situation faced Jenny Randles when investigating the ufological experiences of Gaynor Sunderland. Once again, a seemingly simple saucer scenario became infested with unacceptably occult overtones which provoked the investigator to write: 'There is something to be said for not excluding potentially valuable data, but when the floodgates open it is much harder to shut them again. Just where do you draw the line?'[5] A good question, but not really germane to the issue, as it is quite clear that any line that is to be drawn, has already been drawn by the phenomenon itself. Therefore, any line drawn by ufologists in defence of a preferred paradigm might only serve to exclude them from a proper appreciation of the complexity of the mystery they have set themselves to solve. The fact that a solution is no nearer after over 40 years of sterling efforts by many dedicated individuals must be some indication of the truth of the above observation. So what is there to be done when, according to John Keel, if taken as a whole, the data cancels itself out?

It has been said that the beginning of wisdom is the acknow-ledgement of ignorance. So, before proceeding further, it is time for ufologists who insist on investigating UFOs from a neo-Victorian 'scientific' viewpoint to finally understand that 'The clockwork universe has in any event run down, and the hoary metaphysics which propelled it lies in ashes.'[6]

Having been a ufologist from day one, I have had ample opportunity to sympathize with the efforts of those who sought to discover patterns in UFO data. The idea was to prove something or other from such patterns: for instance, that the saucers were the Martians on the march, because the influx of their vehicles coincided with the planet Mars's closest approaches to the earth; or that they travelled on a kind of magnetic tramline system, as in Orthoteny. Such efforts have been as regular as they have been ineffectual. So far no pattern has been discovered that has survived the slings and arrows of the scientific sceptics. Yet there is a pattern; a pattern so clear in its evidentiality regarding the real *raison d'être* of UFO appearances, that it is surprising that nobody has yet recognized it for what it is: it is the ufonauts apparent addiction to eschatological initiatives. If the data is to be believed, they are all suffering from terminal apocalyptamania; so much so that the latter-day abductee, Whitley Strieber, could confidently write: 'Throughout the literature of abduction there is a frequent message of apocalypse.'[7] But to what purpose? Why should an alien, if not extraterrestrial lifeform, trouble itself with concepts that one would have to imagine have been exclusively generated by our parochial cosmological concepts? This one illogical theological thread indicates that to continue searching for spacefarers, and similarly unproductive paradigms, is redundant. Investigation should, instead, be concentrated on the entity experience. It is the central mystery – all the rest is ancillary. So what is there to be made out of this most outrageous of human experiences? Are we courting madness by even considering it as a subject fit for serious discussion, or is such a strategy vital to the salvation of more than our collective sanity? The importance of the entity experience (as undergone by countless individuals up to the present time) in relation to the UFO mystery as a whole cannot be overstated. Even at the time the ETH was first being formulated, based on ufologists' obsession with reports of things seen in the sky, there was a strong undercurrent of entity experiences that argued against science-fiction solutions. At the time, it was totally ignored by investigators who seemingly felt that it was less socially suicidal to stick to daylight discs and nocturnal meandering lights, and leave the LGM (Little Green Men) to those they designated as the lunatic fringe. So, despite being clothed in acceptable alien eccentricity by men like George Adamski and Howard Menger, the entity experience was the stone which the builders of modern ufology rejected. If it should now turn out to be the corner-stone, they have only themselves to blame. From the many, and seemingly diverse, contacts with entities documented in the literature of the paranormal, of which ufology can be said to be the quintessence, it is clear that entities who present themselves in the guise of Bhov-Rhyll the Betelgeusian or Kokapi from Uranus are totally preoccupied by earth-orientated cosmologies. In not one case has contact with these allegedly superior intelligences resulted in real material benefits to the individuals concerned, or our race in general. Instead, what has been played out has been a series of non-relevant psychodramas.

The idea central to all these allegedly alien presentations is that of the drastic denouement of the human adventure on this planet. It seems to have escaped the notice of those drawn into these confrontations that the only proof that such a fate was in the offing was contained in the 'warnings' delivered by the manifesting 'intelligence'. Because of the percipients' feeble grasp on competent cosmology, the scenarios got away with dealing in plots that seldom rose above the intellectual level of *The Perils of Pauline*. Yet, despite that deficiency, it has to be admitted that, within the parameters of its own cosmological incompetence, the generator of the UFO phenomenon was a master fabricator of cosmic soap operas, its various presentations carrying conviction due to its ability to seemingly tamper with the percipients' 'objective reality' in ways presently incomprehensible; but, hopefully, not for much longer.

Looked at closely, it can be seen that this phenomeon has been assumed to be superior on the basis of a limited range of special effects. These are somewhat multifunctional in that, depending on the way, and in what context, they are presented, they can be used to reinforce a wide range of human 'tunnel realities'. From a number of sources, it can be shown that very probably angels and aliens are interchangeable. The most evidential case is that of the strange affair at Fatima, in Portugal, in 1917, when a certain sectarian Roman Catholic tunnel reality was reinforced by the blatant use of what today's percipients would instantly identify as UFO technology.[8] Even in more modern times, the distinction between the sacred and the secular is difficult to make, as the description of the UFO entity seen by Mona Stafford of Kentucky demonstrates. She quite unambiguously described the entity as 'looking the way they were described in biblical days'.[9] Yet the entity she was describing was definitely UFO related and had presented itself as such, so it could not be in any way 'angelic' – unless, of course, these creatures are angels pretending to be spacemen, or vice versa; or, more likely, something completely different.

One of the more interesting analogies used in these kind of manifestations is that of being akin to a TV image. Indeed, the main percipient to the encounter at Fatima, in the days well before a TV set became an indispensable household item, described the entity she saw in terms of its brightness and light. She said:

> The light had various tones, yellow, white and
> other colours. It was by the different tones and
> different intensities that one saw what was a hand

and what was a mantle, what was a face, and what
was a tunic.[10]

How much more accurately could a TV picture be described? This
TV picture analogy is further enhanced by the testimony of Mrs
Cynthia Appleton, as quoted by Charles Bowen in his book *The
Humanoids*. Seemingly, this percipient had aliens materialize in
her own front room. According to her, they appeared exactly like
a TV picture: 'at first blurred then clear'. During the contact, she
was apparently warned by the aliens not to try to touch them
because she was 'only witnessing a projection'. According to
Peter Paget, writing in *UFO UK*, a similar experience befell two
ufologists while they were pursuing their interest in Warminster.
On this occasion, only one percipient had both vision and sound,
the other only saw the vision which, interestingly, provoked the
author to this analogy: 'This split of communication media
between two people is interesting. It was almost like tuning a TV
when you can lose the picture but keep the sound, and vice
versa.'[11]

If this TV anology is near the truth, it would go a long way in
explaining the 'high strangeness' in many UFO encounters. The
images the various witnesses see might derive from the UFO
version of a Spielbergian special effects department, and the
holographic interactivity of the image seen be merely a matter of
the quickness of the pseudopod deceiving the human optical
sensory organ. This TV, or monitor, analogy will become even
more evidential when we go on to suggest what kind of intrusion
the UFO phenomenon really represents. Whatever the *modus
operandi*, be it telepathic hypnogogery, or something we shall
touch on later, it is undeniable that the phenomenon is always the
star of its own productions – the human percipients being
relegated to the role of extras (or maybe even props) in what can
be clearly seen to be a series of derivative, and repetitive, cosmic
psychodramas. The phenomenon's success in recruiting otherwise
rational individuals to its various playlets is quite astonishing in
itself, and seems to derive from the manifestations' ability to
reinforce whatever cosmological tunnel reality is subscribed to by
any given percipient. While the basic 'save the world' scenario
never varies, it is capable of being presented in any number of
cosmological disguises, which is probably why those who have
undertaken the investigation of such matters are hard put to derive
any sense from the material they so assiduously solicit. Ufology
would be quite content with ET, theosophy with endless
genealogies, spiritualism with summerland, and theology with

anything it could interpret to its own advantage. But the UFO phenomenon makes a cocktail of all these ingredients, leaving those trying to make sense of it all both stirred, and shaken. Human chauvinism being what it is, the best any exegete has been able to do so far is to emphasize the material supportive to whatever emotionally uplifting paradigm they were pursuing, while ignoring or denigrating anything that argued to the contrary. It is unfortunate that apparently everybody – witnesses, investigators and even the phenomenon itself, if we are to judge by the reported content of its many 'messages' – seems to want the UFO enigma to turn out to be something deeply meaningful and momentous in anthropocentric terms. So, after over 40 years of ongoing interactions, why hasn't it? Can the reason possibly be – because it isn't?

It is something of a truism that to solve any problem you must know the right questions to ask, and if you know the right questions to ask then you already know most of the answer. In applying this to the quest for the UFO truth, it becomes apparent that the right questions have never been asked, as no answer – not even a partial one – has yet been forthcoming. As the scientific approach of the past 40 years has led apparently nowhere, perhaps we should now try the non-scientific one: the kind of approach that holds that 'as above, so below', and try to reason by analogy to see if we can find some common denominator, some recognizable interface, in human behaviour patterns with that observed, and documented, in regard to UFO entities. What we must find in human society is an activity that makes no sense except in terms of itself: something which, to the uninitiated, would seem the height of folly, but which, for those engaged in any way with it, would make complete sense and totally absorb their interest. There is such an activity: it is called a game.

All games, for spectator and player alike, create their own microcosm within the larger macrocosm of objective reality. In terms of the demands of the natural order, they could be seen as something short of essential. Their objectives and outcomes have no permanent effect on anything – even themselves – and they can be played over and over without reaching a lasting conclusion. It would seem that it is this very repetitiveness which is their main attraction. Games have been played by generation after generation without losing any of their novelty along the way. They are as much fun now, in this science-fiction century, as they were in the days of *Fanny by Gaslight* – and before. But there is one game, the basic format of which has transcended time and the collapse of civilizations to emerge triumphant today in the form of the electronic arcade game. This kind of game is very simple in its parameters. All it embodies is the idea of good guys v. bad guys, and gives the operator the chance to play god with the interactive internal reality programmed into the computer. In arcades world-wide, these games are played repetitively by individuals, usually immature, who have become addicted to their attractions. I would venture to suggest that, in the face of the eschatological evidence in the UFO documentation, there is every possibility that we might have been invited by the UFO phenomenon to play in what must certainly be the greatest interactive, holographic, technicolour arcade game in the universe. There is no other way of explaining the repetitiveness of the 'save the world' scenario purveyed by entities of all varieties, or the fact that they seem to recruit those individuals most vulnerable to such blandishments, using the frame of reference to which the percipient is most susceptible. Percipients are not chosen because they have ESP: they are chosen for their innate gullibility; the ESP faculty is an ancillary effect of the contact.

For anyone who has taken the trouble to read the contactee/abductee literature with prejudices locked away for safekeeping, it should be abundantly clear that the various 'save the world' scenarios purveyed by entities are almost Monty Pythonesque in their satirization of prevailing human cosmological tunnel realities. Perhaps the most serious question to ask in the circumstances is if our religious impulse is merely a side-effect of UFO/entity manipulation, or if they plagiarize, and pervert to their own ends, mankind's most uplifting spiritual aspirations. At one time, I would have thought the answer to that would have been a foregone conclusion: UFO entities, and others of their ilk, were merely hypnogogic hooligans, entertaining themselves at the expense of the more gullible of the human population. But now something else has entered the picture which puts a whole new complexion on things, and helps in large measure to explain the 'how' if not the 'why'.

For me, as with Adam, it all began with an apple. I went to an exhibition of scientific curiosities and saw my first hologram. It was an image of an apple suspended in mid-air which, if you walked around it, could be viewed in its entirety as if it were real: a neat trick, which seemed to be the consensus at the time. However, now some years on, there is a growing body of evidence that indicates that everything we think of as real could be a hologram – even you who read this page. According to the holographic model, there are no such things as time and space, nor is there a dichotomy between mind and matter, simply because these things do not exist as discrete phenomena, but are merely part of something that gives the impression of being either or both or whatever – depending. The proponents of this new occult interpretation of reality are not the usual wide-eyed cultists, but two extremely sober scientists: one is Einstein's former protégé, David Bohm, and the other is Karl Pibram, a noted neurophysiologist. At an increasing rate, they are discovering data to bear out their contention that our universe, and everything therein, is a hologram.[12] If they are right – and I think they might be, because their model is an Occam's razor of incredible sharpness, where convoluted cosmology is concerned – then, among many other disturbing things, it becomes probable that it is the UFO phenomeon which is *real*, and we, the percipients, who are not. Or, perhaps, we are both equally 'unreal' in a reality that exists only as a holographic delusion. This probability is enhanced once you realize that what you think of as 'out there' – isn't. Apparently, even 'objective reality' is subjective in so far as it would seem to be a genetically programmed, self-induced, holographic illusion. Any number of experiments tend to the conclusion that our sensory equipment, by means not yet fully understood, receives electromagnetic impulses which, when transmitted to the brain, are decoded according to a genetically pre-determined picture. Seemingly, the decoding has very little to do with what signals are received, but it is dependent on which organ they are received by. In some ways, our brain can be compared to a televisual receiver which: 'In some unknown manner, transforms a barrage of nondescript electrical impulses into our diverse experiences of space, form, substance, colour, sound, odour, and taste.'[13] As a result, we can be forgiven for suspecting that even our 'solid' reality might only be, like a TV picture, a signal of some kind.

In speculating about the probability of a holographic universe, sceptics would be quick to point out that a basic element remains unexplained by the holographic model: that is that the universe we inhabit is interactive, a property denied holograms due to the limitations inherent in the photo-laser process which creates them. As with conventional film images, the elements in any holographic version are 'fixed' at the time the photograph is taken. Even if it eventually becomes possible to produce 'live' holography, the image will still not be truly interactive with the viewer. So, how can you possibly have a reality that is both holographic and spontaneously interactive at the same time, if these two properties are mutually exclusive? The answer is amazingly simple: put it all on disk, feed that into your computer – then jump in after it.

As impossible as this might sound, the process is already in use. People have entered computers and interacted with the contents of the program being run; what they went into is called cyberspace, which, to all intents and purposes, is Virtual Reality (VR). The VR technology grew from a marriage between military and civil computer-simulation training aids, computer graphics and arcade games.[14] Somewhere along the way, it was discovered that if the image was extended to over 80°, the viewer was, in effect, pulled into the picture. The simulation became 'virtually real', and not just an object in the current world, as was the case while the image remained at 60° or under. Although still in its virtual infancy, the state of the art allows people to don an electronic exoskeleton and a 'virtuality' face-mask, and enter cyberspace with full sensory response. Even more startling is the fact that these individuals can be 'networked' into the same cyberspace, and thereby see and co-operate with each other's 'telepresence' in manipulating the elements within the Virtual Reality as if they were real. The elements within the Virtual Reality are just as three dimensional (holographic) and interactive as the objects we use daily, and the only reason they are unsophisticated by comparison is apparently because more powerful computers are needed to give full rein to those who create the graphics. However, as these are on their way, the possibilities seem limitless. Creationism takes on a whole new meaning.

Although VR has many possible uses to which it can be put – from allowing a scientist to walk, *sans* spacesuit, on the surface of a VR Mars, to allowing an architect to build a VR building before going to the expense of laying a brick – it would seem that the area in which the VR concept will have its greatest impact is in arcade games. Already in America, the first VR arcades are in operation, and primitive though the graphics might still be, those who have experienced them have testified to their addictiveness. VR games are, by all accounts, the ultimate in boredom relief. Individuals networked together co-operate in cyberspace to save the world from whatever the computer program tells them is menacing it: it is all unbelievably immature, but players apparently can't get enough of it. The best part of these games, as in all computer games, is that the telepresence of the player is invulnerable. This aspect of the telepresence reminds one of the Hopkinsville Goblins who were apparently able to absorb a point-blank shotgun blast without detriment. The analogy might even explain the absence of any hard evidence of UFO crashes. If these objects are indeed telepresences, any such object would, after crashing or exploding, leave no trace of itself, for the same reason that objects which are spectacularly destroyed in computer games leave no trace of themselves on the monitor screen. In our own computer games, especially the newly burgeoning VR versions, the internal cyberentities react to the telepresence of the player interactively. Depending on the skills of any player, this limited free will on the part of the cyberentities allows for a range of outcomes. Also in VR, these cyberentities, and other networked individuals, 'see' the telepresence of the players in whatever form the program dictates. They could, therefore, appear as balls of light, lenticular flying machines, strange bipedal beings, or even, perhaps, as a female with a penchant for standing on top of holm oaks while delivering messages of gloom and doom. All the games are conducted with several levels of difficulty, or dimensions, and the only limiting factors are the sophistication of the software and the exigencies imposed by that which gives substance to their existence . . . light.

So, to think of our universe as being, perhaps, something else's VR is not as outrageous as some might at first suppose. The fact is that, given a computer of sufficient power to service a program of the required complexity, everything that makes up our universe could be replicated within the confines of that computer, because we already know that our universe is an 'information universe': which is to say that its many facets are amenable to the kind of mathematical description that facilitates computer programming. So what's the difference? None, I dare to suggest, that you or I would notice.

To explain the UFO phenomenon, with its attendant entities, in terms of telepresences in a universal VR is fairly easy. The way they appear and behave is analogous to the way human telepresences interact with the VR inside a computer, which itself is analogous to the way we operate in what we think of as objective reality. In pursuit of whatever game strategy is running, human telepresences can 'distort' the VR in which they are operating in ways not available to the native cyberentities. To find the analagous situation in ufology, all one has to do is consider the ramifications inherent in John A Keel's cautionary observation that:

> today it is apparent that the same force that answers some prayers also causes it to rain anchovies and is behind everything from sea serpents to flying saucers. It distorts our reality whimsically, perhaps out of boredom, or perhaps it is a little crazy.[15]

No, not crazy, more likely just a little immature, playing for all its worth a game that Brad Stieger once designated the Reality Game.[16] Those who might still feel that the generalization in connecting religious experience with UFO experience to support the contention of a VR universe is too diffuse, only have to turn to the works of Jacques Vallee, among many others, to find a plethora of material to uphold the connection; not only with accepted religious experience, but also with what are known as occult experiences as well. One noted ufologist, in particular, sealed the connection with Superglue when he wrote about the results of two statistical surveys conducted by two different investigations (one was Gilbert Cornu, who correlated visions of the Virgin with UFO appearances in the years 1928–75, and the other was a reputable Italian UFO group) on completely different samplings, that:

> this much is certain: no explanation of the one (BVM or UFO) will be complete unless it accounts for this bizarre correspondence; whatever UFO sightings are, they are something which is related to visions of the Virgin, and vice versa[17]

Yet, perhaps, the most telling argument in favour of ours being something else's VR is the way the concept clarifies, and reduces to understandable proportions, the act of creation itself. 'In the beginning was the word', makes that much more sense if it is understood in a computer-programming context. By accepting the VR model, we can easily conceive of creation in technological terms. All the manipulations described in Genesis are explained by the computer-programming analogy. What is more, if a human programmer can create something virtually real from nothing, that is create within a computer a cybernetic universe the elements of which can be manipulated as if they were 'real', then what is to stop Someone Else thinking of it first? On this basis, the real answer to what is outside our expanding universe might be God's Little Arcade. Perhaps the only thing that should disturb us about this concept of our universe is whether we are cyberentities (i.e., pawns) or telepresences (i.e., players) in the Game of Life. Fortunately, due to the way our sensory organs operate, the answer is ego sustaining. In the human-generated version of VR, the telepresence is able, by virtue of the electronic exoskeleton and virtuality face-mask, to use the telebody to manipulate the elements within cyberspace in the same way as we use our 'natural bodies' to manipulate the elements in 'objective reality'. There is a similarity between the way the telebody's 'senses' are at its surface, and the way our 'real senses' are also at the surfaces of our bodies, leading to the suspicion that the bodies we inhabit, and think to be 'real', are in fact just another form of telepresence. This could mean that UFOs and entities of all varieties are just a matter of degree: that is, they are the telepresences of individuals who have accessed to a greater degree of difficulty in the game into which we all are apparently networked.

For those who might feel that to refer to Life, the Universe and Everything as a 'game' is unnecessarily facetious, it must be pointed out that, even if the VR model is untrue, that is just what it is: there are rules (Laws of Nature) which must be accommodated; there is an element of risk (coincidence); and there are prizes to be won (success, longevity, etc.). The analogy is capable of almost infinite expansion. But just because it is a game does not mean that life is not serious. Many of life's most important lessons are learned by playing games.

To digress for a moment into theology: if the VR model is correct, it puts beyond the shadow of a doubt the existence of God. It also removes the actuality of life after death from pious hope to unavoidable experience. And for those who merely like to play with grandiose concepts, it expands the possible parameters of reality beyond any infinity so far conceived. And for this reason, given the escalating expertise of those who create human VR, it is possible that, at some future time, they will be able to place in cyberspace elements that will enable the telepresence to make a cybercomputer into which can be programmed another subcyberspace. Talk about 'many mansions'. World without end with a vengeance. And if, as is hypothesized, Someone has beaten us to it – well, I leave that line of speculation to you.

To return now to the UFO mystery and the possibilities for explaining this multi-faceted phenomenon in terms of an already existing VR. As our own computer games have recognizably repetitive parameters, based in large measure on what is known as good guys v. bad guys – a notion that is capable of an infinite variety of interpretations – then to deduce that our own objective reality is a virtually real construction subsisting in a cyberspace, we should have to identify within it a similar repetitiveness of parameters. It seems singularly synchronous that our entire history should, in effect, be a playing out of the good guys v. bad guys scenario. Indeed, our mythology, even our theology, depends for its very existence on the 'truth' of this concept by insisting – each in its own way – that this earth is a gigantic arena for the ongoing battle between Good and Evil. The Christian ethic – with which the entity experience has the closest ties, even in its UFO guise[18] –

goes even further by insisting that it was for this very purpose that we were brought into existence. It all goes to indicate that – as Sherlock Holmes might say – the game's afoot, and it is about time we found out if it really is the only game in town.

I take comfort in the fact that, to investigate properly the possibilities inherent in the holographic VR model, it will take all the resources science has presently at its command. It is a concept that is capable of scientific investigation – and only scientific investigation. The occult can never come to grips with it, simply because it is going to take hardware derived from maths finally to put the issue beyond question, in the same way as it took hardware derived from maths to put the possibility of controllable (well almost) nuclear fission beyond doubt. The clues must be in the data, just as it has been with every other scientific discovery from Galileo onwards. What entity data there is should now be combed for clues, and reputable scientific types, from mathematicians to computer programmers, should be encouraged to approach the investigation in a pragmatic way. Those who know me will know that I have always maintained that the solution to the UFO mystery would solve more than just the mystery itself. I now feel it will bring about a cosmological paradigm shift much greater than that brought about by the realization that the earth wasn't the centre of the universe. I can hardly wait, as I for one would be tickled pink to discover that I was a player in God's Little Arcade Game, for the inevitable corollary would be that, as I progressed, I too could hope to someday access to a different degree of difficulty, and perhaps become a ufonaut – and wouldn't that be fun?

REFERENCES

1   Keel, J A   *Operation Trojan Horse* (Souvenir Press, 1971)
2   Wilkins, H T   *Flying Saucers on the Attack* (Ace Star Book A–11, 1967)
3   Steiger, B   *Gods of Aquarius* (Granada, 1980)
4   Fowler, R E   *The Andreasson Affair* (Bantam Books, 1980)
5   Randles, J & Warrington, P   *Science and the UFOs* (Blackwell, 1985)
6   Finlay Hurley, J   *Sorcery* (Routledge & Keegan Paul, 1985)
7   Streiber, W   *Communion* (Arrow, 1988)
8   Barclay, D   *Fatima: A Close Encounter of the Worst Kind?* (Mark Saunders, 1987)
9   ibid.
10   ibid.
11   Paget, P   *UFO UK* (New English Library, 1980)

[12] Talbot, M   *The Holographic Universe* (Grafton, 1991)
[13] Finlay Hurley, J   op. cit.
[14] Keel, J   op. cit.
[15] BBC TV 'Horizon' presentation
[16] Steiger, B   *Gods of Aquarius* (Granada, 1980)
[17] Evans, H   *Visions, Apparitions, Alien Visitors* (Book Club Associates, 1984)
[18] Dione, R L   *God Drives a Flying Saucer* (Corgi, 1973)

FURTHER INFORMATION

Readers who wish to report UFO encounters, or to study the subject for themselves, are invited to contact the undermentioned organization:

The British Earth Mysteries Society
46 Prospect Walk
Shipley
West Yorkshire
BD18 2LR
House magazine: *The UFO Debate*

INDEX